future changes

Reorganization   134

STUDENT DEVELOPMENT

PROGRAMS

IN THE

COMMUNITY JUNIOR COLLEGE

STUDENT DEVELOPMENT PROGRAMS IN THE COMMUNITY JUNIOR COLLEGE

Edited by

TERRY O'BANION
University of Illinois, Urbana

ALICE THURSTON
Garland Junior College

Prentice-Hall, Inc., *Englewood Cliffs, New Jersey*

ISBN: 0-13-857003-5

Library of Congress Catalog Card Number: 78-172402

10   9   8   7   6   5   4   3   2   1

Printed in the United States of America

Prentice-Hall International, Inc., London
Prentice-Hall of Australia, Pty. Ltd., Sydney
Prentice-Hall of Canada, Ltd., Toronto
Prentice-Hall of India Private Limited, New Delhi
Prentice-Hall of Japan, Inc., Tokyo

To those who have taught us
about community junior college student development programs—
students and colleagues at:

CENTRAL FLORIDA JUNIOR COLLEGE

SANTA FE JUNIOR COLLEGE

MONTGOMERY COLLEGE

CUYAHOGA COMMUNITY COLLEGE

THE METROPOLITAN JUNIOR COLLEGE
    DISTRICT OF KANSAS CITY, MISSOURI

THE UNIVERSITY OF ILLINOIS

THE UNIVERSITY OF MISSOURI AT KANSAS CITY

Contents

Preface

Community junior colleges are responding increasingly to the needs of a troubled society. Recent commitments by the American Association of Junior Colleges to help disadvantaged persons of all ages have not only opened the "open door" even wider but also have forced a reexamination of the kinds of experiences students receive inside the door. New instructional approaches and more meaningful ways of relating to students are being explored. Community outreach programs are developing. Community junior colleges are becoming leaders rather than servers.

In this decade, our institutions face enormous challenges which can be met only when student personnel work becomes, as Dr. Edmund Gleazer once said, ". . . a senior partner in the junior college." Otherwise, individuals will be lost in the thrust for new facilities, in shrinking budgets, in the growing stacks of behavioral objectives, in nerve centers of instructional systems, and in the disparate demands of faculty, boards, citizens, administrators, and students to make the college into what each group feels it should be.

This book is about student development programs at the outset of the Seventies: the clientele, the roles, the problems, the future of student development programs. The authors examine where we are now and where we should be heading, look at critical issues, and present some action models.

That there is a dearth of literature about community junior college student development programs is understandable. In terms of professionalism it is still very young. In fact the dear old dean who signed students' programs of study and the faculty advisors who said "your trouble is you don't study hard enough" are in our very recent past—perhaps they are

still with us. Both the Student Personnel Commission of the American Association of Junior Colleges and Commission XI, the Junior College
Student Personnel Commission of the American College Personnel Association, were established in the Sixties. And as recently as 1965 in the
Carnegie Commission Study of Junior College Student Personnel Programs "woefully inadequate" was the final judgment regarding these programs. Moreover, student personnel workers in the community junior
colleges are task-oriented rather than research-oriented. They are the doers
confronted with daily problems of admitting, enrolling, and enabling: they
allocate financial aids, administer to health needs, place students on jobs,
organize student activities, and test, typically with not enough resources
or support or even expertise. In frustration and fatigue they too often con-
fuse means with ends. Who has time to write? Or strength to seek the long
view?

Now community junior college student development programs must
take on the added task of deepening and humanizing the educational experiences of increasingly diverse, disoriented, disinterested, and often dulled
students nurtured by a confused society, ambivalent about violence, un-
sure of their values and directions, but wanting desperately to know who
they are and where they are going. And wanting a share of the action.

In conceiving this book the editors wished to present a comprehensive
view of community junior college student development programs as the
Seventies begin. We withstood the temptation to put together a collection
of already published and therefore aging materials and instead invited
colleagues to share their insights and their hopes in original chapters. The
result is not a blueprint; too much was undone in the past and too much
is in flux in the future. (While we have used the newer term *student development programs* to title the book, most authors still use the more
common term *student personnel services;* at least no one is using the old
term *guidance services.*) We believe, however, that this book is a significant
first attempt to bring into focus the current state of the art and to forecast
the challenges to which it must respond.

We feel that the programs and philosophies described in this book
can be applied to most two-year colleges in various settings. However,
these chapters have been written by authors whose experiences have been
primarily in the comprehensive, public, community junior college in states
with well developed systems.

We have purposely not included extensive materials on the functions
or services of student development programs. Such descriptions are generally available in the professional journals of student personnel work.
Three monographs provide a good review of functions and services: *Essential Student Personnel Practices for Junior Colleges,* J. W. McDaniel;

Junior College Student Personnel Programs: What They Are and What They Should Be, Charles C. Collins; *New Directions in Community Junior College Student Personnel Programs,* Terry O'Banion.

We are greatly indebted to our many colleagues who shared this venture with us. We thank the authors whose thoughtful contributions have made this book possible. We wish also to express our appreciation to David Cox, James Gulden, and Robert Young of the University of Illinois who have provided invaluable editorial assistance.

TERRY O'BANION

ALICE THURSTON

STUDENT DEVELOPMENT
PROGRAMS
IN THE
COMMUNITY JUNIOR COLLEGE

Making Programs Relevant   1
for Students

The crucial role of community junior college student development programs is explored in Part 1 in relation to the kinds of students who come through the widening admissions door. Meeting their diverse needs, providing opportunities for their responsible participation in college governance, and helping them find what is real and meaningful to them as persons are among the basic tasks discussed in this section.

Two chapters deal with the organization, administration, and evaluation of student development programs. The section concludes with a broad challenge to revitalize junior college education as a means of reconstructing society.

The Crucial Role
of
Student Personnel Services
in the Junior College

LELAND L. MEDSKER

Director, Center for Research and
Development in Higher Education
University of California at Berkeley

For decades society has asked the question, "Who shall be educated
and for what?" Perhaps no query is more difficult to answer partly because any response is heavily value-laden and also because any appropriate resolution of the problem changes over time as changes in society itself occur. It was once said, for example, that a major overriding
goal of formal education was that of transmitting the culture. Now it is
recognized that mere transmission of a heritage is not enough, that culture is an evolving state to be modified and improved by individuals as
they come to understand their inheritance, and further that in the final
analysis it is the capability of the individual as a member of society that
is of most importance. Thus the emphases now are more on process than
on form, on the affective than on the cognitive, on change than on the
status quo, and on the ultimate capacity of man to dominate his environment than on the assumption that he may be circumscribed by indomitable
human and physical forces.

These emphases have special meaning to older youths at the post-
secondary education level who today emerge into young adulthood confronted not only by all the normal psychological problems of maturity and
responsibility, but also by new conditions which shake many of their youth-
ful ideals and tend to constitute roadblocks to their self-identity and development. They come bewildered by an era in which knowledge and
technology are explosive, by a visible degree of continuous occupational
obsolescence, by a change in mores which tends to separate them from
their elders, by a war that is hard to explain, by a nation plagued with difficulty in achieving civil rights, by "mass" in all their encounters, including their schools and colleges, to name only a few of the forces of con-
sternation. Most of them are sobered but not subdued, concerned but

collected, and socially conscious, though also highly individualized. They want a place in an improved society and they expect their educational experiences to be meaningful under present conditions.

It is in such a context that the junior college must function. Destined as it has become to serving an ever-increasing percentage of young high school graduates as well as older youth and adults, many of whom come from backgrounds that have hitherto been underrepresented in higher education, this institution faces enormous problems in making education meaningful to its diverse student body. For although the students will tend to have all the general concerns enumerated above, they will vary tremendously in their motivations and their personal and occupational goals.

Three factors help to establish a perspective for the junior college. The first is the well-recognized fact that not all "education" takes place in the classroom, but instead learning and development occur as much through informal peer group association. The second is the realization that students insist on being involved in planning their educational experiences with a view of identifying what seems relevant. Finally, it is recognized that even though each student must integrate and synthesize his total educational experience while in the junior college, the college itself has a responsibility for assisting him to do so. Simply stated, all this suggests that a junior college cannot be content with its attention to physical facilities, updating its curriculum, and appointing a faculty that is dedicated to teaching, important as all these items are. It must also be concerned about what "turns students on" and keeps them turned on, what it can do to assist them in establishing a personal philosophy in disconcerting times, how it can contribute to their personal growth and development, how it can ease tensions that may block learning and growth, how it may facilitate their desire to participate in socially meaningful activities, and a host of other factors that make the difference between the cognitive and the affective approach.

As suggested by these and other factors, the junior college must be concerned about how to direct its total effort toward the end of serving the many different needs of students. And as implied by what has been said thus far, there are widespread implications for services which for want of a better term have come to be known as those related to student personnel. In some respects this term is ambiguous since it tends to connote a separate function which, as will be discussed presently, is not exactly accurate. More realistically one might conceive this function as an institutional attitude—a realization that there must be a multidimensional approach to helping students make the most of their junior college experience and that unless there is a college-wide, conscious effort toward that end, something will be missing.

Once such an attitude is institutionalized, the role of student personnel services begins to take shape. The "program" for these services must naturally be built around the concerns that students bring with them, together with the manner which the college perceives as its best means of helping students to *grow* as contrasted with a concern merely about their performance while in school.

In further delineating this role, it is necessary to pause briefly to consider the position of the junior college, particularly the public community college, in the American educational system. Its several primary characteristics including its open door, its diverse student body, its multiple functions and programs, its closeness to its community, and its avowed dedication to student interests place a heavy burden on it. To the extent that it will increasingly occupy a central position, as students flow from the high school on the one hand to employment or education in the four-year college on the other, it really must be adept at helping students make educational and vocational choices that appear consistent with both their characteristics and the era in which they live. Yet in this day of open-endedness there is a great danger in having students finalize plans that would reduce their flexibility in future years, thus the task of helping them is made even more difficult.

Assisting students to make educational and vocational choices and thus of enabling the junior college to serve as a "distributing center" ostensibly means appropriate testing and counseling activities which are discussed in subsequent chapters of this volume. Suffice it to say that, while these are functions to be rendered with expertise, they cannot be performed in a vacuum and must generally draw on the resources of all that is known about the student.

But important as pragmatic decision-making with respect to the students' vocational and educational objectives may be, it is no more so than the responsibility faced by the junior college in helping students come to grips with the many philosophical and social questions which concern them. In fact, this task tends to overshadow the others; unless students learn to take this plunge they cannot learn to swim. This by no means implies that there are fixed answers to the various issues raised above, but it does suggest an approach that enables students to voice their concerns as well as their interests, and to initiate activities that seem important to them. Those engaged in student personnel work can assist in two ways: they can help students plan activities outside the classroom and they can perform a catalytic role with the teaching faculty in identifying issues for consideration inside the classroom as well as outside. More than ever before, the total human resources, including staff *and* students, must be joined in a partnership relationship if the college experience is to be meaningful. This obviously goes back to the goals of education and to an emphasis on the impact of the educational experience on student behavior.

If student personnel work is to be regarded as that extra force within the junior college that insures a concern about the students' concerns, then there are many issues and questions to be raised as a means of identifying a functional relationship between this force and various institutional parts. While no list of such issues could possibly be complete, the following questions are considered highly important to student personnel workers as they face the coming decade.

1. What new techniques are available or can be developed which will enable students better to articulate their emotional and philosophical problems?
2. How can outside resources best be utilized in giving students an opportunity to participate in community activities in a meaningful way?
3. What techniques can be employed to help students deal with the tendency to indulge in escape mechanisms?
4. How can the "generation gap" between students and staff (faculty, counselors, and administrators) be overcome? (As a matter of fact, how can such a gap among staff members be overcome?)
5. How can members of the teaching, counseling, and administrative staff best work together in determining the goals of education?
6. What type of staff member is needed to relate to the interests and background of students from ethnic minority groups? Where can they be recruited? Can men and women from middle-class backgrounds be prepared for this task?
7. How can institutions at the junior college level instill in students a sense of inner security and self-reliability?
8. How permissive can junior colleges be? Do their close ties with the community and their conspicuous place in community life permit them to encourage the same freedom of expression that tends to characterize four-year colleges which are farther removed from public influence? What implications does this problem pose for student personnel workers?
9. How can junior colleges compensate for the loss of new experiences and potential growth occasioned by students living at home while attending college?
10. Is participation in student activities something to be pushed or cultivated? How much initiative should a junior college take as an "organizer" of these activities? Is the role of the personnel worker that of a "supervisor" or more that of a "monitor"? How can activities be organized to provide maximum personal and intellectual growth?
11. What kinds of information are needed about students and about what happens to them during and after junior college?
    a. What kinds of data about student characteristics should the open-door college compile on its own students? To what extent can and should junior colleges

collect data on nonintellectual characteristics of students? Can such data be used advantageously?

b. What types of information about students and their outcomes should be made available to the faculty and how can this be done in a way which facilitates use of the data?

c. Can research projects be designed which will evaluate the impact of the junior college experience on the personal development of students with varying characteristics?

d. To what extent and how may a junior college maintain contact with students after they leave the institutions?

12. How may counselors and other personnel workers keep up-to-date on occupational trends in a rapidly changing technological society and how may they best disseminate this information to students?

13. How are students of low ability to be counseled with respect to their occupational and educational goals in a period when the types of work which such students might normally enter are rapidly declining in importance?

14. How can student personnel workers expedite and enrich the instructional program?

15. How should junior college student personnel services be organized and administered? Should they be highly centralized? To what extent should classroom teachers be used in the counseling and advising process and what should be their relation to the professional student personnel staff? How can a dichotomy be avoided between personnel workers and the faculty? To what extent is group counseling a feasible procedure?

16. How may junior colleges organize their total program and group their students in a way that maximizes the influence of the peer group on student growth and development? What implications does this have for working with the very able and creative student? The less able student?

17. To what extent should the customary student personnel services offered during the day be available to evening students? To what extent should the junior college extend counseling services to the community?

18. What are the most effective methods of articulating the work of the junior college with that of the high school? How can student personnel workers specifically aid in this function? What can be done to improve the image which high school students, as well as high school teachers, have of the junior college?

19. What are the most effective methods of articulating the work of the junior college with that of four-year institutions and where can student personnel workers best serve in this process?

20. How can a student health program be made just that, namely a *health* program and not merely a plan which takes care of emergencies and administers first aid?

21. Is it possible that junior college students are overcounseled? May they rely so much on counselors and advisors that they cannot stand on their own

after they transfer to a four-year college where there is likely to be a minimum of counseling assistance?

22. What new avenues of research and service are open to student personnel work through the advent of the new mechanical technologies?

23. What is to be the source of personnel workers in the future and what type of professional preparation should they have?

24. How can the public (as well as administrators and boards of control) be convinced that student personnel work is essential and that the cost of it must be met?

25. How can the total student personnel program be evaluated?

The above list is long and it is unlikely that there are common answers to any one of the questions since resolutions depend on circumstances. It seems appropriate to turn now to some requirements for such a program with the thought that they suggest a response to some of the questions.

The first requisite of a good student personnel program in a junior college is a favorable climate of opinion concerning both it and the junior college as an institution as reflected in the attitudes held by staff members and students. Unfortunately, the perception that many counselors and teachers have of the junior college is not in accord with the role which such a college is presumed to play in today's society. Studies at the Center for Research and Development in Higher Education at Berkeley have revealed the extent to which teachers of academic subjects, for example, look more favorably on that part of the junior college program which serves high-ability students and which involves a transfer program rather than upon the many other services which a comprehensive institution is presumed to render. One might assume that this more narrow view would seldom be held by counselors, but research has shown that even among them there is not always complete acceptance of the open-door, multiple-purpose college.

A favorable climate of opinion toward student personnel work is more likely to exist if the program has grown out of the basic institutional philosophy and objectives of the college and if the entire staff has been involved in determining or reviewing the stated philosophy and objectives. When placed in the context of the overall mission of the junior college and of what the institution seeks to accomplish in effecting changes in the behavior of students, it is difficult to see how any staff member—even the most classroom-minded—can fail to agree that students require services and assistance outside the classroom. It is important to remember that student personnel work not only involves the performance of services to students, but is as much concerned with *attitudes toward students*.

But even assuming that the staff can agree on the general purposes of the two-year college and on the fact that personnel services are important in helping this institution achieve its many objectives, it is still possible that in the day-by-day operation there will be differences of opinion on the extent to which and how personnel programs should be emphasized and implemented. For example, those who are in charge of student activities or those who are professional counselors may become suspect by classroom teachers. Frequently such workers are perceived more as administrators than as members of the faculty with the result that close and harmonious relationships between the faculty and the personnel staff are jeopardized. Unfortunately, personnel workers themselves often do not help the situation. On this point T. R. McConnell, in an address at the University of Minnesota, had this to say:

Perhaps instead of stressing the autonomy and separate organizational status of student personnel services, it would be better to create an atmosphere in which counselors are thought of as ranging from teachers who have acquired considerable understanding of the dynamics of human behavior to highly trained professional counselors whose services are actually extensions of the services of their faculty colleagues. . . . However, this status may not be acceptable to all student personnel workers. I think I have detected a desire on the part of some of them to establish a "priesthood." As members of the order they speak with authority, and do not want their authority questioned, either as to substance or as to the methods by which they arrived at their conclusions. Furthermore, they act as if their knowledge were esoteric . . . The knowledge possessed by the professional staff may be as specialized and requisite to their particular callings as that in other professions or as that of any academic specialty. But for the purpose of establishing rapport with faculty members, there is no value in making this specialized knowledge appear any more recondite than necessary . . . Presumably professional personnel people want intensely to acquire status, if not as much for themselves individually as for their profession. But it might be better strategy for them to share their special knowledge as fully as their academic colleagues are able to understand or appreciate it.[1]

Where wide differences exist between the faculty and personnel workers, the fault can often be attributed to top administrative leadership. If in the interest of administrative efficiency some members of the staff are employed to work primarily inside the classroom and others are engaged in services performed outside the instructional area, it is the function of the top administration to coordinate the activities of both groups and to see that each supplements the other in a unified program which is best for the student.

The attitude of the governing board of the junior college toward student personnel work is also important. Too often the board's awareness of what goes on in the college is limited to the business aspects of the enterprise or, at the most, to the instructional program. True, the board members may realize that a few counselors are at work or that someone is in charge of student activities and student government, but they may not be cognizant of the total scope of student personnel activities and their importance. Again, the chief administrator is responsible for acquainting the board with the need for the wide range of services to students and in informing the board about the performance of such services.

A second requirement—and an obvious one—is that of qualified personnel. Much could be said about the skills required of counselors and other personnel workers, but this is an item generally understood and its importance assumed. The gains made each year in improving the techniques of individual assessment and counseling make it necessary that those engaged in the counseling process keep up-to-date.

There are, however, some more intangible aspects of the work of those engaged in personnel services which should be considered. An important characteristic is the willingness to admit deficiencies, to inquire, and to experiment. After all is said and done, so little is known about careers in a swiftly changing society; about the characteristics of students which are of aid in predicting performance and growth; about those characteristics of a college environment which have an impact on students; about the extent to which and how students should be paired with institutions and with curricula within institutions. All this suggests that counselors and other personnel workers have heavy responsibilities and that they can never accept the *status quo*. This will be more true than ever before during the decade of the 1970s as junior colleges are called upon to recruit and serve an ever-increasing number of students from various ethnic minority groups. Recruiting and preparing a staff that can relate to these students and be of assistance to the teaching faculty in doing so is one of the most difficult problems ahead in the student personnel area.

Junior college personnel workers have another peculiar responsibility. They must be concerned about the growth and development of students from many backgrounds and with various levels of ability and attainment. Yet junior colleges no less than their four-year counterparts must be concerned with academic excellence. Due to the heterogeneity of the student body, this must be excellence in terms of the individual and not according to a standard norm. Each student must be given assistance in developing according to his peculiar set of abilities and background.

A third and last requirement is that student personnel services be organized in a manner that enables them to permeate the entire campus. This is an issue on which there is considerable difference of opinion. Many advocate that student personnel services be organized on a highly centralized basis. Others believe that structure is less important than function and that decentralization can in fact be more effective, particularly if it involves the participation of or at least a close association with teaching faculty members. New and different models are beginning to emerge, and it is likely that in the current decade many radical changes will occur in both concept and practice with respect to implementing the "program" of student personnel services. Suffice it to say here that overall direction of a personnel program, in whatever way it is achieved, is extremely important. No longer can junior colleges afford to leave the implementation of personnel services to change. The parts of the program must be looked upon as a total program with general direction and sufficient administration to insure coverage of the field, implementation of the services, continuous in-service training of workers, and continuing evaluation of the program's effectiveness.

The burden of this statement as both expressed and implied is that junior colleges cannot fail in their efforts to make their program meaningful to students. No longer can they indulge in a "school as usual" philosophy. Students will either develop intellectually—each at his own level —or the junior college will suffer a reputation of educational carelessness. Students will either be aided in the selection and pursuit of appropriate educational and vocational goals or the idea of decentralization of higher education will be pronounced a failure. Appropriate programs for students not transferring to four-year colleges will either achieve prestige or the junior college will lose support for its unique character. The junior college will either be a distinct break from high school, offering experiences to students which develop maturity or certain critics will be proved correct in their contention that students should not attend college while living at home. Students will either find counsel and understanding to ease their anxieties, or everything that student personnel workers have stood for will become a sham. It would seem that the alternatives leave little choice to those responsible for the junior college.

REFERENCE

1. McConnell, T. R., "The Relation of Institutional Goals and Organization to the Administration of Student Personnel Work," in *Approaches to the Study of Administration in Student Personnel Work,* ed. Martin L. Snoke. Minneapolis: University of Minnesota Press, 1960.

Student Characteristics
and Their Implication
for Student Personnel Work

CHARLES C. COLLINS

Associate Director, Junior College Leadership Program
Center for Research and Development in Higher Education
University of California at Berkeley

The eminent biologist, Thomas Henry Huxley, once told his students, "The great end of life is not knowledge but action." And W. H. Auden said to all who read his poetry,
"Act from thought should quickly follow: What is thinking for?"
Facts, left in isolation, are inert. Drawing implications from facts, though hazardous, creates a ferment with a potential for thrust toward action. Thought centered on these implications should give direction to this potential thrust. The sequential order, then, is: facts $\longrightarrow$ implications drawn from facts $\longrightarrow$ thought on suggested options and their consequences $\longrightarrow$ action. Or, related to the subject at hand: facts on junior college students $\longrightarrow$ implications of these facts for student personnel services $\longrightarrow$ thought on the consequences of the options these implications suggest $\longrightarrow$ development, innovation, change, action.

Facts, even in the social or behavioral sciences, can be hard, neat, precise, objective. Implications grow out of the perceptions of the person drawing them; hence they are softer, perhaps a little messy, somewhat imprecise, and admittedly subjective. It might be comforting could it be otherwise, but it cannot. The validity of the implications will depend on the breadth and depth of the contextual knowledge of the person who draws these implications—and upon his unstated assumptions and the internal logic that follows from these assumptions. Step 3 of the sequential order, thought on the consequence of the options suggested by the implications, and step 4, action, go beyond the responsibility of the gatherer of facts or the drawer of implications. At least in matters pertaining to curriculum or student personnel, step 3 and step 4 must be taken by those who know all the complexities and nuances of the local situation and who will have to carry out and live with the action which is taken.

ACADEMIC CHARACTERISTICS

For an opener, take the fact that more and more people are going to college: the 3 percent of high school graduates going to college in 1900 has grown to 50 percent in the 1960s; an average of one new junior college is created every week; presidents of the United States as well as presidents of colleges have said that everyone who wants and can profit from higher education should have it. What are the implications of this colossal fact?

When 60, 70, and 80 percent of high school graduates are enrolled in college, most will not be going to such institutions as Stanford or Yale or the University of California. These millions will be swelling the ranks of the community colleges. In California, for example, 60 percent of California high school graduates now enter a two- or four-year college. In 1968, total enrollment was 878,580 students of whom 568,147 were in California's 86 community colleges as opposed to 98,780 students in the eight campuses of the University of California.[7]

When higher education is almost as universal as secondary education, the college population will, in nearly all respects, be the same as that found in the high schools. On the scale of academic aptitude, the junior college average may actually be lower than that of the high school, for the people's college will have abandoned whatever selection processes they may have had, while the state and private four-year colleges and universities will continue to skim off the academic cream. Of course, both junior and senior colleges may come to see that man is not one-dimensional, that he is a lot more than just his academic aptitude. The community colleges may make a reappraisal, recognize that academic aptitude is only one of the many facets of man, and realize that by opening the door to everybody, they have allowed all the plural riches of humanity to flow in.

If community colleges make such a reappraisal, they may decide to go off the academic gold standard. They may begin looking for more valuable gems: social ethics, human understanding, ethnic subcultures, affective wisdom. They may tell the senior colleges that they are not looking for academic excellence alone and therefore refuse to use the single A-to-F yardstick to measure a student. Junior college instructors and student personnel workers may teach their more rigid senior college colleagues that the plural qualities of man require plural modes of cultivation and call for plural criteria of evaluation. As a more and more diverse population swarms into the junior colleges, there will have to be an institutional reordering of priorities with some de-emphasis on the academic, on cognitive learning, and a new valuation of affective learning, a new concern with human relationships and with the morality and ethics involved in those relationships.

The valuation of human qualities by counselors and other student personnel workers has already undergone significant reappraisal. Those in the vanguard have sought means (course work, self-analysis, encounter groups) to broaden their knowledge of meaningful ways to release and develop the varied qualities they find in their students. They have disabused themselves of the single-standard definition of college and find it arrogant, if not absurd, when others speak of a course being "college level" or of a student being "college caliber."

RESISTANCE TO TESTING

The antagonism toward testing has grown so strong that testmakers have become anxious about loss of handsome profits. Community college professionals in student personnel are asking, "Who needs selection devices in an open-door college?" And their few counterparts in the more selective senior colleges are asking, "Are we not measuring that which happens to be measurable rather than that which is significant?" Some student personnel people in the junior colleges are objecting that the tracking system should be allowed to die a well-deserved death, but that testing props it up and makes a moribund system look viable. Those professionals most disenchanted with testing claim that the achievement testmakers become the curriculum committee, determining what will be taught, and that the academic aptitude testmakers jerry-rig a facade of scientific legitimacy to justify the one-eyed view that the cognitive, the academic, is the be-all and end-all of the college experience.

Criticism of testing by the professionals is genteel and decorous compared to the bad-mouthing by disadvantaged blacks, browns, and whites who feel they have been victimized by testing. To many of those with rising educational and vocational expectations, testing has been used by the *haves* to make the *have-nots* doubt their own competency, to make their self-image ugly, to pile failure upon failure, and to make school a foreign game where the ground rules are fixed to make them lose. Much of this negative feeling toward testing has rubbed off on the counselors, contributing significantly to the low esteem in which they are held by many blacks and others from the third world. The upshot of all this is that student personnel people find themselves in a professional quandary: They know that some testing, particularly in the affective areas of attitudes, interests and values, is of real worth, and they do not want to discard the good with the bad. At the same time, they know they will be obliged not only to remove the threat from testing, but to demonstrate its positive values, if they are ever to recapture the trust of blacks, Chicanos, and others who see tests as the switch used to shunt them off onto dead-end tracks.

SOCIOECONOMIC BACKGROUND

Junior college students, as a group, come from families in the lower socioeconomic classes; specifically, the educations, incomes, and occupations of their fathers are lower than those of fathers of most four-year college students.[2] If this is true now, it is going to be more true in the future, for the middle and upper classes have always sent their children to college, while the children of the lower-middle and lower classes make up the bulk of the astonishing number and percentage increase in enrollment in higher education. Third world militancy on the issue of education may beat down closed doors and may throw a wedge into those revolving doors designed to make exit follow hard on the heels of entry.

This palpable fact of socioeconomic class has some subtle and perplexing implications for student personnel. The junior colleges have with pride staked a claim on the democratization of higher education. Community colleges allege, although Burton Clark and others have questioned it, that they are the escalator upon which those students who can hang on, can ride to whatever class level they choose.[4] Even if this is true, it becomes an area of concern for counseling. Those who move out of their class divorce themselves somewhat from the parents, family, and friends they leave behind. This cannot be done without some feeling of guilt and some emotional losses.

Students who are upwardly mobile need, in a self-conscious way, to take a hard look at what is happening to them and to make some studied choices in class values. It does not necessarily follow that the student must first learn and then adopt the values of the higher class to which he is moving. A strong case could be made for his learning a greater appreciation of the values, mores, and traditions of the class, or caste, or subculture, from which he comes. Perhaps this is what the struggle for ethnic studies is all about. Maybe the black student does not want to divorce himself from his black heritage, and maybe the Chicano student wants to hold to the values of La Raza. Maybe, too the white student should undertake his own ethnic studies by casting a critical look at the life style of the middle and upper class WASP.

The college experience, the whole academic ethos, is so foreign to those parents who have had no contact with it, that it is difficult for them to give understanding and encouragement to their college-bound children. In a general way, they want their children to "get ahead" and even to surpass them. However, they find moment-to-moment encouragement difficult: like an American trying to cheer enthusiastically at a British cricket match. They also find a widening gulf between themselves and their children, who may correct their grammar, reject their politics, and scoff at their religion. But to return to the point at hand: Encouragement of influential and understanding adults is a vital factor in the motivation of college students.[13] If the psycho-logic of circumstances disqualifies the parents as the significant adults, then the student personnel staff should conjure up some parent surrogates to provide this intelligent encouragement.

Although social mobility does not necessarily require rejection of existing values and on-going cultural patterns, college as the vehicle for social mobility should lead to broader interests, to more catholic tastes, to partaking in a richer cultural fare. The formal curriculum can only take the student part way toward this goal. Junior colleges, even more than senior colleges, should develop and financially underwrite such an attractive co-curricular program that it will seduce even the practical-minded, working, commuting student. As a matter of fact, it is just such a student who should be exposed to an enticing motley of new ideas and life styles, and lured into new cultural and intellectual experiences.

FINANCES

It is an irony that many students select the junior college because of its low cost and then discount the education they get because it is "on the cheap." Further, 63 percent of junior college students, as opposed to 18 percent of senior college students, work while attending college. The basis for their dividing time and energy between work and college is partly need and partly this discounting of the seriousness of the enterprise.[2]

At the moment, it is part of black and third world rhetoric to label junior college education second-rate because the junior college is lower in cost and because it admits virtually everyone. This reflects one of the neurotic valuations of a materialistic society: if it is cheaper and if it is not selective, it must not be very good. Some counter must be made to the materialistic tendency to judge things good or bad, valuable or worthless, on the basis of what they cost. Since it is among the functions of student personnel to interpret the college to the student, and to help the student explore the effect of his value system on his behavior, this whole problem falls directly in the laps of the various student personnel workers, particularly the counselors.

Financial assistance officers have an even tougher job. More academically disadvantaged students from poorer families, particularly black and other third world students, are entering the community colleges. Helping them find jobs does not solve the problem, for time on the job is time away from study. If they work enough to earn subsistence, they are likely to flunk out of college. There are only token amounts of grants-in-aid to meet the need, and the scramble for the few dollars thrown out by the federal government is both humiliating and cutthroat. The issues of financial aid—insufficient funds, unmet promises, sudden cutbacks, withholding of aid as a punitive measure—have already resulted in the eruption of violence on some campuses and, predictably, will be the source of many confrontations in the future.

The notion that a student who works his way through college gets more out of it and appreciates it more probably never was true. Now, for most junior college students, it is a grim joke. There is no evidence that working while enrolled in a junior college builds character, but there is evidence that it results in lower academic achievement and a higher drop-out rate.[10] No doubt, student personnel should include an employment office, and the more able student probably can handle 15 or 20 hours of work per week. Nonetheless, major attention must be turned to campaigning for adequate financial aid, perhaps on a work-study program where the academically strong student is paid for being a tutor and the academically weak student is paid for being a tutee. Community fundraising drives may generate a thousand dollars or so for an emergency loan fund, but the kind of campaign being suggested is a political one where the stakes are for millions of federal or state dollars. Failure on this issue may indeed make the revolution of rising expectations into a bloody one.

VALUES, SELF-CONCEPT, AND PERSONALITY

As a group, junior college students are not committed to intellectual values; they do not seek an intellectual atmosphere, nor do they find it.[8] This is true despite the fact that most junior colleges serve the academically oriented (transfer) better than the vocationally oriented (terminal). The typical junior college student's outside work, his commuting, his high school background, the interests and value patterns of his family—all of these are contributing factors. The fact remains, however, that values are a strong determinant of behavior, and unless a student does come to value intellectual pursuits, his moment-to-moment motivation in enterprises of the mind is not likely to be strong.

To a large extent, what is described here is a restriction of freedom. The usual junior college student does not seek option B (intellectual-cultural activities) because he is much more aware of option A (practical-materialistic activities). To increase his freedom, he needs to be made more aware of the alternatives open to him. And these alternatives need to be experienced as pleasure, to bring him reward, not just present themselves as onerous requirements he must meet to get the ticket to a better job and to more material benefits. What is being suggested is that the co-curriculum within the student personnel function can more than supplement; it can be an equal partner to the formal curriculum in the development of intellectual-cultural values. The co-curricular program can so fascinate with intriguing personalities, can so delight with the pleasures of the arts, can so broaden the student's world with its diversity, and can so stimulate the imagination that only the case-hardened know-nothing will be able to escape its lure. Further, those student personnel people involved in the co-curriculum can encourage students to band together for the pleasure of shared experience in the intellectual-cultural realm. They can help create on the junior college campus what spontaneously arises on the university campus, namely, little communities of people who feel comradeship and pleasure from the shared experience of a common interest.

Junior college students more or less comprise a cross-section of the general population, and hence should not be thought of as a homogeneous group. Even so, there are some measurable group differences between them and senior college students. They appear to have a more practical orientation to college and are less likely to value humanitarian pursuits. They are more cautious and controlled, lack confidence in themselves, are less likely to venture into new and untried fields; they seek more certain pathways to the occupational success and financial security which they value so highly. They are, from the research evidence, less autonomous and more authoritarian.[8]

As might be guessed, junior college students appear to be more unsettled about future plans than either four-year college students or than youngsters who do not go on to college. Actually, they are eager for guidance regarding future planning even though they may not have the initiative, the confidence, or the know-how to seek it out. It is congruent with all the other facts that those planning and effecting transfer to senior colleges make more use of the counseling services and are more pleased with them than the nontransfer students.[8]

All these statements should carry a rather loud and clear message to student personnel workers. Certainly there is agreement on the goals of helping the student to become more autonomous and less authoritarian, of increasing his self-confidence, of helping him to see and be willing to consider bolder options. There is a need to take counseling, particularly the value analysis involved in vocational counseling, to the student. If the students won't come to the counselors, then let the counselors go to the students. One way to assure this is to decentralize so the counselors must leave the security of the fort, the barrier of their little cluster of offices, and team up with their faculty colleagues in divisional centers spotted throughout the campus. Or if this is not the way to put the counselors where the action is, then let them find some other natural clustering so they are readily accessible to the students who need and want their help.

Counselors should help keep junior college students from settling too quickly for the commonplace. They need to help them live with ambiguity: to help them see that vocational choice should begin with an imaginative look at a host of options and should then proceed toward a progressive narrowing of choice as the person analyzes the congruence of his own values, interests, and abilities with those demanded by various occupations. The most valuable thing the student can learn in this whole process is the attitude, the posture, of commitment within a wider frame of tentativeness.[6] But this is difficult.

Almost all students and some counselors will expect a definite, almost irrevocable, occupational decision as the end result of vocational counseling. Considering the truth that, "There is nothing permanent except change," this is an impossible, and really foolish expectancy. The whole concept of work is going to change. The nature of occupations will change even more rapidly than in the recent past. The prediction that 50 percent of all jobs a decade hence will be jobs that are not known today, will come to pass. In such a changing environment, the individual himself is going to change, to be transformed, to undergo a veritable metamorphosis. Yet, like all before him, he will have to live the days of his years; he will need to be committed for today yet remain tentative for tomorrow.[5]

Junior college students are often quite uncertain of their interests and doubt if they have the motivation to sustain them through a full college program. Many do not feel confident that their high school work prepared them adequately for college. They are more critical of the high school courses and teachers than are those who go directly to four-year colleges. They estimate their teachers would rate them lower and, in fact, agree that their teachers should rate them lower.[8] All of this, of course, adds up to a self-fulfilling prophecy. Too frequently, the junior college student begins with doubts, sinks to depression, and then stops trying in areas where he experiences little, if any, success. The vicious cycle can only be broken if instructors, counselors, and other student personnel workers begin to insist that self-judgment and evaluation by others be made on a more pluralistic basis.

Obviously, those with high aptitude and lots of experience in manipulation of verbal and mathematical symbols are going to shine like Day-Glo if the learning experience is all at the highest level of abstraction. But symbol manipulation is not the only form of learning. Perceptive blacks living in the ghetto understand the sociology of that subculture in a different and probably more significant way than the white student who has read all the books on it. John Dewey called for learning by doing, and Paul Goodman appears ready to write off most of learning at 2nd or

3rd or Nth level abstraction and substitute a 20th century version of the apprenticeship system.[9]

Of course, student personnel workers cannot wait for a radical revamping of higher education; in the long meantime they must arrange for a goodly portion (25 to 35 percent) of junior college students to develop skill in handling the written and spoken word and the mathematical symbols. In accommodating themselves to this reality, they should still keep pointing to the absurdity of a college which accepts all comers but maintains the narrow learning system and an even narrower evaluation system designed to serve elitist colleges. Junior college students could learn psychology and sociology and government and ecology and ethics and all the arts and a lot of other subdivisions of man's knowledge by experiencing them, by participation, by doing; if learning were this real, they would not tolerate for long an evaluation system as one-dimensional and as meaningless as *A* to *F*.

EDUCATIONAL ASPIRATIONS

"Generally speaking, junior college students have lower educational and occupational aspirations than their peers who begin their education in four-year colleges." [8] Most observers find this understandable, although they might ask what is meant by "lower." What they cannot find understandable is that 70 to 75 percent of junior college freshmen assert their intention to transfer to a senior college and earn a bachelor's degree or more. Most observers of the junior college scene echo the statement made by K. Patricia Cross, "We know, of course, that the educational aspirations of both junior and senior college students are unrealistically high." [8] And they agree with what Burton Clark called the "cooling out" function of higher education, junior colleges using the soft response: ". . . to let down hopes gently and unexplosively. Through it, students who are failing or barely passing find their occupational and academic future being redefined." [3]

It is a fact that 70 to 75 percent of beginning junior college students label themselves as transfer students, whereas 35 percent or fewer of these students actually transfer.[1] Is the implication of this fact that counselors should disuade all but top academic students from taking transfer courses? Let the charge be loud and clear: on this issue, junior college staff, including those in student personnel, fall into their own semantic traps. They ask a premature, value-loaded, badly phrased question and then give face validity to the answer. When a student is asked if his major is terminal or transfer he is really being asked, "Are your vocational and educational aims highly specific and limited or are they still rather general and unlimited?" If the student is uncommitted, or if his commitment is to general education, or if he doesn't know whether he will eventually be a data processor or a teacher of data processing, or if he likes the sound of saying he is going on to Princeton, or if he wants to keep the options open or if, in hard fact, he fully intends to transfer—under all these conditions, the student is likely to label himself as a transfer student. When the terminal/transfer dichotomy really means low-prestige-specific versus high-prestige-general, it should not be so astonishing that 70 to 75 percent are smart enough to make the second choice.

It is also a fact that junior colleges, like senior colleges, "cool out" their students, perhaps more gently but just as effectively. To say that junior colleges use the soft response ("let down hopes gently and un-explosively . . . students who are failing or barely passing find their occupational and academic future being redefined") is to indulge in conscience-soothing euphemisms. It should be put more harshly: out of every 100 students who enter junior colleges, 65 to 70 say, "Oh, to hell with it!" or, by means of probation/disqualification, are told by those who piously espouse universal higher education to get out! Either way, this is somewhat analogous to hospitals discharging the sick and keeping the well.

Part of the error in this thinking begins with the assumption that there is a clear-cut distinction between terminal and transfer. This is a myth without foundation. Most terminal courses in vocational training are as difficult and demanding as transfer courses: industrial electronics is every bit as tough as History 17 A-B. Most courses with terminal numbers are, in fact, transferable to one senior college or another, and since this is true, instructors teaching these courses apply what they think to be transfer grading standards. Add to these points the fact that the general education function of the junior college is, with few exceptions, met by transfer type courses. The logic of these assertions leads then to this: if transfer courses are unrealistic (too difficult) for two-thirds of junior college students, if most technical-terminal courses are as difficult as transfer courses, if most general education courses are really designed and graded as transfer courses, then for two-thirds of the students the transfer, the terminal, and the general education functions of the junior college are all unrealistic. By this reasoning, it would make more sense—and would be cheaper—for the academically able students to be sent directly from high school to the senior colleges. The junior colleges would then be left as remedial schools trying to do what the elementary and secondary schools failed to do.

Again, it comes to this: the idea of universal higher education demands a plural, not a single, absolute definition of what college is. Student personnel workers should be the first to exorcise that devilish mind-set that transfer is unrealistic for many, if not most, junior college students.

What is really unrealistic is for an affluent society to fail to educate each of its citizens to his highest potential, for it is self-evident that this serves both the individual and the general welfare.

Counselors and other junior college staff members should first resist and then reject this artificial distinction between transfer and terminal. Student personnel staff members should work with curriculum committees and with instructors on disabusing students, and their parents, of the vision of step-ladder prestige in society's job structure. They should actively set out to instill a higher valuation for para-professional and for all mid-level jobs in management, in technology, and in the social services, for in the economy of the future that is where most junior college graduates are going to be. If all the above reasoning is essentially sound, then the most important implication is the necessity of convincing senior colleges to broaden their range of curricula to accept a much broadened range of transfer students. They should find, as the junior colleges are finding, that the definition of college has to stretch to fit the new societal goal of universal higher education.

BLACK AND THIRD WORLD STUDENTS

The head-count facts on black and third world students are not yet documented, but it would take an hysterical blindness to fail to see that the junior colleges, patricularly urban community colleges, are getting and will get more black, brown, yellow, and red students. The militancy of those already in will force changes in admissions, retention, financial aid, and other such barriers, so the way will be cleared for the brothers who are out. Many will enter with very hostile feelings about the kind of counseling and the kind of teaching they received in high school and will look upon the junior college as another tracking system where they get shunted on to the lowest track. They are not going to be very tolerant of dead-end tracks or of those that fail to lead to the senior colleges.

It is an open question whether it takes a black counselor to counsel a black student or a third world financial aid officer to handle the explosive issue of assistance to third world students. Caucasian student personnel workers whose racial awareness is as white as their skins would be well advised to limit themselves to white students. Most student personnel staff members have basic understanding and empathy, but even these people will need to learn lots more about third world students than can be got from reading *Soul on Ice* or *Black Rage* or from taking another sociology course or so. They will need to work with and for these ex-colonials in their communities and with and for them in their struggle on the campus.

This kind of involvement is not without its dangers, and not too many have a strong enough stomach for it. Those white professionals who are involved enough in mankind to respond to this challenge may have to accept the rebuff of a self-imposed segregation and be tolerant of strident ethnocentrism during the transitional identity crisis. Interracial relations will remain up-tight and often irrational until the WASPs prove themselves worthy of trust and until the third worlders no longer feel compelled to shout, "I am me and I like what I see me to be!"

An example to develop the point: California's population is about 25 percent non-Caucasian, but something less than 5 percent of students in California institutions of higher learning are non-Caucasian. If racial equity were to be achieved tomorrow, as it almost has to be, old standards would simply have to be changed, dropped, circumvented. The logic must be faced that the same academic admission, retention, and graduation standards cannot be applied to students who have been singularly disadvantaged in academics, who have marched to the beat of a different drummer, who are rich in other dimensions of the human genius. The argument here is for multiple criteria, not for lower standards. The logic also has to be faced that during all those years of disadvantagement, third world counselors, instructors, and other professionals were not being prepared, certainly not at a 25 percent rate. Now they are desperately needed, and some personnel selection standards are going to be bent and broken to get them in. The purist who sees all this as a lowering of the barriers, as a watering down of education, should have shown his concern long ago when gradualism was still an option. Again, this is not to say that the standards should be lower, but that the criteria should be different, should be plural, should have latitude in interpretation. Besides, staff members who come in through the side door are likely to enter unencumbered with many of the hang-ups typical of those taking the orthodox path; en route they will have picked up some different forms of wisdom that will enrich the whole college community.

SENSE OF COMMUNITY

The community college student does not have much sense of community, on campus or off. There does not seem to be much of a "we" feeling among most junior college students, and there is, therefore, only faint loyalty to the college and even a more pallid identification with the wider community. In a study of junior college dropouts, Jane Matson came to the conclusion that a lack of community feeling was one of the factors distinguishing between those who dropped and those who held on.[11]

Though junior colleges are often called community colleges, some question exists about whether there is real *community* out there or only some businesses and some families who happen, geographically, to live next to each other. And on campus, for many students, there is no little universe in which they find they can revolve. Part of the difficulty stems from the fact that students are usually commuters and often part-time workers. "For the usual student in a commuter college, his office, his file cabinet, his locker, sometimes his lunch room, and sometimes his trysting place, is his car. The reason for this is very simple: he has no home base on campus. The confused bedlam of the student center serves this need no better than the quiet hard-chaired decorum of the library. The student is not likely to work out his problems of personality identity sitting in his car waiting for his next class. Neither is the college, nor the intellectual and cultural values for which it stands, likely to become the object of his identification." [5]

One of the best ways to establish a "we" feeling is for "us" to do some significant things together. Projects in the outer community, aide work in some types of social service, discussion in small student-faculty retreats, participation in co-curricular activities of an active, nonspectator, type, involvement in sensitivity groups—all these fall in the category of doing significant things together, and all fall within the scope of student personnel. Instead of relying only on the typical first semester orientation class, counselors might consider voluntary continuation of encounter or other types of group sessions for student exploration of the self and the significant other; these sessions would be open to the student for the duration of his enrollment in the community college.

As suggested before, the counseling function might be profitably decentralized and in the process become the hub of little universes to which the student could attach himself. There are any number of models for this: William Rainey Harper College in Illinois and Monterey Peninsula College in California are among those having decentralized counseling along divisional lines. De jure recognition of de facto clustering by color or ethnic origin might tie in neatly with current demands for separate ethnic studies. Even arbitrary clusters, as long as they allowed for mobility, might be worth a try.

AGE AND SEX

In age, students in junior colleges are more senior than students in senior colleges. Only 15 percent of entering four-year college students are over 19 years old, whereas over 30 percent of junior college freshmen have left their teens behind them. Actually, Leland Medsker reported almost 50 percent of junior college students had reached and passed their majority, but his data of the late 1950s may have been skewed to the high side by the veterans of the Korean War.[12] If all part-time students in the junior college evening divisions were included in the computation, the 50 percent figure would be a conservative estimate. An aggressive campaign by student personnel staffs to take vocational and educational counseling to the adults in their communities (now being done in some ghetto areas) would actually make those under 21 a minority in the junior colleges.

The implications of this age factor seem to have been largely ignored. Only a few junior colleges have counseling programs specially designed for older students, and many do not even have regular counseling services available for the thousands of adults in evening divisions. Older students returning to school after many years of absence have fears, aspirations, and attitudes different from those of the recent high school graduate; they doubtless require a kind of orientation different from the stock "ease-them-out-of-puberty" introduction to college. They also need a different approach in counseling, one that recognizes their greater maturity, experience, and definitiveness of purpose and one that affords them not only respect but the dignity of being peers with the counselor.

Although some older students may want to merge completely with the younger students, most find themselves a little uncomfortable in any facilities outside the classroom and the library. Perhaps they deserve and would enjoy a special lounge within the student center, a retreat which would be quieter and less bouncy, where they could feel free to show their age. It is a rare junior college indeed which has any kind of organization for evening division students, and only the more aggressive adult students in the day division involve themselves in student politics. These older students are often shining lights in the classroom but have little to say and, consequently, feel little involvement in the co-curricular program. This is unfortunate, for they would add richness to it and would gain richness from it. They are a large segment in a college system which claims to be student-centered. To be more or less blind to their presence in the total student personnel function is to negate a cardinal premise of the junior college philosophy.

No doubt there are other significant characteristics of junior college students that have implications for junior college student personnel programs. Even so, an end must be called at some point, and in this instance conclusion will be reached with brief mention of the factor of sex ratio. In studies done during the 1950s and reported by Leland Medsker, the ratio varied from 3 to 1 to 2 to 1 in favor of men over women.[12] This ratio, without question, reflects social values; education is highly valued for men and not so highly valued for women. Values can, of course, be taught, and if student personnel people believe that what is good for the gander is good for the goose, then it is encumbent upon them to try to recruit more girls among high school graduates and more women from the community. Beyond recruitment, counselors and other student personnel workers must look critically at what the junior college has to offer women. If the curriculum is oriented towards male occupations, male interests, male predelictions, then why should women enroll in numbers equal to men? The same goes for the co-curriculum. Too often the major role for girls in student activities is that of sex-symbol, which is rather limiting both as to numbers who qualify and as to scope. The budget, the nature of activities, the ease of involvement, and every aspect of the co-curricular program should be co-sexual, should reflect the fact that there are as many women as there are men and, more to the point, that as many women as men should be in college.

REFERENCES

1. American College Testing Program, *College Student Profiles: Norms for the ACT Assessment.* Iowa City: American College Testing Program, 1966.

2. ASTIN, A. W., R. J. PANOS, and J. A. CREAGER, "National Norm for Entering College Freshmen—Fall, 1966," *ACE Research Reports.* Washington, D.C.: American Council on Education, 1967.

3. CLARK, BURTON R., "The Cooling-out Function in Higher Education," *American Journal of Sociology,* 65 (1960), 569–76.

4. ———, *The Open Door College: A Case Study.* New York: McGraw-Hill Book Company, 1960.

5. COLLINS, CHARLES C., *College Orientation: Education for Relevance.* Boston: Holbrook Press, 1969.

6. ———, *Junior College Student Personnel Programs: What They Are and What They Should Be.* Washington, D.C.: American Association of Junior Colleges, 1967.

7. Coordinating Council for Higher Education, "Fall 1968 Enrollment in California Higher Education," *California Higher Education,* 3 (June, 1969), 3.

8. CROSS, K. PATRICIA, *The Junior College Student: A Research Description.* Princeton, N. J.: Educational Testing Services, 1968.

9. GOODMAN, PAUL, "The Present Moment in Education," *The New York Review of Books,* April 10, 1969, pp. 14–24.

10. KNOELL, D. M. and L. L. MEDSKER, *From Junior to Senior College: A National Study of the Transfer Student.* Washington, D.C.: American Council on Education, 1965.

11. MATSON, JANE E. "Characteristics of Students Who Withdraw From A Public Junior College." Unpublished doctoral dissertation, School of Education, Stanford University, 1955.

12. MEDSKER, LELAND L., *The Junior College: Progress and Prospect.* New York: McGraw-Hill Book Company, 1960.

13. TRENT, J. W. and L. L. MEDSKER, *Beyond High School: A Study of 10,000 High School Graduates.* Berkeley: Center for Research and Development in Higher Education, University of California, 1967.

Higher Education's
Newest Student*

K. PATRICIA CROSS

Director, College and University
Programs Educational Testing Service

College students have long been a source of fascination to the American people who are alternately proud, angry, amused, baffled and bewildered by each succeeding college generation. The protesting activist of the 1960s appeared in startling contrast to the silent generation of the 1950s. The veterans of the late 1940s brought new academic intensity to the campuses that had coped with the enthusiastic cause-chasers of the 1930s. Such characterizations reflect the changing interests and values within the broader society. But the change in the American college student population of the 1960s is more fundamental. Higher education's newest students are not the traditional college students with new values; they are in fact students new to higher education. The new backgrounds, motivations, and abilities which they bring are challenging time-honored forms of higher education.

Higher education has just about reached the saturation point for the bright youth from the upper socioeconomic levels, since 80 to 90 percent of this group are now in college. The newest college student is necessarily going to come from the second and third quartiles in ability and the lower socioeconomic strata of our society.

Unlike the protesting activist who casts an image of new values for the 1960s, the coming generation represents a quite different segment of our society. The activist is in reality the traditional college student—albeit perhaps in wolf's clothing. He is the bright child of liberal, affluent, college-educated parents, and he is a product of the culturally and educationally advantaged environment that has been represented in the college-going

* Permission has been granted by Educational Testing Service to reprint, with adaptations by the author, this article first appearing in the *1968 Proceedings of the Western Regional Conference on Testing Problems.*

population of this country for a hundred years. Furthermore he attends the oldest and most selective of the traditional four-year colleges and universities. In vivid contrast to this student, is higher education's newest student. He represents the American goal of universal higher education. He comes from the lower socioeconomic levels, and he has less academic aptitude and lower motivation for intellectual pursuits than the traditional college student. He is to be found, not in the well-established four-year college, but in the emerging junior and community colleges.

Over the past decade, researchers have collected a vast array of facts about the characteristics of students. I have attempted to synthesize these data into a coherent picture of today's junior college student—giving special attention to the ways in which he differs from the traditional college student for whom the present system of higher education is planned. While both the quality and quantity of research are sufficient to permit useful generalizations, it should be remembered that to generalize is to ignore temporarily the infinite variety of individuals and institutions.

A fundamental characteristic differentiating two-year college students from four-year college students in the 1960s is the socioeconomic background from which they come. In America we have long attempted to perpetuate the folklore that it is not who your parents are or what your background is, but rather what you are and where you are going that counts. It is only recently that we have faced the reality that family background plays a very large role in determining what an individual is and, perhaps to some extent, what he is capable of becoming. We now know, through educational research, that various indices of the socioeconomic status of the parents bear an important relationship to who goes to college, where they go, how long they stay, and even why they go. Let me document that rather sweeping statement with some research data.

In a longitudinal study of some 10,000 high school graduates recently reported by James Trent and Leland Medsker [12] of the Center for Higher Education at the University of California at Berkeley, it was found that most children of upper socioeconomic families entered college regardless of their ability; 84 percent of the upper two-fifths in ability entered college, but 57 percent of those in the lowest two-fifths of the class also went to college. The proportions, for the same ability levels, of those entering college from the lower socioeconomic levels were less than one-half of these. The bright child of a father who worked at a low level job had about a 41 percent chance of going to college, and if he also had low ability, his chances fell to 20 percent.

The figures are just about as dramatic when the question posed is *where* young people go to college. Two large national studies [1, 3] reported that approximately two-thirds of the students attending private universities were the children of college-educated fathers, whereas the proportion of this group in junior and state colleges dropped to about one-third. There are, of course, numerous ways of measuring socioeconomic status, and Project Talent [3] used seven different indices, including mother's and father's education, father's occupation, number of books in the home, whether or not the student had a room, desk, typewriter of his own at home, and so on. They found that the junior college group fell between the noncollege and four-year college group *on every index* of socioeconomic status.

In other words, America's newest college student has spent the first 17 years of his life in a different cultural environment from that of the students we're accustomed to teaching in college. He is less likely to have seen good books and magazines around the home, less likely to have been able to retreat to a room of his own, and less likely to have been exposed to discussions of world affairs at the dinner table. Research to date indicates that students reflect rather faithfully the interest and concerns of their parents.

One of the natural accompaniments of a home which is intellectually oriented is an interest in college on the part of the parents and the students. SCOPE, which is an acronym for School to College: Opportunities for Post-secondary Education, is a longitudinal study of some 90,000 high school students as they enter the adult world of jobs, college, or marriage. The research, sponsored by the College Entrance Examination Board, is presently underway at the Center for Higher Education at Berkeley under the direction of Dr. Dale Tillery. The first wave of data from the SCOPE study is now in, and it offers testimony to the important role played by the parents in the higher education of their children. SCOPE data show that students who entered four-year colleges were much more likely to receive parental encouragement than either those who did not enter college or those who entered junior colleges. Not only were the parents of college students more definitely interested in further education, but they were also more likely to have expressed an opinion to their children. Almost half (47 percent) of the young people who did not enter college perceived no particular parental interest in the matter. Twenty percent of the junior college group and only 14 percent of the four-year college students reported this type of parental indifference.[11]

One might hypothesize that the student who started college despite the relative indifference of parents would be more likely to be highly motivated to complete his college education. But this appears not to be the case. Parental attitudes toward college also bear a strong relationship to *persistence* in college. Seventy percent of the college students who remained in college over the four-year period of the Medsker-Trent [8] Study had stated, as high school seniors, that their parents definitely wanted them to attend college. Only 48 percent of the students dropping out during the four-year period felt that college was important to their parents; for bright high school seniors who did not attend college, only 15 percent reported having received parental encouragement.[12]

The obvious question to be raised in discussing parental encouragement on the part of those in the lower income brackets is, is consideration of higher education stifled because of the expense involved? If so, students appear not to recognize it in their answers to questionnaire items. In the SCOPE survey, only 1 percent of the high school seniors who entered junior or senior colleges and 5 percent of the noncollege youth stated that their parents would like for them to go to college but felt that they couldn't afford it. When asked, "What do you think is the one most likely reason you might not go to college?", only about 14 percent of each group (noncollege, junior college and senior college) picked "too costly." The data collected by the American Council on Education[1] are similar. Roughly one-third of both junior and senior college freshmen said they had *no* concern about finances; only about ten percent of each group confessed to having a "major concern" about financing a college education. To judge from the questionnaire responses, approximately equal proportions of junior and senior college students worry about money for higher education.

And yet, the sources of money for college are quite obviously different for the two-year and four-year college freshmen surveyed by the ACE.[1] Junior college students tended to lead senior college students in the percentages obtaining money through employment during college, summer employment and personal savings. Larger percentages of four-year college students reported receiving scholarships, parental aid, federal government assistance and loans. The sources of financial assistance reflect, in part, the financial aid available in the junior and senior colleges; scholarships and parental assistance are more likely to be available to the four-year college student, whereas the junior college student is forced to rely more heavily on his own resources.

More dramatic behavioral data are provided by Medsker and Trent's study[9] of the college attendance rates in 16 cities which were similar in demographic and industrial features but different in the type of public college available in the community. It was found that the impact of local opportunities for college was most vivid for the high ability students from low socioeconomic levels. Whereas 80 percent of the bright youth from high socioeconomic backgrounds went to college, even if there were none in the local community, only 22 percent of the lower socioeconomic group of the *same level of ability* entered college when there were no local colleges.

The presence of a junior college more than doubled the likelihood of college for bright students whose fathers were employed at the lower occupational levels. In junior college communities, 53 percent of the bright students from lower socioeconomic levels entered college, whereas in communities with no public college facilities, only 22 percent of such students entered college. Between these extremes were the other communities studied by Medsker and Trent.[9] Colleges in the multiple-college communities enrolled 49 percent of bright low socioeconomic youth, state college towns 41 percent and extension center localities 35 percent.

One can argue that the existence of a junior college in the local community attracts new students to higher education because of the reduction in cost, because of the "educational awareness" brought to the community, or because less intense motivation is required for continuing education in the same community. Perhaps all three factors are usually involved.

The fact that low socioeconomic status consists of many interrelated variables—limited financial resources, low parental education, little interest in cultural and educational pursuits—makes any attempt to separate financial considerations from the context in which they occur extremely difficult. The ambiguity between questionnaire responses and college-going behavior raises some rather basic questions. When we ask the student how concerned he is about financing a college education, for example, we don't often know much about his frame of reference when he answers. The wealthy student going to a high-cost private college may state that he has "no concern" about finances, but the same response might be given by the student who is attending a low-tuition junior college in a city where he knows he can work part-time and live at home. Furthermore, the student's motivation influences his perception of the cost of a college education. For some students, college would be worth any price; for others the necessity of giving up a car would rule out college as "too costly."

In evaluating the role of finances, it is also necessary to give some consideration to how much the student knows about the subject. Knoell and Medsker [7] found that many students reported in interviews that they had made very unrealistic estimates of the cost of attending college away from home. They also found that among the junior college students who had completed transfer to a four-year college, financial problems ranked first among the reasons for withdrawal. Forty percent checked "lack of money" as one reason for dropping out.

The relative importance of dollars and cents cost of college cannot be accurately assessed with the research data presently available. Certainly it must be considered a factor related to who goes to college, where they go, and how long they stay. But I also stated earlier that home environment and circumstances had something to do with *why* young people seek a college education.

Most research is in agreement that students entering junior colleges are influenced more by practical considerations and less by intellectual interests than are their peers in four year colleges.[2, 6, 10] "Academic reputation" is the most common reason for the selection of a university, whereas "low cost" and "close to home" frequently lead all other reasons given for attending a junior college. When high school seniors in the SCOPE study [11] were asked what type of college they would *like* to attend even if they were not now planning to enter college, the students who later entered four-year colleges were more likely to select a college description which involved emphasis upon studying, serious discussions with faculty, and the availability of concerts and lectures than were junior college and non-college youth who tended to prefer a college emphasizing vocational training. By and large, junior college students tend to major in the applied fields and Knoell and Medsker [5] found that over half of the junior college students were enrolled in business administration, engineering, and education, even after transfer to a four-year institution.

The business-practical orientation of the junior college student is further illustrated by the personal objectives which he considers "essential" or "very important." In responding to each of 17 objectives in the ACE questionnaire, the percentage of junior college students exceeded that for four-year college students by as much as 7 percent on only two objectives —to be well off financially and to succeed in business. Senior college freshmen were more likely than junior college students to attribute importance to objectives such as helping others in difficulty, joining the Peace Corps or VISTA, becoming a community leader, keeping up with political affairs, and developing a philosophy of life.[1] Whereas young people from the upper socioeconomic levels tend to see the college experience as an opportunity for intellectual stimulation and the development of the mind, the children from lower socioeconomic families are more likely to see a college education as the pathway to better jobs and upward social mobility.

These differing interests of groups of students are quite apparent in their responses to direct questions regarding their educational goals. But more subtle measures of personality characteristics reinforce these findings. Data from the SCOPE study [11] reveal large differences between the intellectual interests of noncollege youth and junior and senior college students. Dale Tillery and his colleagues in the SCOPE research used a short experimental intellectual disposition scale. This scale, which was derived from the Omnibus Personality Inventory, measures characteristics such as flexibility, openness to new ideas, interest in ideas for their own sake rather than for their practical application, and the like. The scale clearly differentiated among the four-year college students, junior college students and noncollege youth. Fifty-nine percent of the four-year college students, 36 percent of the junior college students and only 23 percent of the noncollege group scored in the top third on this measure of intellectual interest.

To no one's surprise, intellectual interests tend to parallel intellectual ability. The SCOPE study also involved the administration of a brief test of academic aptitude to the high school seniors in the sample. When the test scores were grouped into the top, middle, and lowest thirds, it was found that 71 percent of the students who entered four-year colleges scored in the top one-third compared with 36 percent of the junior college students and only 16 percent of the noncollege youth. While virtually all research is in agreement that across broad samples, four-year college freshmen make higher mean scores than two-year college students on almost any of the traditional tests of academic ability, it should be remembered that there are individual junior college students who score very high, indeed, on tests of intellectual ability and there are junior colleges in this country whose students make higher mean scores than those in some four-year colleges.

It should be quite obvious, by this time, that today's junior college students are not seeking what we have come to regard as quality in traditional higher education. The problem, I submit, is not in the students but in our singular model for excellence in post-secondary education. There is some evidence that our secondary schools have also adopted an academic model that may be quite inappropriate for large numbers of students. Worse yet, rather than implementing the educational goal of helping young people to develop their potential, we may be doing considerable damage to the self-esteem and feelings of worth of the majority of young people.

It is painfully obvious that higher education's newest students do not fit the academic mold in their concepts of themselves. The SCOPE data [11] show that 57 percent of the four-year students felt that they were "definitely able" to do college work, but only 29 percent of those entering junior colleges expressed such confidence. Students' estimates of their teachers' ratings of them followed the same pattern; 75 percent of the four-year college group felt that their high school teachers would rate them good or excellent students, whereas this confidence dropped to 41 percent for junior college students. Junior college students were more likely than four-year college students to feel that their high school teachers went too fast and they were less likely to feel that their teachers understood them.

The feelings of academic inferiority of the junior college student were also expressed in the ACE questionnaire [1] which listed 17 traits and asked students to indicate the abilities on which they felt they were "above average."

The pattern of different abilities in the two-year and four-year college groups was apparent in the students' answers. Large proportions of senior college students rated themselves above average on traits such as academic ability, drive to achieve, leadership ability, mathematical ability, intellectual self-confidence, and writing ability. The *only* traits on which larger proportions of junior college students than four-year college students rated themselves above average were: athletic ability, artistic ability, defensiveness, and mechanical ability.

The SCOPE questionnaire [11] used a somewhat different form of question for studying student perceptions of their abilities. Whereas the ACE questionnaire asked students to indicate the abilities on which they felt they were "above average," the SCOPE questionnaire asked for their "best" abilities. The differences between percentages for junior and senior college groups were extremely small in both approaches, but the patterns were consistent. High school seniors in the SCOPE study who later entered four-year colleges reported that their best abilities were in reading, mathematics, writing, music, conversation, and public speaking. The junior college group had large proportions stating that their best abilities were: working with tools and machines, painting and drawing, sports, and cooking or sewing. Both the ACE and SCOPE data suggest a tendency for the more academically oriented senior college students to feel competent in the academic and verbal pursuits, whereas the junior college students perceive their strengths in the nonacademic tasks.

Certainly we need to explore further students' feelings about their own abilities. Is the school experience so pervasive that the nonacademically oriented student learns to respond generally with "below average"— or are there areas, perhaps not related to present school activities, in which he could experience success and feelings of personal worth?

One cannot help observing that there is little in most elementary and secondary school programs which is designed to help the less academically oriented achieve a more successful school experience. And this observation is reflected in the responses of the students. The SCOPE noncollege group showed the greatest dissatisfaction with the amount of freedom which was permitted in selecting high school courses, whereas the four-year college students indicated the least desire for change in this area. It is also of interest to observe that 83 percent of the four-year college group found their high school courses "very useful" as preparation for college; a much smaller proportion (48 percent) of the noncollege group found the courses useful for their immediate futures in the labor market.

One thing stands out clearly in this review: we possess only traditional measures to describe a student who does not fit the tradition. The inevitable result is that we picture America's newest college student as being less adequate than his peers at the tasks of higher education—*as those tasks have been developed over the years for a different type of student.* We must conclude that intellectual dimensions sharply differentiate junior college students, as a group, from senior college students. The junior college student is less able—on our *present* tests; he is less intellectually oriented—on our *present* measures; and he is less motivated to seek higher education—in our *traditional* types of colleges. If we pose the same tasks for all institutions of higher education, then we run the risk of having the junior college become a watered-down version of the four-year college. Such an eventuality, of course, would subvert the purpose and concept of the junior college, one of the most challenging innovations in higher education of this century.

It hardly seems likely that we will "help each student develop to his fullest potential" by offering a single scheme of opportunities, rewards, and punishments. The great future task is to investigate the ways in which the junior college student differs in *kind,* or in pattern of abilities, rather than in *degree* from the traditional college student.

Arthur Jensen [4] notes that: "Literal equality of educational opportunity—if interpreted to mean that we treat all children exactly alike—makes as much sense as a doctor giving all his patients exactly the same prescription. Even giving every patient different amounts of the same medication would be disastrous. The parallel in education is to be avoided also."

If we wish to avoid offering a weak senior college prescription to the junior college student, then we must begin the long and difficult search for new measures and new programs specifically designed for higher education's newest student.

REFERENCES

1. ASTIN, A. W., R. J. PANOS, and J. A. CREAGER, "National Norms for Entering College Freshmen—Fall, 1966," *ACE Research Reports.* Washington, D.C.: American Council on Education, 1967, 2(1).
2. BAIRD, L. L., "Family Income and the Characteristics of College-bound Students," *ACT Research Reports.* Iowa City: American College Testing Program, February, 1967, p. 17.
3. COOLEY, W. W. and S. J. BECKER, "The Junior College Student," *Personnel and Guidance Journal,* 44(5) (January, 1966), 464–69.
4. JENSEN, A. M., "How Much Can We Boost IQ and Scholastic Achievement?" California Advisory Council on Educational Research, Research Resume No. 35, Burlingame: California Teachers Association, November, 1967.
5. KNOELL, D. M. and L. L. MEDSKER, *Articulation Between Two-Year and Four-Year Colleges.* USOE Cooperative Research Project No. 2167.

Berkeley: Center for Research and Development in Higher Education, University of California, 1964.

6. ————, *Factors Affecting Performance of Transfer Students from Two- to Four-Year Colleges: With Implications for Coordination and Articulation.* USOE Cooperative Research Project No. 1133. Berkeley: Center for Research and Development in Higher Education, University of California, 1964.

7. ————, "From Junior to Senior College: A National Study of the Transfer Student." Washington, D.C.: American Council on Education, 1966.

8. MEDSKER, L. L. and J. W. TRENT, *Factors Affecting College Attendance of High School Graduates from Varying Socioeconomic and Ability Levels.* USOE Cooperative Research Project No. 438. Berkeley: Center for Research and Development in Higher Education, University of California, 1965.

9. ————, *The Influence of Different Types of Public Higher Institutions on College Attendance from Varying Socioeconomic and Ability Levels.* USOE Cooperative Research Project No. 438. Berkeley: Center for Research and Development in Higher Education, University of California, 1965.

10. RICHARDS, J. M., JR. and L. A. BRASKAMP, "Who Goes Where to Junior College," *ACT Research Reports.* Iowa City: American College Testing Program, July, 1967, p. 20.

11. SCOPE, "School to College: Opportunities for Postsecondary Education." Unpublished data from Center for Research and Development in Higher Education, University of California, Berkeley, 1968.

12. TRENT, J. W. and L. L. MEDSKER, *Beyond High School: A Study of 10,000 High School Graduates.* Berkeley: Center for Research and Development in Higher Education, University of California, 1967.

Student Personnel Work
and Minority Groups

JOHNNIE R. CLARKE

Assistant Dean of Academic Affairs
St. Petersburg Junior College

The community junior college has included student personnel services as one of its major functions. Implementation of student personnel programs differs from college to college, but the emphasis on services to facilitate effective student development remains constant.

All the functions of student personnel services, as generally agreed upon, are as essential for minority group students as they are for the junior college population as a whole. The thesis of this chapter is that these services must be extended in order to meet the special needs of minority group students.

The open-door admission policy has made the community junior college the most important avenue to higher education for minority group students. Although present enrollment of these students is low, the community junior college will increasingly receive a larger proportion of them. As employment demands for persons with post-high school education increase and university requirements for admission continue to become more selective, more and more minority group students will enter the junior college. The import of this is almost alarming. The Carnegie Report of 1965 pointed out that "not many junior colleges have student personnel programs whose adequacy even approaches the importance of the task to be done." [5] Added to this needed improvement in the present services offered is the special need to make provisions to minority group students who also must be served. The resultant strain on personnel and resources will be a test of the commitment of the administration and of the staff to the philosophy of the junior college and to the philosophy of personnel services.

Minority Group Defined

The term "minority group students" is used in this chapter to designate those groups of students who differ from the majority group in some identifiable ethnic or racial traits. In other words, such groups as Negroes, Indians, Mexicans, and Puerto Ricans can be classed as "minority group students." The term also includes the status assigned these groups and the resultant effects of this designation. Such groups usually are composed of persons who have had no opportunity:

to grow up in home, neighborhood, and school environments that might enable them to utilize their ability and personality potentials fully; they are at a disadvantage in school, and in after-school and out-of-school situations. It is because of these disadvantages, reflecting environmental deprivations and experiential atypicalities, that certain children may be referred to as "minority group children." [7]

Although minority group students will be discussed in general, special reference to black or Negro students will be the dominant theme. Since this group represents the largest and most visible of the minority groups, concern for this group is more intense.

At this point it should be made clear that the labels "black" and "Negro" will be used interchangeably. It should be noted that there is little or no agreement among or within any of the minority groups on labels of reference. Many minority groups have arrived at a point of adjustment in the mainstream of American life to feel that they are Americans and resent any racial or country-of-origin labels. The American Indian, on the other hand, regards his label as a source of pride. Until recently, the Negro's racial referent was considered by him and others as a stigma of inferiority. The practice of assigning group referent labels is in itself odious. It serves to perpetuate differences and traditionally these differences serve as a status reference of superiority and inferiority.

In the case of the Negro, it is postulated that the label "black" serves to produce in-group feelings of confidence and pride. Whether the term is successful in doing this is questionable. Many Negroes feel that it is a popular term serving to produce superficial evidence of race pride. Those who feel this way have been through the "nigger," "colored," and "Negro" cycle. The label "black," when used by advocators of the term, is not a racial or color designation; it is used to designate persons who have some African ancestry; it includes in its meaning a people with a past, with a history of kings and thieves, glorious kingdoms and hovels, successes and failures. If referent labels are used in dealing with this minority, and it appears that such labels will be a part of American society for a long time to come, the student personnel staff should ascertain from the group what label they prefer.

If student personnel workers in the junior college are to assist minority group students in operating effectively in the social and academic environment of the college, they will need to plan for purposeful environmental intervention. Each area of service, therefore, will be discussed in terms of its structuring in order to assist these students to achieve the highest possible realization of their potential. Student personnel functions as delineated in the Carnegie Report will serve as the frame of reference for this chapter.

ORIENTATION FUNCTIONS

PRE-COLLEGE ORIENTATION

Most minority group students receive secondary education in schools which support the expectations and values of the majority middle class. The schools do little to raise their level of aspiration, to furnish models for identification, and to develop deferred gratification.[3] Most of their experiences and their communication have been informal. The informality of their life-style leaves them ill-prepared to cope with the formal aspects of admission requirements, registration procedures, and the sophistication of financial aid applications. The very strict, orderly procedures for college inquiries and the subsequent impersonal relationships which accompany college enrollment discourage the minority group student from seeking admission.

The environmental influences of minority group students far too often deprecate the value of college education. To desire post-high school education for these students is often beyond the expectations of their families, their peers, and their teachers. In fact, these groups tend to depress the educational aspirations of the students. The school, with its poor record for assisting minority group students, plays a major role in setting their aspiration level.[1, 8, 6] Malcolm X, in his autobiography, recalls that he wanted to be a lawyer but his teacher suggested that he aspire to do something with his hands.

When a student from a minority group, in spite of his environmental conditions, manages to attain senior high school status, it is significant evidence that the student has a great deal of mobility. It is at this level that the junior college counselors can have great influence in directing his striving toward post-high school education.

A first step is for those persons on the student personnel staff responsible for recruiting, orientation, program planning, career guidance, and personal-social counseling to secure from the administration a commitment to provide programs which will help minority group students toward their educational goals. The staff must ascertain whether the administration is willing to provide the personnel and other resources which will be required to help these students to move into the academic mainstream.

A second step is to develop a working relationship with the high school counseling staff and with other agencies in the community concerned with high school and college students. The nature of these relationships should be one in which each group can define its group role as a team member working for the mutual benefit of students and the team.

A third step is to set up a counseling arrangement either in the high school or at some easily accessible place within the community. The selection of an off-campus counseling operation is dependent upon the location of the junior college. If the college is located in an area where it can be easily reached by the students the college wishes to help, then this step would be unnecessary. An off-campus counseling center would require that a student personnel team, including students, be available at the high school for assisting prospective students in making application, requesting financial aid, planning programs, and acquainting them with registration procedures. Counseling functions related to testing and career planning could also begin at these centers.

This type of organization would have the advantage of close contact with the high school counselors, easy access to student records, and a familiar atmosphere in which to work. Further, by using junior college students who are graduates of the high school as team members, the college can demonstrate its effectiveness and its interest. As a by-product, this center may serve as a source of motivation for post-high school education, influencing in a positive way the dropout rate.

Another type of recruitment operation can be achieved by setting up a counseling center in the community. Some of the junior colleges near urban areas have set up centers in the inner-city. The junior colleges can maintain counseling personnel and students at the center to carry on all the student personnel functions related to pre-college orientation, admissions, registration, and financial assistance. Students are contacted by the staff wherever they can be found. Some walk in, some are sent in by various agencies, and others are solicited from local student gathering places. This type of operation involves a more elaborate organizational structure and requires additional funds, but where it has been used, it has proved to be an effective means of pre-college recruitment and orientation.

Pre-college orientation using either of these plans tends to help the minority group student overcome his antipathy toward the formality of college procedures. Pre-college orientation makes movement into the college a more familiar process, and helps the student to develop feelings of self-confidence. This increase in his ability to cope as a result of his knowledge of college programs and procedures tends to enhance and sustain feelings of academic mobility. It is expected that students who have been exposed to pre-college orientation as proposed here and who have experienced the attendant interest manifested by such an experience will move toward the development of the motivation desired.[15]

COLLEGE ORIENTATION

Minority group students are less familiar with the formal atmosphere of the junior college. They are less apt to explore the unfamiliar environment. They are uncomfortable in the presence of so many unknowns. They are reluctant to ask directions for fear of betraying their lack of information.[1] Therefore, the college orientation period which is usually sufficient for other students should be extended for a longer period of time for minority students. This extension does not have to be and should not be a formally organized group activity for minority group students exclusively. This would accentuate their differences and defeat the purpose of orientation.

It should be, if at all possible, a counselor-initiated activity designed to acquaint the student with those aspects of college life which most students discover by themselves. Directives and procedures which are usually given in large orientation sessions should be reinforced in informal casual settings. Continuous contacts with these students in structured or unstructured situations should be deliberately sought. Informal introductions to student activities such as encouraging visits to meetings of those organized groups which are open to all students should be made. Informal introductions to staff persons in charge of various operations of the college such as the bookstore, the registrar's office, the financial aid office, and the library should be arranged by the counselors. These types of purposeful activities help the student to personalize his dealings with these offices and assist him in broadening his perception of the college. When the minority group student is enabled to bring the routine operational aspects of the college within his perceptual field and develops the ability to cope with these routinized operations, he becomes more and more accepting of other experiences at the college.

The student personnel staff should be aware that students seldom read college catalogs and student handbooks. Much of this information is communicated (correctly or incorrectly) from student to student. Counselors can become a part of this mainstream of communication if they will leave their offices to spend part of their time with students in casual sessions around the campus. Both counselors and students can learn much from each other in informal exchange in the lounges and other areas where students gather. It is in this type of exchange that the minority group student becomes more communicative and begins to develop feelings of belonging.

APPRAISAL FUNCTIONS

RECORDS

Assessment of secondary school records of minority group students requires knowledge of the type of high school, the type of curriculum offered, and the type of experiences students had at the school. The usual criteria used for assessing records of other students are insufficient for making judgments about minority group students.

It is in the area of record evaluation that the minority group student is dealt one of the cruelest blows. Where the nature of the secondary school academic experience is unknown, a "good" record may be over-rated, while a "fair" record may be underrated and the student may find himself with a program of studies which is either too boring or too difficult.

The student personnel staff should study the nature of the secondary school experience and the nature of the environment of the minority group schools in order to make a more accurate assessment of the records of these students. Some junior colleges have solved this problem by employing members of minority groups as a part of the personnel staff. The success of this practice is dependent upon the personality and competency of the person employed and the type of atmosphere provided within the employment situation.

Other junior colleges have used the results of research, both nationally and locally, for the prediction of success of minority group students. The results of such data gathered from follow-up studies, predictive measures, and other studies of behavior have been used as the basis for making record appraisals. A combination of the two approaches is far more successful than either of them alone. When the staff of the college designs its own research for use as a basis for appraisals, a more accurate assessment of its students can be made. It should be noted that whatever method of appraisal of records is used, the person making the judgment should be familiar with the background of students who are being appraised.

TESTING

Testing and the use of test data have been severely criticized as a means for making decisions about minority group students. It is claimed that standardized tests: "(1) may not provide reliable differentiation in the range of the minority group's scores, (2) may have quite different predictive validity for minority groups than for the standardization and validation groups, and (3) strongly depend for their interpretation upon an adequate understanding of the social and cultural background of the group in question." [7]

It is also claimed that the cultural bias of standardized tests makes them unsuitable for use with minority group students. Admittedly, the tests are culturally biased, but so is the whole educative process. The academic degree or certificate which the student is pursuing is a culturally determined symbol of the attainment of a culturally developed set of objectives. Therefore, a testing program designed to determine the academic needs of students as a means of assisting them to move more successfully toward their objectives is educationally sound. "In spite of their typical cultural bias, standardized tests should not be sold short as a means for making objective assessments of the traits of minority group children." [7]

Caution should be taken in making normative interpretations of the scores of minority group students. Special cautions should be taken in interpreting the scores of these students on personality inventories, interest inventories, and tests of values or beliefs. Here the cultural differences will be more pronounced and a thorough understanding of the student's background should be known before conclusions are drawn.[11]

Testing programs designed to gather both cognitive and affective data about students will provide a better index for advising or programming minority group students, and other students as well, than data gathered from either of the areas alone. Behavioral research has revealed that a student's academic progress is influenced by affective factors as well as cognitive factors.[12]

Non-intellective factors appear to be positively related to student success and should be considered by junior colleges as an added factor in the placement of remedial students. Measurements from different kinds of tests, surveys, and inventories can aid in the prediction of college success, aid the counselor, and designate needed objectives.[18]

A recent study conducted by the writer showed that the way in which the junior college student perceives himself and the school environment is an essential factor in academic success. In the case of Negro males, it appeared that predictors of academic success can be based solely on affective measures.[4]

Courses of study based upon both affective and cognitive data will expose the student to a more relevant curriculum. Relevance, in this case, means that the curriculum will be suited to the needs, objectives, and abilities of the student. Thus, successful academic adjustment at the junior college is almost assured not only for minority group students but for other students as well.

When test data are collected to make judgments about a group's behavior, extreme caution should be taken in drawing conclusions and applying them to individual cases. Good counseling techniques require each individual to be appraised in terms of his own potentialities. What is good for one minority group member is not necessarily good for the entire group.

One means of assisting the student personnel staff in the use of test data is to develop local norms.[16] Such norms serve as a more secure basis for making comparisons both for the minority group student and for other students. They also provide a more adequate base for prediction.

APPLICANT APPRAISAL

When the staff has collected all the data concerning students—records, tests, interviews—and the final steps are made to assist the student in the choice of curriculum, it is necessary to note the hidden motivation of many minority group students. Membership in a minority group and the rigors of the life-style of the group often appear to develop an ability to "jump gaps." Many of these students who do not meet the regular criteria for placement seem to overcome discrepancies in background and are able to compete successfully with other students.[2] Although there is little or no research to support this position, the records of many students who have succeeded will attest to the validity of this assumption. This seems to occur whether the school environment is accepting or rejecting.[9]

Appraisals of minority group students should always be as objective as that of other students, but should also take into account the life-style of the group as well as the demands of the academic community. There should be an open, frank discussion of the appraisal with the student, always focusing on the truth of the situation. Claude Brown in his autobiography of a black boy growing up in Harlem recalled that there was one man the gang could trust because he would not lie to them. When the counselor takes on the function of appraisal, he should be aware that he becomes for the minority group student the mediator between the student and the curriculum as well as between the student and the college as a whole. Therefore, he should always assist the student in seeing the reality of the total appraisal process.

CONSULTATION FUNCTIONS

STUDENT COUNSELING

Counseling minority group students is no different than counseling other students. Problems occur when the cultural bias of the counselor enters into the situation. Minority group students often complain that the counselor doesn't understand them or that the counselor regards them as all alike. The complaint is more often true than not. A counselor often has little knowledge of the background of minority group students and tends to order the counseling session in terms of his own value orientation. Even when the counselor attempts to be unbiased, minority group students take their cues from visible gestures such as a raised eyebrow, a frown, a smile, and so on. These students are adept at reading visual signs.

If the real premises of counseling are employed, the counselor will recognize that each student brings to the counseling conference a different set of values, attitudes, interests, and abilities regardless of his group membership.[12] When the counselor has some knowledge of these differences and takes them into account during the counseling sessions, all students can benefit from the counseling services.

Many junior colleges have felt it necessary to employ Negro counselors to whom the minority group students can relate. To hire a counselor from a particular minority group in order to provide an identity figure for students from that group is no assurance that the purpose will be achieved. All Negro students do not relate to a Negro counselor. The counselor may be "whitewashed." An American Indian counselor does not necessarily become an identity figure for American Indian students at the college.[21] In many cases the counselor from the minority group is rejected by the group.

What is important is the ability of the counselor and the nature of the counseling situation. Good counselors can provide beneficial services for all students. Counselors who have no knowledge of the life-style of minority group students and who are unable to structure a warm and accepting, help-giving relationship will fail in their services to minority group students and will, in all probability, fail with other students.

In the case of the Negro student, it is essential that counselors exert special efforts to help create an academic environment in which these students can develop feelings of personal worth.

It may be extremely difficult to upgrade the academic achievement of the disadvantaged Negro child without first providing an atmosphere in which the child can more fully discover and respect himself. The probelm is of such magnitude as to warrant a concerted attempt to train prospective teachers and counselors in the mechanics of self-theory and methodology of changing self-esteem.[20]

Much of the defensiveness of Negroes, especially the males, can be attributed to the lack of feelings of personal worth and dignity. Therefore, it is imperative that counselors use every means they can to help create a climate which will foster the academic and social growth of minority group students.

A look at the counseling services presently provided by the junior college to minority group students will reveal that many more of these students are benefiting from the services than the popular media would lead one to believe. The demand for black counselors, black teachers and black curricula is a reaction of a vocal few to the behavior of a few poor counselors, poor teachers, and a nonrelevant curriculum. To meet the demands does not necessarily mean that the needs will be met. The underlying cause for the protest is just as legitimate for the other students as for the black students.

It must be noted that counselors are often caught between the needs of the students and the institutional offerings. Attempts to fit the needs of the students into the existing curriculum have produced academic misfits and college "push-outs." The student personnel staff in these cases should become the initiators of curriculum change; the staff should make known the curriculum needs of the students, and should become involved in curriculum development to meet these needs.[13] Often the source of student discontent is found in the inability of the college to serve the real academic needs of the students. The necessity to meet these needs is even greater in the junior college than in the senior universities and colleges. With an open-door policy, the college obligates itself to make provisions for the successful pursuit of its programs to all persons who are admitted.[14]

CAREER COUNSELING

Minority group students, especially Negroes, are often limited in career choices. They know very little about career opportunities other than the traditional careers of the members of their group. Aspirations for other types of careers, until recently, were usually stymied by the school and society. Knowledge of new careers should be an essential part of career counseling for minority group students. They need to know what career opportunities are available; they need to identify their own areas of interest; they need to know what is involved in career choices; they need to know how to plan a goal attainment strategy; and, they need to know what alternatives they have. Such knowledge will help the minority group student make realistic, attainable goal choices.[19]

Career planning for minority group students involves more than the traditional interview, testing, and advisement. It should include explorations of occupational clusters, the skills and knowledges needed for the pursuit of these occupations, and opportunities for future success in these jobs. More time will be needed for extensive and intensive testing and for student-counselor contacts. Foremost in the process should be a clear exploration of the reality of the student's capabilities. The counselor should make certain that the student understands his own potentialities, understands the choices involved and realizes the consequences of his choice. The counselor, on the other hand, should be certain he understands the background of the students, the pressures which come from the student's membership in a minority group and how all these affect his aspirations.

A few junior colleges have provided career planning assistance through special credit or noncredit courses designed to assist the student in personal and social planning. Some of these courses have used a system's approach to plot the steps from goal conception and analysis to goal attainment. Extra help has been given to minority group students in these courses in specially scheduled counseling sessions. Some junior colleges have attempted to meet this need through an orientation course. The success of either approach has yet to be assessed. But whether or not the college uses an individual or group approach, the need is so severe that any in-depth method used to assist minority group students in making realistic career decisions is justifiable.

PARTICIPATIVE FUNCTIONS

Participation by minority group students in student activities as an extension of the curricular activities are noticeably lacking. This is to be expected since the possibility of elected leadership positions are very slim and since many club memberships are solicited by invitation only or have requirements which minority group students often cannot meet. There are instances where a member of a minority group has been elected to office but these instances are so rare that they receive wide coverage by both student and national publications. The paucity of numbers and the lack of political acumen often depress the interest of minority group students.

Responsibility for involving students in co-curricular activities has been abdicated by the college in the name of student rights and freedom. In the case of minority group students, the assumption is made that they prefer to be left alone with their "own kind." It appears that somewhere in this dilemma the student personnel program has a significant responsibility. A minority group student will not generally participate in co-curricular activities without some extra push. This is not to advocate taking him by the hand and leading him, but it does suggest that some type of appropriate action should be taken by the personnel staff.

In many cases black student organizations have come into being as a result of feeling left out. The militancy of these organizations is often an attempt to seek recognition and to compensate for a lack of involvement. Within the context of a given college, such organizations may be of constructive value to black students, but the necessity of having organizations for various ethnic or racial groups should never exist.

The difference between a student's involvement or noninvolvement may be a suggestion from a sponsor or a counselor. The extent to which the staff wishes to assume responsibility for student involvement has to be determined within the context of the philosophy or the commitment of the department, but whether or not there should be involvement is a moot question.

The student personnel staffs of some junior colleges have encouraged involvement by purposely seeking out minority group students to invite them to certain student activities. Some have used tutors as liaison persons for the student activity program. In junior colleges where student activities are primarily related to the academic departments, involvement of minority group students will be more open, the students involved will have more person-to-person contacts, and the department activities can be based upon a more immediate bond of relationships. The most difficult task is to devise a plan which will establish with these students the idea that all students have equal access to student activities and that all students are needed and wanted.

REGULATORY FUNCTIONS

The regulatory functions of the student personnel program which apply to other students should affect the minority group student in the same manner. In the area of social regulations, special assistance may be needed by the minority group student. In individual counseling sessions, the counselor can help a student understand the accepted patterns of social ethics and can assist him in acquiring a pattern of social behavior which will be acceptable to the student and to the college.

FACILITATIVE FUNCTIONS

Because of the low incomes of most minority group students, many of them will need financial assistance. Analysis of financial need will reveal many aspects of family life which are different. Counselors assisting students with applications for financial assistance should be aware that the life-style of a minority group family will differ from his own and that the evaluation of financial necessity should be within the context of the applicant's family pattern. Further, these students may need assistance in completing the application forms. When giving such assistance, special care should be taken so that questions which may prove to be embarrassing to minority students will not harm the counseling relationship.

ORGANIZATIONAL FUNCTIONS

In order for the student personnel services to provide effective assistance to minority group students, there must be a philosophical and financial commitment. The administration must show a definite expression of concern for the welfare of minority group students at the junior college. Too often, the affairs of the junior college are so organizationally oriented that the student is the last to be considered. Therefore, in order to develop an atmosphere in which the minority group student will receive the necessary attention for adequate development, the administration must show a definite commitment to this point of view. Further, the administration should periodically ask for progress reports to insure that the college is responding to the needs of minority group students.

Provisions for appropriate and adequate student personnel services for minority group students are dependent upon staff knowlege of the needs and problems of these students. There must be an understanding of the culture of these students and an appreciation of the contributions of their culture to the general society. Where there is inadequate information, the staff should plan some type of in-service program to increase its understanding.

Administrative provisions should be made for the student personnel department to influence curriculum development.[17] There should be a helping relationship between the student personnel staff and the instructional staff. The student personnel staff is most knowledgeable about the academic needs and problems of the students. Their appraisals of students and counseling contacts focus attention on these areas. Therefore, the staff should have orderly and continuous influence upon curriculum development and curriculum change.[10]

In order for the student personnel department to make the necessary adjustments to better serve all students, adequate financing must be available. To service the minority group student in an effective manner requires additional financial resources. Often the staff must be increased in order to provide more individual attention. Institutional philosophical commitment should be accompanied by the necessary financial commitment. It is by far a better policy to support an effective program of student assistance than to create disgruntled students.

More and more minority group students will be coming to the junior college in the future and the problems of their minority status will be more and more acute. There is no choice to face these problems and attempt to develop effective solutions.

REFERENCES

1. BERKOWITZ, LEONARD, *The Development of Motives and Values in the Child*. New York: Basic Books, Inc., 1964, p. 67.
2. CLARK, KENNETH and LAWRENCE PLOTKIN, "The Negro Student at Integrated Colleges: Summary," *Education of the Disadvantaged*, eds. A. Harry Passow, Miriam Goldberg, and Abraham Tannenbaum. New York: Holt, Rinehart & Winston, Inc., 1960, p. 116.
3. CLARKE, JOHNNIE R., "A Curriculum Design for Disadvantaged Junior

College Students." Unpublished dissertation, University of Florida, 1966.

4. ———, "Identification of Disadvantaged Junior College Students and Diagnosis of their Disabilities," St. Petersburg, Florida, 1968. (Mimeographed)

5. COLLINS, CHARLES C., *Junior College Student Personnel Programs: What They Are and What They Should Be.* Washington D.C.: American Association of Junior Colleges, 1967, p. 41.

6. DEUTSCH, MARTIN, "Social Psychological Perspectives on the Development of the Disadvantaged Learner," *Journal of Negro Education,* XXXIII (Summer, 1964), 238.

7. ———, *et al.,* "Guidelines for Testing Minority Group Children," *Journal of Social Issues,* XX (April, 1964), 130.

8. DOUVAN, ELIZABETH, "Social Status and Success Strivings," *Journal of Abnormal and Social Psychology,* LII (March, 1956), 222.

9. EGERTON, JOHN, *Higher Education for "High Risk" Students.* Atlanta: Southern Education Foundation, 1968, p. 50.

10. GARRISON, ROGER, *Junior College Faculty: Issues and Problems.* Washington, D.C.: American Association of Junior Colleges, 1967, p. 66.

11. GOLDBERG, MIRIAM L., "Factors Affecting Educational Attainment in Depressed Areas," *Education of the Disadvantaged,* eds., A. Harry Passow, Miriam Goldberg, and Abraham Tannenbaum. New York: Holt Rinehart & Winston, Inc., 1967, p. 45.

12. HUMPHREYS, J. ANTHONY, ARTHUR E. TRAXLER, and ROBERT D. NORTH, *Guidance Services.* Chicago: Science Research Associates, Inc., 1960, p. 58.

13. LAHTI, ROBERT, "A President's View—Student Personnel Services in the Community College." Paper presented at Student Personnel Workshop William Rainey Harper College, Palatine, Illinois, October, 1968, p. 18.

14. MATSON, JANE, "Trends in Junior College Student Personnel Work." Paper presented at Student Personnel Workshop, William Rainey Harper College, Palatine, Illinois, October, 1968, p. 29.

15. McCLELLAND, DAVID C., "Toward A Theory of Motive Acquisition," *American Psychologist,* XX (May, 1965), 330.

16. RAINES, MAX, "A Last Chance Talk on Student Personnel Work." Paper presented at Student Personnel Workshop, William Rainey Harper College, October, 1968, p. 35.

17. ROBERTSON, GLEN, "The Counselor and the Curriculum," *Junior College Journal,* XXXIX (March, 1969), 74.

18. ROUCHE, JOHN E. *Salvage, Redirection, or Custody?* Washington, D.C.: American Association of Junior Colleges, 1968, p. 48.

19. ——— and David M. Sims, "Open-Door College or Open-Door Curriculum?" *Junior College Journal,* XXXVIII (February, 1968), 19.

20. WILLIAMS, ROBERT L. and HARRY BYARS, "Negro Self-Esteem in Transitional Society," *Personnel and Guidance Journal*, XLVLL (October, 1968), 124.

21. ZINTZ, MILES, "Problems of Classroom Adjustment of Indian Children in Public Elementary Schools in the Southwest," *Education of the Disadvantaged*, eds. A. Harry Passow, Miriam Goldberg, and Abraham Tannenbaum. New York: Holt, Rinehart & Winston, Inc., 1960, p. 88.

The Student's Role
in the Affairs of the College

RICHARD C. RICHARDSON, JR.

President, Northampton Area
Community College

The question of the relationship between an institution of higher education and those who comprise its student body deserves the most careful thought and judgment of all concerned. There is no exact model representative of this relationship. The college is a creation of society designed to serve a number of distinct purposes; chief among these may be included the transmission of culture, the socialization of the individual, and the legitimation of ability, particularly with respect to occupational competencies. In order to achieve these objectives, the institution must create the kind of atmosphere which will ensure the active cooperation of those who are being served in the process.

The act of belonging to, or being served by, an organization involves relinquishing a part of the member's individual freedom of action in order to advance the common welfare and to avoid infringing upon the rights of others. From this statement we may conclude that it will be necessary for any institution of higher education to establish a framework within which students may operate, just as it must establish a framework within which teachers and administrators may interact, since a method of structuring relationships among individuals is an indispensable condition for an ordered society.

The issue that has developed concerning the student's relationship to the institution has resulted from a tendency of institutions of higher education to structure a separate category for students. This view involves some basic assumptions concerning student characteristics that seem, in many instances, to no longer be true. We must examine, then, the philosophy out of which the definition of the student's role in the governance of the institution should develop. At issue must be the nature of the limitations that should be imposed upon students with respect to their relationship to the institution and the structures through which students should relate to other constituent bodies within the college.

It is pointless to talk solely of self-regulation, since such an approach fails to consider human nature adequately and could result in the isolation and alienation of the student body from other members of the college community. It is dangerous to talk of power struggles among various groups within the institution who should be working to promote the common cause. It is obsolete to talk of students as if they were children to be guided by the benevolent dictums of an all-wise and all-powerful administration and faculty.

The students of a community college are characterized by extreme diversity with respect to age, family responsibilities, income, interests, aptitude, and most other attributes of comparison. They are bound together, however, by other important distinctions. They have a common interest in pursuing higher learning and they do not reside on the college campus. Hence, they are each citizens of their individual communities and responsible for their actions off campus to others—family and civil authorities, for example.

The community college exists to serve this diversity of students through a broad range of programs and to encourage the development of maturity. It exists to provide an environment which will enhance the transition from school to community. Finally, it exists to serve the needs of society which brought it into existence and to do so as efficiently as possible. In order to accomplish these goals, the college must preserve a certain independence of thought and action, for a failure to do so renders the institution vulnerable to the pressures of small but vocal groups who may claim to represent the community, but who are, in fact, bound up in their own individual interests.

It is imperative, then, that the college community define the relationships which shall exist between its constituent members and the rights and prerogatives of each. These must be so defined and so expressed that every member of the college community from the student body to the board of trustees both comprehend and endorse them fully. To accomplish this task, development must take place in an atmosphere that is uncharged by conflict conditions. The failure to substitute considered solutions in a calm atmosphere can only lead to intemperate solutions when crises occur.

THE INSTITUTION AND THE STUDENT

The college must adopt procedures which are viewed as realistic and hence acceptable to the majority of the student body. A failure to do so will require that the college resort to coercion to ensure student compliance. Authority does not exist unless it is accepted by those to whom it is supposed to apply. There is increasing evidence today that students are rejecting traditional forms and concepts of authority; yet most institutions persist in operating as if the authority once accepted freely still exists. The result of this failure to gauge accurately the effect of changing conditions has been the increasing disaffection and alienation of student bodies, creating in some instances the need for strict measures and disciplinary action to ensure compliance. Inevitably this cycle has become increasingly violent to the point where we must now accept the need for reconstruction of some of our basic concepts and procedures.

The danger of a belated reaction is that we shall seek, in our well-intentioned haste, to create a role for the student that he neither fits nor desires. The two most prevalent formats through which students relate to institutions at present are what might be termed the university model on the one hand and the *in loco parentis* model on the other. Those who accept the university model take the position that there are certain matters which fall within the province of the professional staff of the institution and these should be discharged without reference to the needs or interests of students. There are other matters which fall within the province of students, and here students should be left as much as possible to their own devices since this will result in the least amount of inconvenience for the university.

The *in loco parentis* model follows the dictums of the university model with respect to those affairs that belong within the province of professionals but in addition, seeks to regulate closely the personal life of students through the enforcement of highly questionable regulations based upon the perceptions of those who establish them of the general state of morality prevailing in the community that the institution serves.

There is need for a third alternative, but it would be unfortunate if that alternative should result in an overemphasis on the student's role, to the point that the professional abdicates his responsibility for providing the leadership that should characterize relationships among those who coexist within an institution of higher education. Such an approach can never resolve the real problem, which is integration of the student as a part of the college community, participating in the work of the institution in accord with his level of experience and maturity. Unfortunately, there are varying opinions concerning the level of experience and maturity of the students and frequently these opinions are shaped to the conveniences of those who hold them. It can be readily demonstrated that the experience and maturity of college students today surpasses that of preceding generations and that many of the problems which are experienced develop as a result of this miscalculation.

We need not become champions of student power to justify student involvement in institutional governance. If we accept as our basic premise the concept that some minimum level of student cooperation is essential to the preservation of an orderly community and that without such order all our efforts must be to no avail, then we can concentrate on the means for achieving such cooperation without becoming involved in polemics concerning the needs of developing citizens in a democratic society. To be sure, such needs do exist, and the academic community must take them into consideration. In addition to the philosophic considerations, however, there are many pragmatic reasons for student involvement that need to be cited.

THEORETICAL CONCEPTS

Let us now briefly consider some of the more important reasons why students should be involved in institutional governance. It has been pointed out earlier that the failure to adopt procedures acceptable to the majority of the student body will force the college to use coercion in order to operate. We know that coercion breeds frustration and ultimately, in many instances, rebellion. Essentially, this implies that procedures must be adopted in cooperation with student bodies and then reviewed periodically, rather than being established unilaterally and viewed as immutable.

The reason that this is so rests in part with the nature of authority. Barnard defines authority as the extent to which one individual within an organization will accept the directives issued by another.[1] Duryea has pointed out that the zone of acceptance for policies which result in effective action broadens as those who are affected participate in their determination.[2] From these two statements we may conclude that, if we are to achieve acceptance by students of organizational policies, then we will need to involve them in the development of such policies or risk arriving at conclusions that are unacceptable to those whom they are designed to serve.

The student voluntarily associates himself with the academic community to pursue goals that he perceives as held in common with the institution. More often than not, there is not the correlation between objectives that is assumed. The need exists, then, for either the institution or the student to change. Perhaps there needs to be some accommodation on the part of each, but the institution cannot escape its responsibility to establish standards and to encourage growth. The compelling requirement, then, is for change on the part of the student.

In the absence of accepted authority relationships, the only alternative is meaningful involvement of the student in the real process of governing the institution. As Millett has accurately pointed out, the restraints imposed by the institution ought to be the minimum required to ensure orderly achievement of objectives.[3] All restraints should be directly related to the purposes for which the institution exists. The college has neither the right nor the responsibility to establish itself as a moral guardian, a parent surrogate, or an interpreter of local mores unless it has received a specific mandate from its constituency to that effect. This does not mean that the college does not have the responsibility for exposing students to ethical values and of doing everything in its power to promote the understanding and acceptance of those attributes considered essential to the preservation of our society. The college has no moral right, however, to seek to promote conformity through compulsion.

The college exists to promote growth. Growth requires a certain freedom of action with the right to make mistakes upon occasion, provided that such mistakes do not cause undue harm either to the individual or the institution. The young man or woman of college age who has not yet been emancipated from the home stands on the threshold of this experience. In adult society, the only effective controls are those from within the individual. The role of the college, then, must be to encourage the development of internal controls through providing freedom to the individual, subject to the rights of others involved in the life of the academic community.

The adoption of a philosophy of individual freedom as a conscious policy to encourage the growth of self-control carries with it certain inherent problems which the institution must be prepared to face. It is inevitable that some students will carry such freedom to an excess which will occasion criticism of the institution for its failure to have rules against such behavior. With all due allowance for this point of view, it needs to be emphasized that rules never prevent undesirable behavior; they simply protect the institution at the expense of the transgressor. The absence of regulations makes possible the use of excesses as learning experiences for the institution and the individual.

The college then may be regarded as a microcosm of society with students assuming the role of free citizens under the leadership of faculty and administration. The professional members of the staff have the responsibility of developing procedures, standards, and reasonable limitations with respect to matters that fall within the area of their particular competencies, primarily the instructional program. In so doing, they need to be informed of the probable consequences in terms of student behavior for the alternatives they consider. The students have primary responsibility for developing procedures, standards, and reasonable limitations with respect to socialization experiences including student activities and non-classroom conduct, but they also have an extremely important stake in the nature of their instructional experience. In order to make the maximum contribution in both of these areas, they need to receive the mature guidance of those whose own experience will provide answers to the probable results of alternative courses of action.

Thus it may be seen that students and faculty need to play complementary roles, each learning from the other, and each making a unique contribution in the area of greatest competency. Finally, and perhaps more pragmatically, it may be observed that those institutions that have the strictest regulations and the least amount of student involvement normally experience the greatest degree of difficulty, and the regulations themselves seem more of a hindrance than a help in solving the problems that arise.

TOWARD IMPROVED INVOLVEMENT [4]

It must be recognized that there are two fundamental prerequisites to student involvement in institutional governance and to the guarantee of student rights. The first of these is the presence of an active faculty organization that possesses real authority as well as a sense of security in its own prerogatives. If faculty are not actively involved in institutional governance, there is little hope that any attempt to involve students more actively can succeed.

A second barrier to meaningful involvement is the current reliance upon representative student governments which are neither representative nor governments and which have been completely disavowed by most of the student body who do not even bother to vote in the elections. The report of the Study Commission on University Governance of the University of California at Berkeley is a shocking indictment of student governments, but similar statements of lack of effectiveness have been appearing with increasing frequency during the past ten years.[5] The truth of the matter is that many student governments have no real authority, are not integrated with the mechanisms for institutional governance, and are not respected by the student bodies. They serve primarily as popularity contests for those so inclined and to convince accrediting associations of student involvement.

It is not possible, however, for ongoing institutions to escape the necessity of basing any attempts to move in new directions on those which currently exist. The following recommendations are based on the concept of reform of existing structures rather than the establishment of new frameworks. New institutions unburdened by past follies might do well to give serious consideration to more radical reforms.

1. Each community college should have a student organization with defined powers and responsibilities and an established place in the machinery for the development of institutional policies.

2. To improve communication between the student organization for policy formulation and the faculty organization for policy formulation, there should be representatives of each sent as observers to the other. It would be the responsibility of such observers to comment on the point of view of their organization upon request and to keep their organization informed of the activities of its counterpart.

3. Joint faculty-student standing committees should be established to deliberate and make recommendations to the faculty and student policy-formulating bodies. Faculty members should predominate and there should be a faculty chairman for those joint committees where the matters considered involve areas that are primarily a faculty concern. Student members should predominate and there should be a student chairman of those committees involving matters of primary concern to the students.

4. An attempt should be made to ensure the representativeness of student policy-formulating organizations by the election of candidates from defined constituencies as opposed to the at-large elections which are frequently the case at present. It is suggested that the division or department might serve as a basic reference point in defining constituencies.

5. Divisions and departments should be urged to consider students majoring in their disciplines as viable subgroups of the college and to create student advisory committees that would meet with faculty members in these areas to foster communication and planning for improved student life. These advisory groups might also be involved in faculty meetings of the department or division whenever possible.

A flow chart for policy formulation illustrates the relationships described. Dotted lines indicate channels of communication. Solid lines are lines of communication and authority. Policy matters of concern to faculty and students would require action by both student and faculty organizations prior to action by the board of trustees. Recommendations of both organizations would be reported to the board of trustees when appropriate. Joint committees would provide the structure through which solutions acceptable to both groups might be obtained.

STUDENT RIGHTS AND FREEDOMS: ADDITIONAL CONSIDERATIONS

Given the philosophy of encouraging the development of maturity and self-control by providing the least amount of regulation essential to the objectives of the institution, it follows that there must be definition of what constitutes the minimum of regulation and how the academic community shall proceed in the establishment and enforcement of the limitations to be imposed. The following guidelines are intended to amplify the responsibilities of the student policy-formulating body and to provide suggestions as to what its principal areas of concern ought to be.

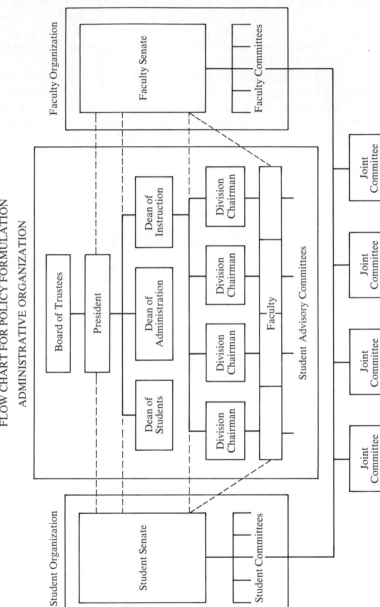

FLOW CHART FOR POLICY FORMULATION
ADMINISTRATIVE ORGANIZATION

Faculty Organization

Faculty Senate

Faculty Committees

Board of Trustees

President

Dean of Instruction

Dean of Administration

Dean of Students

Division Chairman

Division Chairman

Division Chairman

Division Chairman

Faculty

Student Advisory Committees

Joint Committee

Joint Committee

Joint Committee

Joint Committee

Student Organization

Student Senate

Student Committees

There should be a college community approach to all matters that involve students. The approach should be so structured that students have at least an equal voice in determining the recommendations that shall be made to a governing body in matters that affect them most directly. The total institution, including faculty, students, administration, and governing body, should work together to establish the purposes and minimum standards of conduct necessary to ensure the existence of an ordered system with academic freedom for both students and faculty.

The institution has the responsibility of making its standards and ideals clear to all who apply for admission. Care should be taken, however, to ensure that the freedom of students to accept or reject standards or ideals not essential to the main purpose of the institution is preserved.

The recommendations of representative student governments or other recognized student groups in areas defined as being appropriate for student involvement should be reported to appropriate officers or committees in the administrative organization of the college. In the event of a disagreement between a recognized student group and the official or committee to which that group normally reports, an appeal procedure should be available to ensure that such conflicts of opinion receive hearings at which students are represented at successively higher levels within the institutional framework. In areas of significant disagreement, provision should be made for carrying an appeal to the governing body.

APPROPRIATE AREAS FOR STUDENT INVOLVEMENT

A case can be made for some student involvement in most areas of college policy formulation, since students are directly or indirectly affected by the results of such policies. However, there are some areas which are more central to student concern than others, and in like manner, there are areas in which a greater student contribution can be anticipated. The following distribution of institutional activities is suggested with respect to the degree of student involvement indicated.

AREAS WHICH SHOULD BE PRIMARILY OR TOTALLY UNDER STUDENT LEADERSHIP:

1. Student publications.
2. Allocation of student activity fees.
3. Student conduct and discipline unrelated to the classroom situation.
4. Recognition of campus student organizations.
5. Approval of guest speakers invited by students.
6. Distribution of student-initiated literature on campus.
7. Distribution of off-campus literature on campus.

To say that a matter should be primarily or totally under student leadership should not be interpreted as conceding absolute autonomy to student leadership in matters of proper concern to the college community as a whole.

AREAS WHICH SHOULD BE GOVERNED BY AGENCIES INVOLVING EQUAL STUDENT AND FACULTY REPRESENTATION:

1. Coordination and approval of co-curricular activities.
2. Alterations in the academic calendar.

AREAS WHICH SHOULD BE CONSIDERED FOR SOME DEGREE OF STUDENT INVOLVEMENT:

1. Faculty reappointment, promotion to higher rank and tenure.
2. Admissions standards for curricula and courses.
3. Class size.
4. Allocation of instructional funds.
5. Curricula or course revision, addition, or deletion.
6. Administrative structure of the college.
7. Staff salaries, fringe benefits.
8. Teaching loads.
9. Provision of services to the community.
10. Requirement for degrees and certificates.
11. Selection of the president.
12. Selection of college officers directly related to student life.

It should be noted that the form of student involvement may vary greatly depending upon the area that is concerned. In some areas such as curricula or course revision, such involvement will be obtained by placing students on appropriate standing committees. In areas such as faculty reappointment, promotion to higher rank, and tenure, student involvement may come through the distribution of evaluation forms which are then used by appropriate committees and administrators in making the necessary decisions. With respect to administrative structure of the college, staff salaries, and fringe benefits, student involvement is likely to be peripheral unless it becomes necessary for the college to take significant steps in order to improve the availability of resources in these areas. For example, students might be mobilized through their interest in the college to participate in a campaign to raise a tax levy or pass a bond issue intended to relate to these particular areas.

JOINT STATEMENT ON RIGHTS AND FREEDOMS

On January 17, 1968, the Association of American Colleges endorsed the Joint Statement on Rights and Freedoms of Students with certain enumerated qualifications. Previously the Joint Statement had been drafted and endorsed by the United States National Student Association and the Council of the American Association of University Professors. It may be fairly contended that the statement as originally drafted was not entirely applicable to community colleges because of the predominantly university orientation of those who were involved in its development. The following statements concerning student rights and freedoms represent an adaptation of the joint statement for purposes of community colleges. Wherever possible the original language of the joint statement has been retained.

The governing body, the administration, the faculty and the student body have, as their joint responsibility, the establishment and preservation of the following essential rights for all students:

1. *Freedom in the Classroom.* The instructor in the classroom and in conference should encourage free discussion, inquiry, and expression. Student performance should be evaluated solely on an academic basis, not on opinions or conduct in matters unrelated to academic standards.

2. *Confidentiality of Student Records.* To minimize the risk of improper disclosure, academic and disciplinary records should be separate and the conditions of access to each should be set forth in an explicit policy statement. Transcripts of academic records should contain only information about academic status and should not include any institutional action such as suspension or expulsion for academic or disciplinary reasons which affects a student's ability to re-register at the institution. Information from disciplinary or counseling files should not be available to unauthorized persons on campus or to any person off campus without the express consent of the student involved except under legal compulsion or in cases where the safety of persons or property is involved. No records should be kept which reflect the political activities or beliefs of students. Provision should also be made for periodic routine destruction of noncurrent disciplinary records. Administrative staff and faculty members should respect confidential information which they acquire about students in the course of their work.

3. *Freedom of Association.* Students bring to the campus a variety of interests as members of the college community. They should be free to organize and join associations to promote their common interests.

   a. The involvement of a student organization in controversial activities should not be considered as adequate justification for the removal of recognition from the organization or for disciplinary proceedings against members or officers of that organization unless it can be proven that such controversial activities are in direct violation of college regulations or civil or criminal laws.

b. If faculty advisors are required, each organization should be free to choose its own advisor. Institutional recognition should not be withheld or withdrawn solely because of the inability of the student organization to secure an advisor, provided that the organization has made an honest attempt to do so. The degree to which faculty advisors should exercise authority with respect to the activities and policies of the student organization should be determined by each college, but the approach used in determining the degree of control should be so structured that students have at least an equal voice in making the determination.

c. Student organizations may be required to submit a statement of purpose, criteria for membership, rules of procedures, and a current list of officers. They should not be required to submit a membership list as a condition of institutional recognition.

d. All campus organizations should be open to all students without respect to race, creed, or national origin, except for religious qualifications which may be required by organizations whose aims are primarily sectarian.

4. *Freedom of Inquiry and Expression.*

a. Students and student organizations should be free to examine and discuss all questions of interest to them and to express opinions publicly and privately. They should always be free to support causes by orderly means which do not disrupt the regular and essential operation of the institution. At the same time, it should be made clear to the college and the larger community that in their public expressions or demonstrations, students or student organizations speak only for themselves.

b. Each institution should develop a written policy concerning the procedures required by an institution before a guest speaker is invited to appear on campus. Students should have a major role in the development of the policy and in the determination of those to be invited. The policy should clearly define restrictions concerning the appearance of guest speakers and should make clear to the college and larger community that the sponsorship of guest speakers does not necessarily imply approval or endorsement of the views expressed either by the sponsoring group or by the institution.

5. *Freedom of Expression in Student Publications.* Student publications and the student press are a valuable aid in establishing and maintaining an atmosphere of free and responsible discussion and of intellectual exploration on the campus. They are a means of bringing student concerns to the attention of the faculty and the institutional authorities and of formulating student opinion on various issues and in the world at large. Institutional authorities, in consultation with students and faculty, have a responsibility to provide written clarification of the role of student publications with standards to be used in their evaluation and the limitations on external control of their operation. At the same time, the editorial freedom of student editors and managers entails correlary responsibilities to be governed by the canons of responsible journalism such as the avoidance of libel, indecency, undocumented allegations, attacks on personal integrity, and the techniques of harassment and innuendo. As safeguards for the editorial freedom of student publications, the following provisions should apply:

a. If institutional policies provide for advance review of copy, a review board should be established to arbitrate the differences of opinion. At least half of the members of the review board should be students.

b. Editors and managers of student publications should be protected from arbitrary suspension and removal because of student, faculty, administrative, or public disapproval of editorial policy or content. Only for proper or stated causes should editors and managers be subject to removal, and then by orderly and prescribed procedures. The agency responsible for the appointment of editors and managers should be the agency responsible for their removal.

c. All college published and financed student publications should explicitly state on the editorial page that the opinions there expressed are not necessarily those of the college or the student body.

6. *Freedom to Exercise the Rights of Citizenship.* Two-year college students are both citizens and members of the college community. As citizens, students should enjoy the same freedom of speech, peaceful assembly, and right of petition that other citizens enjoy, and as members of the college community they are subject to the obligations which accrue to them by virtue of this membership. Faculty members and administrative officials should ensure that institutional powers are not employed to inhibit such intellectual and personal development of students as is often promoted by their exercise of the rights of citizenship both on and off campus.

Activities of students may, upon occasion, result in violation of law. In such cases, college officials may apprise students of sources of legal counsel and may offer other assistance. Students who violate the law may incur penalties prescribed by civil authorities, but institutional authority should not be used merely to duplicate the function of general laws. Only where the institution's interests as a college community are distinct and clearly involved should the special authority of the institution be asserted. The student who incidentally violates institutional regulations in the course of his off-campus activity, such as those relating to class attendance, should be subject to no greater penalty than would normally be imposed. Institutional action should be independent of community pressure.

7. *Guarantee of Procedural Due Process in Disciplinary Proceedings.* In developing responsible student conduct, disciplinary proceedings play a role substantially secondary to counseling, guidance, and admonition. At the same time, educational institutions have a duty and correlary disciplinary powers to protect their educational purpose through the studying of standards of scholarship and conduct for the students who attend them and for the regulation of the use of institutional facilities. In the exceptional circumstances when the preferred means fail to resolve problems of student conduct, proper procedural safeguards should be preserved to protect the student from the unfair imposition of serious penalties.

The administration of discipline should guarantee procedural fairness to an accused student. Practices and disciplinary cases may vary in formality with the gravity of the offense and the sanctions which may be applied. They should also take into account the presence or absence of an honor code and the degree to which the institution officials have direct acquaintance with student life in general, and with the involved student, and with the circumstances of the case in particular. The jurisdictions of faculty or student judicial bodies, the disciplinary responsibilities of institution officials, and the regular disciplinary procedures including the student's right to appeal a decision should be clearly formulated and communicated in advance. Minor penalties may be assessed informally under prescribed procedures.

In all situations, procedural fair play requires that the student be informed of the nature of the charges against him, that he be given a fair opportunity to refute them, that the institution not be arbitrary in its actions, and that there be provision for appeal of a decision. The following are recommended as proper safeguards in such proceedings when there are no honor codes offering comparable guarantees.

a. *Standards of Conduct Expected of Students.*

The institution has an obligation to specify those standards of behavior which it considers essential to its educational mission and its community life. These general behavioral expectations and the resultant specific regulations should represent a reasonable regulation of student conduct, but the student should be as free as possible from imposed limitations that have no direct relevance to his education. Offenses should be as clearly defined as possible and interpreted in a manner consistent with the aforementioned principles of relevancy and reasonableness. Disciplinary proceedings should be instituted only for violations of standards of conduct formulated with significant student participation and published in advance through such means as a student handbook or a generally available body of institutional regulations.

b. *Investigation of Student Conduct.*

1. Except under extreme emergency circumstances, premises occupied by students and the personal possessions of students should not be searched unless appropriate authorization has been obtained. For premises such as residence halls controlled by the college, an appropriate and responsible authority should be designated to whom application should be made before the search is conducted. The application should specify the reasons for the search and the objects or information sought. The student should be present, if possible, during the search. For premises not controlled by the college, the ordinary requirements for lawful search should be followed.

2. Students arrested or detected in the course of serious violations of college regulations or infractions of ordinary law should be informed of their rights. No form of harassment should be used by institutional representatives to coerce admissions of guilt or information about conduct of other suspected persons.

c. *Status of Student Pending Final Action.*

Pending action on the charges, the status of a student should not be altered, or his right to be present on the campus and to attend classes supended except for reasons relating to his physical or emotional safety and well-being or for reasons relating to the safety and well-being of students, faculty, or college property.

d. *Hearing Committee Procedures.*

When misconduct may result in serious penalties and if the student questions the fairness of disciplinary action taken against him, he should be granted, upon request, the privilege of a hearing before a regularly constituted Hearing Committee. The following suggested Hearing Committee procedures satisfy the requirements of procedural due process in situations requiring a high degree of formality.

1. The Hearing Committee should include faculty members or students, or if regularly included or requested by the accused, both faculty and student members. No member of the Hearing Committee who is otherwise interested in the particular case should sit in judgment during the proceedings.

2. The student should be informed in writing of the reasons for the proposed disciplinary action with sufficient particularity and in sufficient time to ensure opportunity to prepare for the hearing.

3. The student appearing before the Hearing Committee should have the right to be assisted in his defense by an advisor of his choice.

4. The burden of proof should rest upon the officials bringing the charge.

5. The student should be given an opportunity to testify and to present evidence and witnesses. He should have an opportunity to hear and question adverse witnesses. In no case should the committee consider statements against the student unless he has been advised of their content and of the names of those who made them, and unless he has been given an opportunity to rebut unfavorable inferences which might otherwise be drawn.

6. All matters upon which the decision may be based must be introduced into evidence at the proceeding before the Hearing Committee. The decision should be based solely upon such matters. Improperly acquired evidence should not be admitted.

7. In the absence of a transcript there should be both a digest and a verbatim record such as a tape recording of the hearing.

8. The decision of the Hearing Committee should be final, subject only to the student's right of appeal to the president, or ultimately to the governing body of the institution.

STUDENT RESPONSIBILITIES

When we talk about student rights and freedoms, it is necessary to recognize that with rights and freedoms must go responsibilities. Such responsibilities as a minimum include:

1. Compliance with and support of duly constituted civil authority.

2. Respect for the rights of others and cooperation to ensure that such rights are guaranteed, whether or not the views of those exercising such rights are consistent with the views of the majority.

3. Cooperation to ensure that the will of the majority is implemented after due consideration has been given to contrary points of view. Such cooperation, however, does not include the suppression of minority points of view.

4. The exercise of dissent within a framework compatible with the resolution of differences.

5. Knowledge of college regulations established through the joint efforts of students, faculty, and administration.

CONCLUSION

Recently, increasing consideration has been given to the role of students in institutions of higher education. As a result of unrest at Berkeley and other major centers, administrators and faculty members alike have sought the meaning of the new student activism. The issue has been brought most clearly into focus by publication of the Joint Statement of Rights and Freedoms of Students and its subsequent endorsement by a number of national organizations.

Now the issue confronts two-year colleges, even though many administrators and faculty members might prefer to cling to the thought that "It can't happen here." In one sense it is unfortunate that the issue of student rights and freedoms must be considered at a time when the rights and freedoms of faculty in the two-year college are still far from clear in the minds of many, but changing times produce issues that must be recognized and considered. This much at least is clear. *In loco parentis* is dead and no one has as yet named a successor.

By the same token, students have indicated an increasing disaffection and alienation with the "hands off" impersonal policy of the large university. The time has come when an alternative must be sought which will provide to students the opportunity for meaningful involvement in the affairs of their institutions.

Such involvement must not be limited to social and behavioral considerations that do not impinge upon the educational process itself. Students have made it quite clear through the thrust of their activism that their major concern lies with the content and implementation of the instructional program. It is essential that the community college, which is providing leadership in so many areas of educational innovation, recognize its responsibilities with respect to the important area of student role in the governance of the institution.

REFERENCES

1. BARNARD, CHESTER, "Functions of the Executive," as quoted in Parsons *et al., Theories of Society,* Vol. 1. Glencoe, Ill.: The Free Press of Glencoe, 1961, note p. 633.

2. DURYEA, E. D., "The Theory and Practice of Administration," in Gerald P. Burns, *Administrators in Higher Education.* New York: Harper & Row, Publishers, 1962, p. 32.

3. MILLETT, JOHN D., *The Academic Community.* New York: McGraw Hill Book Company, 1962, note p. 180.

4. RICHARDSON, RICHARD C., "Recommendations on Student Rights and

Freedoms," *Junior College Journal,* American Association of Junior Colleges, February, 1969, pp. 34-42.

5. Study Commission on University Governance, *The Culture of the University: Governance and Education,* University of California, Berkeley, January 15, 1968.

Helping Students
Search for Values

DOROTHY LEACH

Counselor, California State
College at Long Beach

"Helping students search . . ."

This phrase points to an ongoing process. Values will be found, and found anew, discovered and rediscovered, within the life of each individual, as well as by his generation and his time. The search is not only for new values or ends, appropriate to a new age, but also for new means, or new forms to express, embody, and exemplify the enduring values.[6]

In the student unrest of the past few years, there have been signs which have generated optimism in such observers as Erikson, Rockefeller, Riesman, Schlesinger, Halleck, and numerous others. However, the so-called radical students often demonstrate that they are "rebels with a cause, but without a program." [7] Negative goals often appear to outnumber and outweigh positive goals. Many young rebels seem to know only what they don't want. Either they cannot or are not prepared to be nearly so explicit with regard to the next step: what they *do* want. The absence of an integrated value system was revealed as characteristic of today's college student in a recent national student survey.[9]

Harry S. Broudy has tried to ascertain what students really love and hate, and what they would do if the freedom they demand were really given to them. He reports that "only on the most rare occasions have they been willing to accept real liberty to shape their own studies or their lives, especially when the price of liberty was accountability for the wrong choices." [6]

This is perhaps the point where faculty, administration, and student personnel workers need to help the most: in moving beyond rebellious discontent to new specifications and clarifications of goals and their implementation.

Helping students search for values will not be accomplished by those who feel that they are in possession of some body of wisdom which they may offer the young. Rather, effective help will consist of demonstrating the ongoing nature of our own search, of mutually sharing our experiences in the process, and as far as our roles in the college permit, of providing those kinds of experiences which lead to the clarification of values.

It is of great importance that student personnel workers who share the student's search should represent an appropriate diversity. Various religious and nonreligious philosophies, varying political persuasions, differing intellectual and practical orientations, broad ranges of aesthetic and economic values would ideally be represented. This provision of divergent points of view to which the student can react will be of the utmost help in stimulating and aiding his own value-structuring process.

Students are, or should be, in the process of becoming persons. This means that an important obligation of the college is to provide stable models and supportive persons who will accept the transitional character of the student's value system as appropriate and desirable for this stage, and will in turn, help the student to feel this desirability.

Can we convey to the student: "You are growing; this is good. Your feeling of insecurity is a normal expectation. It's all right to be uncertain at this point. Whether or not you will grow as a person depends in part on your tolerance for a period of uncertainty."

We can further help him by understanding his emergent values not as rejections of his background, for which he must then feel disloyal, but rather as expanding opportunities for understanding more deeply, and accepting the differing value systems of others, including his parents.

The junior college student, because he ordinarily moves daily between these two "cultures" of home and campus, may be kept more aware of the transitional state of his value structure than those students who live on campus. He can hardly avoid (or postpone until Christmas vacation) the recognition that he is changing in important ways.

Not all value challenges are in the direction of acquiring new values that conflict with those of the home (although if the student is the first of his family to go to college, this may be a very important aspect of his situation). More often the changes will represent clarification and increased internalization of values. If we in the colleges are doing our job, his changing will provide both the challenge and the occasion to make his conceived values operative in his behavior.

College years as a time of value change have been demonstrated in numerous studies in the past decade, despite the fact that in the Fifties the college generation was notably apathetic. In 1968, the C/R/M Inc. national student survey found that two-thirds of their sample felt that college "had changed their whole view of themselves." [9]

The author conducted an informal survey in the summer of 1969 in two classes of fourth and fifth year students who were working toward teaching credentials. After determining that 85 percent of these students had attended a junior college for two years, they were asked what had been their chief concerns during each of those years, and whether or not they perceived their values as having changed by the time they came to the state college for their junior year.

Their chief concerns on entering college had been social conquest of various kinds (acceptance by the "right" group, or by the opposite sex in general) and making good grades. The overwhelming majority felt that their values had changed by the end of junior college. They described themselves as having become more tolerant of people who differed from themselves, as discovering the intrinsic rewards of learning for the first time, as becoming concerned about defining vocational goals, and as being able for the first time, to develop values different from their parents'.

It is not implied that these were "typical" junior college students. But the personal value changes they experienced are very common.

STUDENT VALUES TODAY

Attention has been called to some major shifts in the value systems of today's youth. They have moved toward values which lead to immediate gratification, challenging any arbitrary structure that is imposed on them.[10] Both autonomy and immediate experience have taken on great significance for them. Frequently labeled "the NOW generation," they have shown great urgency to do "their own thing." At one extreme, the militant student's cry "is for action now, not preparation for action later. In this real sense he is no longer a student at all, since he clearly rejects knowledge as a precondition of any meaningful activity." [3]

On the other hand, present students seem more informed, more aware, more personally and socially responsive than earlier ones. Affluence offers freedom and choice of meanings, choice of what shall be worth a man's commitment and endeavor. The Depression may have urged on our generation a more narrow and more materialistic meaning; struggles born of poverty have no necessarily ennobling virtue. Today's youth must work out their own meanings, from which their own values may be derived, and that asks much more of them. The Depression and its subsequent focusing on economic security may have served a whole generation poorly as preparation for parenthood in which wider and more enduring values could be inspired in their children. When the chief needs of security are met, human concerns rise to higher levels; to intimacy, human relationships, integrity, authenticity, autonomy, and self-actualization. These are major concerns of today's students.

It has been suggested that students' sense of urgency today reflects a profound uneasiness; perhaps they are not even sure they have a future. How much of a chance have they to live, "not to go down in history as the apocalyptic generation?" [16]

It is obvious that they do not view the future as guaranteed, in any sense. This uncertainty is echoed in the bitter eloquence of the student speakers at the June 1969 commencements. This generation confronts all previous generations not only with regard to time, but to the other core values of our culture enumerated by Kluckhohn.[12] These students reaffirm the intrinsic worth of the individual human in the face of the most threatening mechanization and depersonalization of contemporary life. They reassert their freedom, their choice, their mastery of their environment. They reject the earlier activity-orientation of our culture, denying that work is intrinsically virtuous, or that material goods are worthy ends as well as means. They reject competition as the primary basis for human relationships.

Kluckhohn, in her formulation, did not deal with the question of acceptable sources of knowledge, or the question of how value or worth shall be established. Neither has this generation answered these questions; but they have indicated that tradition or other arbitrary authority cannot be that answer.

If this generation seems unappreciative of the "tried and true ways of the past" it should hardly surprise us, inasmuch as "a greater cultural evolution has occurred within this century than in the whole history of man combined." [5]

A decline in respect for authority is, in Halleck's opinion, "best understood in terms of the psychological impact of our new media." Television is acquainting youth "with the cynical facts of life at a time when such truths may be indigestible . . . The hypocrisies of the older generation have always been with us. What is new today is that it is ridiculously easy to expose them. The effect on our youth . . . has been to create a deep skepticism as to the validity of authority." [11]

The young have seen too clearly, perhaps too painfully, the gap behind the "generation gap": a striking discrepancy between the conceived values (publicly stated ideals) and the operative values (those effective in the choices that are spelled out in action). They have seen for themselves that values do not function in abstract form, that ". . . complicated judgments are involved, and what is really valued is reflected in the outcome of life as it is finally lived." [13]

WHAT IS THE PROCESS?

Allport uses "values" to refer to "meanings perceived as related to self," or "matters of importance" as distinct from mere matters of fact.[1] These matters of importance, he believes, are not acquired by drill, indoctrination, or reinforcement. Instead, they are those matters, which out of the rich web of experience, claim our attention, then our genuine interest, and are thus incorporated into our self-concept where they "utilize the basic energy, the basic spontaneity, that the organism itself possesses."

A useful analysis of the process of effectively obtaining values has been offered by Louis E. Raths, who sees the process of valuing as depending upon the meeting of seven conditions.[13] The first three are essential qualities of choice: choosing freely, choosing from among alternatives, and choosing after thoughtful consideration of the consequences of each alternative. (Impulsive choices do not lead to values.) The fourth condition is prizing, or cherishing; the fifth, open affirmation of our choice. Sixth, by acting upon choices, we allow values to give direction to actual living. Seventh, this acting upon the choice will be repeated, as values tend to form persistent patterns in our lives.

WHERE AND HOW DOES THE PROCESS OCCUR?

I am going to suggest three general contexts of encounter which frequently occasion new or restructured values for the student. He encounters himself, the valuing person, in each of them, and emerges more clearly defined to himself. They are not clearly separable; there will necessarily be overlapping functions.

THE ENCOUNTER WITH THE WORLD ABOUT HIM

The urgent growth task which confronts every adolescent may be understood as consisting of two interdependent parts. One half of this task is to search out his personal identity from among the many alternatives that lie before him. This means the definition of himself spiritually, physically, vocationally, socially. "The other half is defining a cognitive map of the universe so that the self, when developed, will have a place to stand." [4] To do this, the student must both encounter the world and get some perspective on that encounter. Formal education by definition, should be productive in both of these phases. Every increase in knowledge furnishes the potential for a richer phenomenal field and a better basis for intelligent choice. The student will have to consider abstractions and absolutes as he examines his own relationship to nature, to learning, to justice, to the scientific method, to religion, and so on. By sorting out these relationships, he also sorts himself out, and thus asserts for himself the significance of his cognitive understanding of the nature of things.

This engagement of the self with the world about him will have been a lifelong process. In childhood, his very naïveté, and its corollary curiosity serve as the greatest stimulus. But the college years, for students of whatever age, represent another new impetus to a sustained encounter in depth with the marvels of earth and the life processes on it. Never before, and perhaps never again, will such active and intense stimulation to learn the objects and ways of the world be packed into a relatively short period.

"The capacity to become interested in the totality of any object and not merely in the immediately need-satisfying aspects of need-related objects is the source of the richness of the human perceptual world." [14] This richness which comes about because man can free himself temporarily from perceiving the world only in terms of his needs, "extends in two dimensions: (1) the great variety of objects significant for man, and (2) the depth and richness with which he can perceive each single object. Both dimensions distinguish man's perceptual world from the animal's." [14]

Thus the human animal, in his course of development, moves within and beyond his roles as user of tools, manipulator of his environment, to the roles of appreciator and celebrant. The shift from *knowledge* to *acknowledgment* marks the great event of his selecting certain aspects of his world for prizing.

The student's capacity for this choosing and prizing is favored by the very nature of a college, but it must be recognized (and students themselves have begun to do so) that the responsibility of the college to further this process is not met by merely presenting vast information about this world. The student's appreciation, as well as his information, must be guided and shared by those who already appreciate the complexity, value the intricacy, marvel at the functional efficiency of the natural world. The shift from the extrinsic motivation of grades to the intrinsic satisfactions of discovering more about their universe and its inhabitants is a student trend which is but one illustration of this experience as a producer of values.

Never before have so great a proportion of a people been exposed to the mind-opening experience that is, hopefully, available in college. Not everyone is upset, or even surprised, at the apparently changing values of the younger generation. Much of the current dismay, especially when it is based on a minority who retreat into private experience via drugs, disregards the widening of social responsibility and dedication to service which has marked student values since the apathetic, materialistic students of the Fifties. If we consider education to be a mind-opening process, there is no cause for dismay. Would education be a good investment if the new generation had values and standards identical to ours?

THE ENCOUNTER WITH CONTEMPORARY HISTORY

Value changes may be expected to occur when we feel the direct impact of significant events, and our society has been provided with more than enough of these in recent years. Impact may be felt directly and keenly, even from vicarious experiences. Television has allowed us—indeed has forced us—to participate in tragic, brutal, noble, incredulous, awe-inspiring happenings. Emotionally we have not been able to preserve the spectator's distance that the newspaper used to permit us.

Events of this magnitude have shaken our customary assumptions and forced us to restructure values. More than one person found his comfortable truce with racial injustice exploded by a bomb at a Birmingham church. Assassin's bullets have shattered the complacency of millions. Footprints on the moon have challenged every man's assumptions about life on our planet.

Colleges have long since ceased to provide any refuge from the assaults of contemporary history. There are no sidelines. College students are in the mainstream of events, and their developmental task of finding those concepts, creeds, purposes, and persons to whom they can commit themselves has thus been immeasurably intensified.

THE ENCOUNTER WITH PERSONS

In decrying the deterioration of college teachers into mere knowledge technicians and purveyors of facts, William Arrowsmith has called for a restoration of education to its central purpose: "the molding of men rather than the production of knowledge . . . It is possible for a student to go from kindergarten to graduate school without ever encountering a man—someone who might for the first time give him the only profound motivation for learning, the hope of becoming a better person." [2] The teacher can thus enhance the becoming of a human being "because he possesses the human skills which give him the power to humanize others. If that power is not felt, nothing of any educational significance can occur." [2]

To become human entails the selection and prizing of certain experiences over others. In this process, the college should act as a catalytic agent, bringing the student and the experiences together. Very significant experiences can occur through the *persons* whom the student encounters in the college.

Arrowsmith's assertion that the humanities stand or fall according to the human worth of the man who professes them is hardly less true of student personnel workers, whose real job reaches so far beyond the dispensing and gathering of information. Are the students of community colleges any less in need of teachers, administrators, and counselors with the "power to humanize"? Are instructors in vocational skills, crafts, and technology any less needed as humanizers? Is education that humanizes—education that is directed to the "molding of men rather than the production of knowledge"—an appropriate concern of the two-year college? Does the community college see one of its responsibilities as encouraging students to develop values as a part of their educational experience?

It is to be hoped that the community college's view of the purpose of education is one that encourages value-making as a necessary function. Donald A. Eldridge, while president of AAJC, pointed out that community colleges perform the tasks of vocational and preprofessional training with efficiency, but that such effort constitutes "only part of the need, providing in a sense only the means to the ultimate end, which is education for living . . . Many two-year colleges are giving new importance to the fine and performing arts and all kinds of creativity, meanwhile acknowledging that the liberal arts are and should continue to be valued as the fundamental education for free men." [8]

Not only for its late adolescent students, but especially in its many contacts with mature students, does the community college's role as facilitator of values emerge imperatively. "The value-making activity would appear to be central to the life experience. Primary in importance are values relating to self-discovery." [15] For the adult student, this process of self-discovery may have been interrupted by the early assumption of responsibilities which left neither room nor time for questioning one's values. When such a student resumes, or perhaps even begins, belatedly, this quest for his own freedom and its meanings, he is often the most eager and productive of students. "Education is an agency with the force of a social institution behind it, the main purpose of which is to assist in the process of self-discovery in the world of knowledge, skills, vocation, and—of highest worth—personal values." [15]

Gordon Allport has pointed out that education for values occurs only when teachers teach what they themselves stand for, no matter what their subject is.[1] This observation is no less true of student personnel workers, whatever their specific role.

The finding of a recent survey that "students lack a realistic sense of what their ideals imply in terms of social and public action" is one that we all may observe around us, in many students.[9] Here is a highly significant clue, however, for those of us who accept our responsibility in the student's value-making process. We will not be able to help students search for values if the same can be said of us.

We must know who we are, what we are about, and what we are

for. We must know what our ideals imply in terms of action. For all our inclination and all our training, we are in danger of being vaguely committed to "helping" without a realistic sense of what our ideals and values imply, and without responsible action in their behalf.

The clarity of our values, the integrity of our behavior are visible in our everyday contacts with students. Only thus do we effectively share our own search for values with students. We dare not do less. We cannot do more.

REFERENCES

1. ALLPORT, GORDON W., "Values and Our Youth," reprinted from *Teachers College Record* December 1961 in Esther M. Lloyd-Jones and Herman A. Estrin, *The American Student and His College.* Boston: Houghton Mifflin Company, 1967.

2. ARROWSMITH, WILLIAM, "The Heart of Education: Turbulent Teachers," *Matrix* 1967.

3. BETTELHEIM, BRUNO, "Student Revolt," *Vital Speeches,* April 15, 1969.

4. BLAINE, GRAHAM B., JR. and CHARLES C. MCARTHUR, *Emotional Problems of the Student.* Garden City, N.Y.: Anchor Books, Doubleday & Company Inc., 1966, note p. 104.

5. BOTKIN, ROBERT, "Can We Teach Values?" *Educational Record,* Spring 1968.

6. BROUDY, HARRY S., "Art, Science, and New Values," *Phi Delta Kappan,* November, 1967, note p. 116.

7. BROWN, HARRISON, "Why the Generation Gap?" *Saturday Review,* July 19, 1969, pp. 20-22.

8. ELDRIDGE, DONALD A., "New Dimensions for the Two-Year College," *Junior College Journal,* 36 (September, 1967), 10-12.

9. HADDEN, JEFFREY K., "The Private Generation," *Psychology Today,* 3 No. 5 (October, 1969).

10. HALLECK, SEYMOUR L., "The Generation Gap: A Problem of Values" *Education Digest,* 34 (January, 1969), 32-35.

11. ———, "Hypotheses of Student Unrest," *Phi Delta Kappan,* September, 1968.

12. KLUCKHOHN, FLORENCE, "Value Orientations," *Toward A Unified Theory of Human Behavior,* ed. Roy R. Grinker. New York: Basic Books, Inc., 1956.

13. RATHS, LOUIS E., MERRILL HARMIN, SIDNEY B. SIMON, *Values and Teaching.* Columbus: Charles E. Merrill Books, Inc., 1966, note p. 27.

14. SCHACHTEL, E. G., *Metamorphosis.* New York: Basic Books, Inc., 1959, note p. 85.

15. TRIPP, PHILIP A., "Value Making: A Principal Function of the College Experience," *Journal of the National Association of Women Deans and Counselors,* 30 (Fall, 1966), 1.

16. WALD, DR. GEORGE S., "A Generation In Search of a Future." Speech delivered at MIT on March 4, 1969, and reprinted in *Vital Speeches,* April 15, 1969.

Organization and Administration of Student Personnel Work in the Community College

J. W. McDaniel

President Emeritus,
San Bernardino Valley College

ROBERT A. LOMBARDI

Dean of Students,
Moorpark College

PREVIEW

The campus has moved from the back pages to headlines. No longer just an impressive citadel of brick and lawn to be shown to visitors on the Sunday afternoon drive, the local college draws more eyes than the brewery or the county courthouse, and the searching look of the visitor is for *people,* for students, for professors, for guards—and especially for administrators. Again in its brief history, college governance is being goaded into review of its priorities, programs, and leadership. Since the forces that insist on change are *human* forces, it is essential that review of all college organization patterns and administrative principles begin with basic components—*people* and *relationships between people.* This is especially true of student personnel work.

PEOPLE AFFECT PEOPLE

A college is a community of people. In some colleges—small colleges, specialty schools, highly selective colleges—the people may be very much alike. In community colleges they tend to be very different; at best, as different as the communities they serve.

The most human quality of people is their ability to communicate with each other. They touch, they see, they hear, they smell, they talk, they write, they smile, they scowl, they roar, they cry. They invent symbols and codes and rules, and systems of symbols and codes and rules. They communicate visibly, directly, bluntly. And they communicate under the table and behind the back and on the sneak.

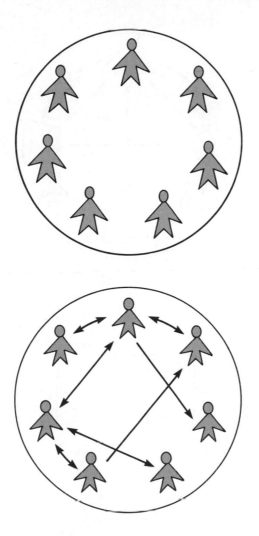

The people in a college community interrelate in many ways. Each person enters the community as an individual and retains his individuality throughout his college years. But he also becomes a member of a group; usually a member of several groups. He acquires the identity of the group and communicates with the symbols and trappings of the group. Signals fly from person to person, from person to group, from group to group. A college community is a hotbed of signals.

Communication is always two-way. Each person and each group receives signals (input) and sends signals (output). Input and output are not necessarily equal, nor in the same media, nor of equal directness. And

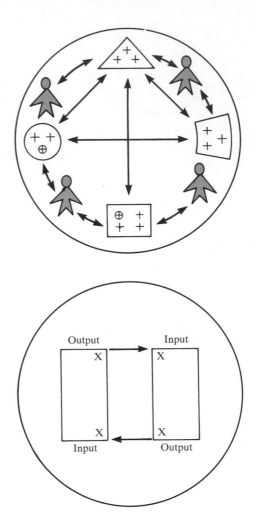

frequently the interpretation by one group of the signals of another group is very different from the intended signal.

In a college community, certain large groups stand out as of particular importance. The students, as a whole group, and in their many subgroups are the largest group and are the group of primary interest to every other group. The faculty, several layers of administration, the Board of Trustees, and a variable assortment of special service workers constitute other usually visible groups. Direct and indirect communication between these groups is constant.

Student personnel services represent a special effort of colleges to bring the findings of behavioral sciences and the artistry of professional

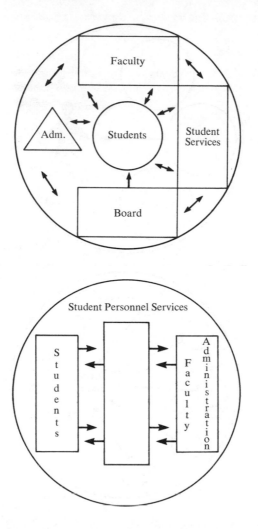

personnel workers to the service of students and all other segments of the college community. The compelling purpose of student personnel services is the individualizing of the total impact of the college community upon each individual student. The curriculum of the college, the processes of instruction, and the total college living experience all aim at making the student capable of freedom.

Effective accomplishment of the goals of a college requires: (1) the provision of services that meet student needs, (2) organization of the services into a pattern that is compatible with the character of the college, and (3) administration of the services in ways that are mutually supportive, and that collectively reinforce college goals.

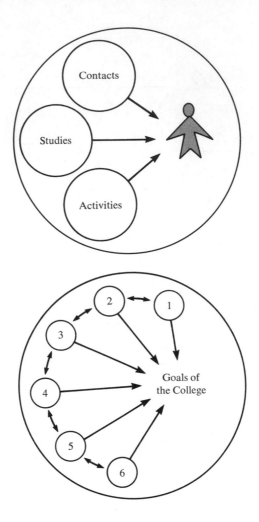

ORGANIZATION PATTERNS FOR STUDENT PERSONNEL WORK

Effective administration of student personnel work is facilitated by accurate analyses of (1) the jobs to be done, (2) the optimal times for doing these jobs, and (3) the roles and relationships of personnel employed to do these jobs.

ANALYSIS OF STUDENT PERSONNEL WORK BY BROAD FUNCTION

1. Routine services *for* students and college.

    Colleges are really run by clerks.

    Catalogues must be assembled, printed, distributed, revised.

Calendars must be made, checked, cleared, printed, posted, distributed.

Schedules must be compiled, checked, printed, distributed.

Information about everything about the college must be assembled, printed, distributed, told.

Records must be designed, printed, distributed, filled out, checked, filed, found, changed.

Registration procedures must be designed, explained, calendared, housed, patrolled, checked.

Transcripts must be evaluated, prepared, posted, checked.

Enrollment lists must be prepared, distributed, revised.

Grades must be secured, recorded, checked.

Books and food must be sold, ordered, records kept.

Money must be collected, kept, banked, accounted for.

Most of the work involved in these, and many more, important jobs is essentially clerical. It can be done more accurately and more rapidly by good clerks than by preoccupied professionals. Colleges are notoriously inefficient in the performance of routine clerical services.

Student personnel offices do most of the clerical work in a college. It is false economy not to provide a core of trained clerks, each with defined duties, and with a line-of-authority pattern of organization for each student personnel office.

2. Professional services for students.

College is a time for making decisions.

Career plans are made, changed, refined.

College majors are chosen, dropped, changed.

Courses are selected, changed, carried, or dropped.

Decisions on the level of scholarship appropriate for the student are made.

Health problems are faced.

Friendships are formed.

Sex needs are encountered—frequently gratified, seldom satisfied.

Personal philosophies are shaped.

Decisions cannot be made *for* students, they must be made *by* students. Helping students in decision-making situations requires the knowledge, the skills, and the time of the professional worker. Counselors, psychologists, physicians, nurses, social workers, placement officers, activity directors, financial aid officers, tutors, and other professionals are provided by colleges *for* students, but in effecting their services they work *with* students.

Working arrangements for professional work are different from those for routine clerical work. Decision-making cannot be timed. It does not flower in a waiting room or in a line at the counter. Quiet offices must be provided. More time control must be extended. Creativity and responsibility must be cultivated by a climate of freedom. Effectiveness rather than efficiency is the goal.

3. College-community activities *with* students.

The concepts of "the college as a community" and of "the total college as a part of the greater community" are of increasing challenge to student personnel work. These long overdue concepts are parts of the insistence by students that they be involved in the planning and management of their education and of their lives during the college years. Colleges are moving, at varying speeds, to accommodate these thrusts, and to harness the strong motivations toward cooperative work of students and faculty. Professors are involving students and townspeople in planning curriculum and instruction. College administrations are vying with each other in identifying and working with their campus subgroups and their community minority populations.

Professional student personnel workers have been slow to develop personnel and procedures for involving themselves in student and community activity movements. The professional tools and the professional habits of most student personnel workers have built in greater competency and greater comfort in working in a "professional" and "client" situation. While the developing situation will continue to need these individualized services, there is need also for the invention of new tools, new services, new professionals. These professionals will work *with* students, and with townspeople in effecting changes in their communities. They will clear out slums, build new parks, tutor slow learners, eradicate rats, convert the alienated, teach cooperation skills. They will plan and build new cities wherein the campus and the city are one and wherein the quality of life for all will be more nearly equal to the quality of life for some. The development of these new dimensions is the most exciting challenge now facing student personnel workers.

ANALYSIS OF STUDENT PERSONNEL WORK BY TIME OF SERVICE

There is a best time for most student services. The phasing of need and service is aided by a flow chart that starts with services rendered before the student reaches the campus and progresses through the entire college career of a class. Exhibit A presents a portion of such a chart developed by Jim Nelson for Orange Coast College that will illustrate the value of this tool.

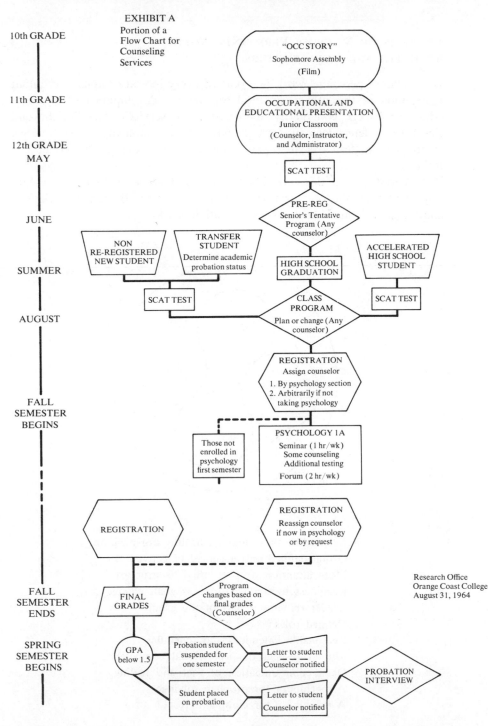

EXHIBIT A
Portion of a
Flow Chart for
Counseling
Services

10th GRADE

"OCC STORY"
Sophomore Assembly
(Film)

11th GRADE

OCCUPATIONAL AND
EDUCATIONAL PRESENTATION
Junior Classroom
(Counselor, Instructor,
and Administrator)

12th GRADE
MAY

SCAT TEST

JUNE

PRE-REG
Senior's Tentative
Program (Any
counselor)

NON
RE-REGISTERED
NEW STUDENT

TRANSFER
STUDENT
Determine academic
probation status

ACCELERATED
HIGH SCHOOL
STUDENT

SUMMER

HIGH SCHOOL
GRADUATION

SCAT TEST

SCAT TEST

AUGUST

CLASS
PROGRAM
Plan or change (Any
counselor)

REGISTRATION
Assign counselor
1. By psychology section
2. Arbitrarily if not
taking psychology

FALL
SEMESTER
BEGINS

Those not
enrolled in
psychology
first semester

PSYCHOLOGY 1A
Seminar (1 hr/wk)
Some counseling
Additional testing
Forum (2 hr/wk)

REGISTRATION
Reassign counselor
if now in psychology
or by request

REGISTRATION

Research Office
Orange Coast College
August 31, 1964

FALL
SEMESTER
ENDS

FINAL
GRADES

Program
changes based on
final grades
(Counselor)

SPRING
SEMESTER
BEGINS

GPA
below 1.5

Probation student
suspended for
one semester

Letter to student
Counselor notified

PROBATION
INTERVIEW

Student placed
on probation

Letter to student
Counselor notified

Analysis of Student Personnel Work
by Roles and Relationships

Student personnel work is a part of every job on campus. Acceptant recognition of this role is essential for optimal development of a totally educative college community. The pattern of services extending beyond this base is determined by size, purposes, and complexity of the college. A frequent pattern has an organization chart like that portrayed in Exhibit B.

Variations on this model are many and are easy to design. More important than the organization chart is the pattern of real-life relationships that determine how the organization works.

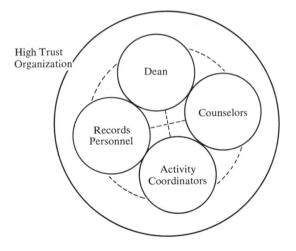

Relations like these make a healthy organization:
Group defined and accepted objectives
More attention to goals than to structure
Readiness to change forms as goals change
Leader remains a part of the group
Defined roles
Reasonable calendars and schedules
Mutual respect of professional competence
Open communication of fact and feeling
A machinery for problem solving
A machinery for complaint resolution

Tight Ship Low Trust Organization

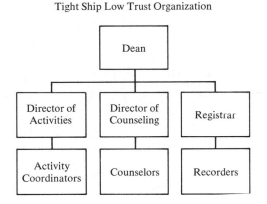

Relationships like these make a sickly organization:

Visible and emphasized lines of authority

Top man definition of roles and practices

Implied but not clearly stated calendars and schedules

Specific orders, not much explanation

Private communication

Formal intragroup relationships

Suspected suspicion of each other

No established problem-solving or grievance procedures

AN ORGANIZATION PATTERN FOR STUDENT PERSONNEL SERVICES

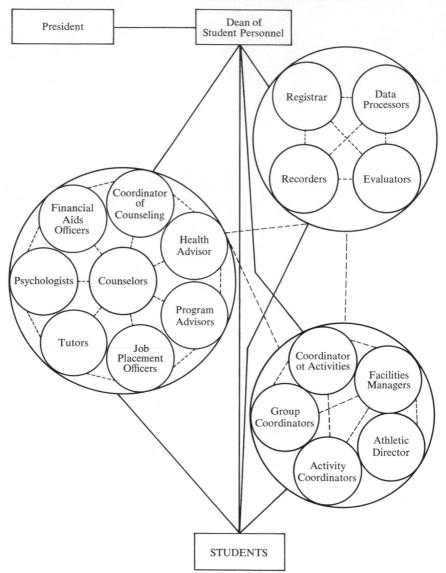

STAFF NEEDS FOR STUDENT PERSONNEL WORK
IN COLLEGES OF VARYING SIZE

In a one-student, one-teacher college, all services would be combined into one position. In a 10,000 student college, the addition of one new service usually requires the addition of a position. Between these extremes the relationship of positions required to services provided is highly variable. In the 1965 AAJC-Carnegie Corporation study of student services needed in colleges of varying size, Max Raines recommended the following positions.[1]

Administrative Unit	Staff Levels	Enrollments			
		500	1,000	2,500	5,000
Admissions, Registration, and Records	Registrar or Admissions Director	1	1	1	1
	Professional	0	½	1	2
	Clerical	2	4	6	8
Guidance and Counseling	Dean of Guidance and Counseling	1	1	1	1
	Head Counselor or Supervisors	0	0	1	2
	Professional Counselors	1	2	8	16
	Clerical	1	1½	2½	5
Placement and Financial Aids	Director (combined)	½	½	1	1
	Professional (placement or scholarships)	0	0	½	1
	Clerical	1	1	1½	2
Student Activities	Dean of Student Activities	1	1	1	1
	Professional	0	0	½	1
	Clerical	½	1	2	3
Administration	Vice-president of student personnel	1	1	1	1
	Administrative Asst.	0	0	0	1
	Clerical	1	1	1	1

ADMINISTRATIVE PRINCIPLES FOR
STUDENT PERSONNEL WORK

Effective student personnel work requires commitment, support, plan, staff, and operational theory. The most essential principles can be implied from the introductory schematics with which this section started. In brief restatement, these principles include:

1. Good student personnel work takes time and costs money. College administrations must provide the budget support and policy support consistent with the level of student personnel program they wish to maintain.

2. Active involvement in an activity is a most effective motivator. The best insurance that faculty, students, administration, or clerks will support an activity is to involve them in decision-making at the time of actual decision.

3. Some student personnel services are of a routine clerical character. There is no excuse for not making these services as efficient as good planning and modern technology can effect.

4. Some student personnel services necessitate a human-to-human relationship. They cannot be done well by machines, by clerks, or by professionals who behave like clerks. Colleges must identify the personal qualities required for these services and must provide the time, a suitable working climate, and the freedom to move required by these services.

5. Effective student personnel services require clear communication through both formal and informal channels. Private communication breeds suspicion and confusion.

6. Student control by inflexible regulation leads to evasion and rebellion. Student control by continuous helping develops suspicion of patronizing and insincerity. Student personnel programs which aim at helping students to become free men must steer between too much regulation and too much compromise.

7. Findings from the behavioral sciences provide guidance for the administration of student personnel work. The authors of this section have found much value in the compressed analysis of "Superiors and Subordinates" by Herbert A. Shepard.[2] Readers will find an uncomfortably close conformity between the military-industry line-of-command pattern spelled out in Shepard's analysis and the administrative practices of many colleges. Yet administrators generally, even those who operate differently, agree with the "high trust" principles enumerated by Shepard. "Wide participation in decision making," "face-to-face relationships," "mutual confidence," open communication, and "internal control of performance," are sturdy attributes of good management. Both their personality characteristics and their professional expertise equip student personnel workers to *lead* their colleagues in the application of behavioral science theory to the improvement of college administration.

SUMMARY

A frequent criticism of colleges during these days of open and critical examination is that students have lost their individuality and have become mere numbers—or holes punched in a card. The student revolution, which reaches the video screen almost nightly, is partly a search for identity and a plea that students are also people. The charge is that college administrators have given higher priority to the efficient processing of data bits than to the expansion of human personalities.

Administrators of community college student personnel programs know that their student bookkeeping must be *both efficient* and *personal*. They know that their counseling programs must support *both* "standards" and individual motivations. They know that the "climate" of their campuses must support *both* order and freedom.

To develop, staff, and manage an organized program of student services, services that bridge these built-in conflicts, calls for a high level of human engineering. It calls for a day-by-day recognition that people are more important than things, that communication involves feeling as well as knowing, and that trust is more motivating than suspicion. It is the thrust of this chapter that effective administration of student personnel services begins with good human relations within the student personnel staff.

REFERENCES

1. COLLINS, CHARLES C., *Junior College Student Personnel Programs: What They Are and What They Should Be.* Washington, D.C.: American Association of Junior Colleges, 1967.
2. SHEPARD, HERBERT A., "The Direction of Research Establishments," *National Physical Laboratory.* London, 1957.

Evaluation of Student Services in Community Colleges

Joseph W. Fordyce

President, Santa Fe Junior College

Perhaps no more important responsibility—nor none more complex —faces the student personnel administrator than determining the means by which a college can measure the efficiency and effectiveness of its own student services. Only by using appropriate evaluative devices can there be a true appraisal of student services and in turn can there be provided an adequate base for further appropriate development of these services and programs. This chapter, therefore, intends: (1) to review briefly some trends in evaluative procedures in student personnel services; (2) to point out some of the challenges and difficulties in this process; and (3) hopefully to point toward some positive approaches that might be available to junior colleges for this demanding task.

TRENDS IN EVALUATION

Until recent years, evaluation of guidance services has generally tended to lag well behind the practices and techniques in the field. Practitioners and theorists have defined their activities primarily on the basis of armchair logic and have expected others to accept their conclusions largely on faith. A review by Froehlich [2] however, pointed to 177 studies published prior to 1948 that began to bring evaluative studies and techniques to maturity. Froehlich's summary no doubt gave impetus to further studies, and this present review suggests some interesting modifications and refinements of the procedures that he uncovered.

Of perhaps major importance in more recent studies has been the development of insight into the complexities of human behavior with resulting increased understanding of behavioral changes, or the lack thereof, as the result of student services. Increased emphasis has also been placed upon an overall approach in terms of an all-college evaluation as opposed to any attempt to evaluate student services apart from the remaining influences of the college environment. An additional trend has been that of discarding the search for a single methodology that is best for all situations, and seeking instead to find that devices, or combination of devices, that seems most appropriate for the particular occasion.

CONTINUING CHALLENGES

Out of these studies and reviews has come recognition of a variety of problems and challenges that must continuously be attended if evaluations are to be more than naive, and perhaps even worthless, recountings of vague generalizations with little or no relation to the situation of the particular college. At the forefront of these challenges is the *problem of goals*. Too frequently, the aims of student personnel services have been couched in terms of a particular technique or activity; for example, "counseling" is frequently listed as an *aim* of guidance. Effectiveness of guidance can be determined only in relation to outcomes that can be isolated and described.

Generally speaking, moreover, these outcomes must reflect the changes in human behavior that the college expects to produce. Certainly we should have no hope of success, nor indeed will we know when success has been achieved, unless the aims are clear, defined in terms of behavioral changes that can be measured or observed, and agreed upon as legitimate aims of the total college. In a very real sense, then, student personnel services do not have aims. They must, if they expect any degree of success, share in the formulation of *college* aims, and provide services and techniques on a cooperative basis with all the other facilities of the institution to help bring about those changes in student behavior that will insure that the aims are met.

Another persistent problem in evaluation has been that of *control of variables;* student personnel services do not operate in a vacuum, but rather within a nexus of interrelated influences upon the individual. Inasmuch as each of these factors, individually or collectively, may compare favorably with the guidance situation in terms of influence, it becomes extremely difficult to attribute to guidance whatever changes may be noted. This problem has been partially resolved in guidance research by the use of control groups that are similar in all important characteristics to the experimental group, with the exception that they do not receive that aspect of guidance in which the researcher is interested. This device is not completely satisfactory, however, inasmuch as the matching cannot be perfect and also because subtle influences will continue to enter in such a way that they may be more disturbing to one group than to the other.

This condition may, in turn, be partially resolved if the experiment or observation is sufficiently replicated. For example, cooperative programs of research could be developed in which similar experiments or observations would be made in a number of different geographical regions and at various times. If the results were sufficiently similar we could begin to have faith that they were indeed causally related to the independent variable.

Another persistent problem has been associated with the *time factor*. Assuming that "good" results are obtained through evaluative studies made immediately after counseling or guidance, what evidence exists that the gain will persist over a sufficiently long period so that the total effect can be considered valuable? Conversely, some research has indicated that, in the long run, counseled individuals made what was considered to be effective adjustment even though immediate evaluation had indicated no significant changes. This would suggest the need for longitudinal studies and, to the extent that guidance proves valuable, for pervasive and continuous counseling programs.

The value of a number of time samples may be illustrated by a rather neat experiment performed by Courts [1] a few years ago. Since he was interested in the effects of tension upon learning, only one aspect of his results is pertinent to this discussion. He found that learning occurred in approximately equal amounts when the individual was under no tension as measured by a dynamometer and when the individual was under tension equal to approximately three-quarters of his capacity. Had Courts been satisfied with observing only at these two points, he would have missed the most important result of his experiment. Actually, he measured also at a number of other points along the tension continuum and thereby was able to arrive at the conclusion that "learning efficiency increases as tension increases up to some moderate tension level and thereafter efficiency decreases."

By far, however, the most persistent and challenging problem that evaluators encounter is that of the determination of *adequate criteria*— the finding of acceptable measuring devices. The challenge here is to find some event or some circumstance of the nonguidance world against which the effects of guidance can be compared or measured. If we use such social criteria, for example, as joining organizations, who is to say that the compulsive "joiner" has actually improved his social adjustment? Job efficiency is excellent as a criterion of the effectiveness of vocational guidance, but who is to say and on the basis of what kind of judgments whether or not a man is operating efficiently and with satisfaction anywhere close to his optimum level? The mere presence of a guidance service, therefore, cannot be used as an indication of the effectiveness of guidance services, nor can one guidance index be used as a measure of evaluation of another until that index has demonstrated its validity. If one guidance index is to be used as a criterion to measure the effectiveness of another index, what evidence have we that the original index has the kind of relationship with the events of the real world that we presume it has? This problem is a complex one which can be resolved only through the cooperative efforts of all who deal with human values and human development.

The complexities of these problems, however, should not in any sense be considered insurmountable barriers either to the continuation and development of the services that we believe to be so vital in meeting legitimate educational aims, or to the evaluation and assessment of these services with the constant goal of improving them. Recognition of the problems and complexities should enable us to pursue our evaluations on a continuingly more effective and sophisticated level, rather than discouraging us from attempting this all-important process.

POSITIVE APPROACHES

It has been suggested that evaluation must start with a recognition of goals. Although each college must determine its own aims, it is suggested that there exists a central core of concerns that a public community junior college would find difficulty in neglecting. These general concerns for each student would include, but would probably not be limited to:

1. Maintenance of good mental and physical health for himself, his family, and his community;
2. Understanding of the cultural heritage to gain perspective of his time and place in the world;
3. Understanding of his interaction with his biological and physical environment;
4. Development of ability to communicate in speaking and in writing;
5. Development of sound moral and spiritual values;
6. Exercising of privileges and responsibilities of democratic citizenship;
7. Utilization of mathematical and mechanical skills effectively for purposes of vocation and of ordinary life situations;
8. Utilization of critical thinking for the solution of problems and for discrimination among values;
9. Development of rewarding social and personal patterns of life;
10. Development of abilities to share in satisfying home and family life.
11. Achievement of optimum vocational adjustment;
12. Development of creativity and the appreciation for creativity.

Similarly, a congeries of services and activities has been developed, which have given evidence, in some college or another, that they can produce effective results in these areas of concern. For an exhaustive list of such services and activities, reference is invited to almost any standard textbook on guidance and student personnel services, but special attention for an easily accessible yet comprehensive list should be given to McDaniel's *Essential Student Personnel Practices for Junior Colleges.*[3] Such a list would usually include the following:

1. Articulation with secondary schools.
2. Orientation of prospective and new students.
3. Selection and admissions.
4. Registration and records.
5. Advisement and educational guidance.
6. Vocational advisement and information services.
7. Counseling.
8. Financial aid.
9. Work programs.
10. Student activities.
11. Placement.

To indicate the use of a statement of aims and services in the evaluative process, there follows a series of paradigms to illustrate positive approaches that hopefully can be used by individual colleges in evaluating their own program of services. It should be noted that this is not a checklist; it is illustrative only and must be adapted by a college to its own individual situation because the basic factor in each case is that of a college aim; obviously, the illustration will be pertinent to a particular college only if that college has indeed adopted that aim as its own. The general pattern of the illustrative material is to list: (1) a college aim; (2) a particular student personnel service that might be considered as contributing toward meeting that aim; (3) an indication of the specific aim, definable and measurable, which presumably is subsumed in the overall aim; and, finally (4) possible indices of success or of accomplishment.

It will be noted that this approach reveals at least two by-products. First, the specific aim of the service in relation to the overall college aim sets forth in each case an assumption that should lend itself to further research efforts of a more intensive and long-range nature. Secondly, the last factor, possible indices of success or accomplishment, will be recognized as criteria, the worth of which, to a very great extent, must be largely a judgmental matter. It will be noted that these indices fall generally under the following general categories: *

* These are essentially the categorization schemes developed by Froehlich.

1. The presence and organization of specific services.
2. Techniques employed and duties undertaken.
3. Client opinion.
4. Expert opinion.
5. Test results, especially "before and after."
6. External phenomena; for example, grade point averages, number of drop-outs, years on the job, number of promotions.

To summarize, then, the following illustrations are examples of a procedure of progressing *from* the general aim of the college *to* a specific aim or purpose of the particular service that presumably is a part or sub-division of the general college aim *to* possible indices of success, ranging in difficulty of collection from very simple number counting to considerably more complex processes of measurement and collection of judgments.

ILLUSTRATION A

1. College aim: "Exercise privilege and responsibilities of democratic citizenship."
   2. Service A: Student government association.
      3. Specific aim: Widespread responsible participation in those affairs of the college that relate to general citizenship.
      4. Possible indices of success:
         Number of students who vote in elections;
         Number of students who participate in student-sponsored activities.
   2. Service B: Educational advisement.
      3. Specific aim: Exposure of students to curricula opportunities in which appropriate learnings take place.
      4. Indices:
         Enrollment in appropriate courses by students judged to need help in this area;
         Scores on tests of related knowledge.

ILLUSTRATION B

1. College aim: "Develop rewarding personal and social pattern of life."
   2. Service A: Course in personal development.
      3. Specific aim: Lessening of prejudice and bias on ethnic or racial considerations.
      4. Indices:
         Scores on tests—commercial and homemade—indicative of attitude and pertinent knowledge;
         "Expert" opinion as to campus climate.

2. Service B: Cultural activities.
   3. Specific aim: Increased knowledge and understanding of and
      appreciation for cultural events.
   4. Indices:
      Number of students attending and participating;
      Faculty judgment of enthusiasm for such activities.

ILLUSTRATION C

1. College aim: "Achieve optimum vocational adjustment."
   2. Service A: Course in occupations.
      3. Specific aim A: Increase knowledge of available occupations.
      4. Indices:
         Scores on tests sampling knowledge;
         Evaluation by teacher of student understanding.
      3. Specific aim B: Improve choice of proposed occupation.
      4. Indices:
         Student judgment;
         "Expert" judgment on before and after choices.
   2. Service B: Counseling and advisement.
      3. Specific aim: Appropriate student selection of program and
         courses.
      4. Indices:
         Numbers of students in various programs;
         Faculty opinion of appropriateness of distribution of students;
         Number of failures in various curricula.

ILLUSTRATION D

1. College aim: "Develop sound moral and spiritual values."
   2. Service: Course in personal development.
      3. Specific aim: Increase ability to formulate appropriate self-
         appraisals.
      4. Indices:
         Self report of students;
         Scores on tests, "before and after."

ILLUSTRATION E

1. College aim: "Share in the development of satisfying home and family
      life."
   2. Service: Counseling.
      3. Specific aim: Increase awareness of self—other relations.
      4. Indices:
         Family opinion;
         Self reports.

ILLUSTRATION F

1. College aim: "Use mathematical and mechanical skills effectively for purposes of vocation and of ordinary life situations."
    2. Service: Job placement.
        3. Specific aim: Improve appropriateness of student selection of initial employment.
            4. Indices:
                Employer evaluation;
                Business community climate for accepting students for employment;
                Student report of job satisfaction.

AIMS AND SERVICES

To repeat, this list of illustrations is obviously not intended to be exhaustive. It is, on the other hand, intended as a suggested series of procedures through which every junior college might guide itself in providing appropriate evaluation of its student personnel services. Each college must determine its own aim within the broad policies, regulations, and legislation under which it operates in its own state or district. It must also determine the educational services, including student personnel services, that it considers will have the greatest chance of producing those desired results.

THE SETTING

One major issue remains. This report has attempted to indicate that eventually the effectiveness of student personnel services can be judged and evaluated only in terms of desired student growth, development, and change. Although this is believed to be a truism, the fact still remains that a number of aspects or considerations in regard to student personnel programs must be recognized as having only an *indirect* effect upon individual students; the importance of these factors is that, well managed, they make it possible for the other more direct services to exist and to flourish. Included among these factors, situations, activities, or services would be:

1. Effective organization and administrative policies of the college;
2. Effective organization and adequate staffing of student personnel services;
3. Clear delineation of responsibilities among the administrative, instructional, and student personnel faculties;
4. Clear delineation of who is "the student" that the college, and therefore student services, purports to serve;

5. Effective procedures for sharing information among any members of the total faculty who may be in a position to help;

6. Clear delineation of the teaching faculty role in guidance (so-called "academic advisement" may well be the area in which the instructor can make the *least* contribution);

7. The maintenance of high morale that permits each segment of the faculty to see and accept its responsibilities while holding in high respect the responsibilities and functions of each other segment;

8. An adequate program of testing and other analytical devices by means of which information necessary to the educational process can be obtained from each student.

The point in regard to these peripheral considerations is that if the individual student is to be served, the "stage management" must be smooth, efficient, and unobtrusive. Too frequently, these secondary services have come to be considered as primary means or even ends in themselves. Witness the tremendous number of elaborate testing programs in which the assumption seems to exist that the actual taking of the test is somehow or other beneficial to a desirable growth pattern in the student so exposed. Services and the evaluation of these services can be meaningful only if the house that provides them is in good order.

HYPOTHESES

Many of the propositions stated throughout this paper are in actuality hypotheses and assumptions needful of proving:

1. Participation in college student activities is predictive of effective adult citizenship.

2. A distinguished academic record in sociology and social psychology indicates freedom from bias and prejudice.

3. The individual most nearly free from racial prejudice is most likely to lead a productive life.

4. Increased knowledge about occupations leads to improved vocational choice.

5. Students who make most appropriate curricular selections make the most appropriate vocational selections.

6. Understanding of self leads to better mental health.

7. Participation in interscholastic athletics leads to improved physical and mental health.

8. Continuity of educational experience insures increased learning.

9. Knowledge of library resources improves academic accomplishment.

10. Accurate self-evaluation is essential to the establishment of satisfying family relationships.

Exploration of the validity of these hypotheses might move forward the science and art of student personnel work.

REFERENCES

1. COURTS, FREDERICK A., *Psychological Statistics*. Homewood, Ill.: Dorsey Press, 1966.
2. FROEHLICH, CLIFFORD P., *Evaluating Guidance Procedure, A Review of the Literature*. Washington, D.C.: Office of Education, 1949.
3. McDANIEL, J. W., *Essential Student Personnel Practices for Junior Colleges*. Washington, D.C.: American Association of Junior Colleges, 1962.

An Outsider's Viewpoint — Friendly but Critical

E. G. WILLIAMSON

Dean of Students Emeritus,
University of Minnesota

I am pleased that, for the third time, I am asked to give an outsider's friendly but critical view of student personnel work as it is developing in junior colleges across the nation. Speaking from my own observation and firsthand experience I shall be glad to make a few comments which are intended to be constructive and perhaps to initiate innovation in areas where it has not yet begun. This statement is also intended as a word of encouragement for those who realize we are in a new decade and that the junior college is, in the best sense of the word, an experimental institution trying to keep abreast of the times as changes occur in society and in the kinds of students who come to the institution.

ACADEMIC ADVISING

I should like to repeat a few points I have made in previous reviews before I enlarge my criticism and extend it to new points of view. I still feel that advising by faculty is outdated because the faculty, while it may know curriculum requirements, usually does not have any more insight into the dynamics and motivation, the aspiration, and the capabilities of students who come for advice than was true a half century ago, when advising based on common sense was first replaced by psychological appraisals of a more sophisticated sort. I acknowledge that we have by no means arrived at solid, reliable, and fully valid appraisal methods. Much more needs to be done by counselors in junior colleges as well as in four-year colleges and universities. But advising by untrained persons, even though they may be expert in their own field of knowledge, is not sufficient; some psychological understanding of the complexities of human relations and aspirations is needed, especially because we are now bringing into the colleges many individuals who a few decades ago would not have been enrolled because they could not have met formal admissions requirements.

What is needed is a sophisticated type of psychological understanding of the individual, so that he himself can better appraise his own capabilities as he proceeds toward his tentatively chosen goals of work and style of living. New experiences often yield data which call for a change of direction and aspiration. Such continuous reappraisal of the individual's capabilities and progress requires a psychological background which the average faculty member does not possess. Without supplemental training, which many faculty are not willing to acquire or are not convinced is necessary, they are not prepared to cope with developmental problems of students.

THE NEW STUDENTS

Many students are now enrolling who do not meet traditional admissions standards; some would have been pushouts or dropouts in former years, while others constitute a large new segment of the population who never considered college before. In America our determination to provide opportunities for everyone to be educated up the limits of his capabilities calls for broad college admissions policies far more cogenial to the junior colleges than to most four-year colleges, which are unprepared to deal with atypical students. Opportunities for continuous reappraisal of aspirations and capabilities are crucial for such students in their efforts to avoid what Myrdahl referred to as the permanent underclass—those who are permanently unemployed because they are permanently untrained.

Corporations are now providing employment and training for disadvantaged persons. Junior colleges in some communities are working closely with industry, especially in urban centers, to provide educational opportunities for every individual who can profit by further training and who can be induced to attempt it.

While the junior colleges have made great progress in educating socioeconomically disadvantaged students, much more needs to be done because there are still so many individuals who do not yet aspire to secure additional education. The open-door admissions policy of junior colleges has resulted in ever-increasing enrollments; two-thirds of these students report that they initially aspire to complete the bachelor's degree although about a fourth of them will actually transfer to four year colleges. Many students still have a four-year college degree as their ultimate goal regardless of their interests or capabilities, and are in great need of counseling and encouragement in redirecting their efforts.

Junior colleges should work aggressively with industry, the United

States Employment Service, and other community agencies in trying to enroll unemployed and sometimes low-aspiring individuals. Through careful appraisal and personal counseling, junior colleges should encourage them to develop their potential. I have great admiration for the progress that has been made in many junior colleges in many states. Much more remains to be done, however, because of the large numbers who appear on relief rolls and who seek employment without adequate training. While the open-door admissions policy presents opportunities for such individuals, aspiration to utilize educational opportunities must be cultivated through counseling and other growth-producing experiences. For the most part, four-year colleges will not attempt this necessary societal reconstruction task. It is mostly the junior colleges that offer hope for large numbers of uninspired individuals who drift from one job to another without any permanent attachment, living marginal lives. Students who can handle transfer level work should not be neglected, because our society is greatly in need of trained specialists. But what of those who because of limited previous educational opportunities or nonacademic bent are unlikely to profit from traditional college education? It is this latter group that seems to me to provide the great opportunity for junior colleges to make a real contribution to societal improvement.

THE COMMUTING STUDENT

We must not continue to neglect the student whom we loosely classify as a commuter. Often he comes to the campus for classes and then goes away, scarcely an integral part of the academic enterprise. Such commuters miss much of the richness of the academic maturing process which many individuals in the four-year elite colleges prize so much: the informal learning which takes place among resident students as they go about their attempts to reform or restructure our society. Only a few institutions are making any serious attempt to reach those who do not voluntarily join in the totality of learning experiences at their academic institution. Unhappily the four-year colleges that have become bureaucratic and tradition-ridden are unlikely to pay much attention to students who come to the school only for formal classwork. Experimentation is needed with regard to the commuter, and it seems likely that the junior colleges, with their flexibility, open-door policy, and lack of ties to the ancient model of Aristotle's academy, can make it possible for such experimentation to take place.

STUDENT UNREST

Today as never before youth is in revolt. And that is as true of students in junior colleges, particularly those in urban settings, as it is of four-year college students. They are revolting against organized society for many reasons which I will not try to analyze in this chapter. But the fact that they are revolting and that some are willing to destroy the schools and many other institutions indicates that this is a very serious matter. Is the junior college prepared, and responsible, for doing something about it? I think that it is. I think that it has a very rich opportunity to help individual students learn how to reconstruct our society in ways which develop the human talents that our citizens possess. This is no easy task because it calls for social engineering which the schools, for the most part, have not been adequately prepared to do, either historically or technically.

Now what are we going to do about it? Shall we sit idly on the side-lines while police and the militia restore order, and force individuals into classes where they will not be motivated to aspire to work for constructive societal change, but rather will hate the society which ignores their individual and collective problems? Or will we work as counselors, teachers, and administrators to help distraught youth mature into the kind of citizens who will reconstruct society in ways which are more humane and more adapted to helping each person achieve his full potential as a human being? Obviously, I vote for the latter attempt even though I know it is a difficult, long-range project. I fully believe that student personnel workers can provide leadership in aiding all students to organize out-of-class activities to attain social goals. Especially is the extracurriculum wide open for creative innovation of this kind of learning. Students are responsive to challenges of unresolved societal problems if student personnel workers are personally acceptable to them and effective in aiding and stimulating them to turn their enthusiasm with compassion toward the causes of human misery.

In the formal curriculum itself I think it is possible for junior colleges to organize new types of courses on current social problems and the need for societal reconstruction. We can teach the content and historical background of how we got this way through depressions and wars, and not merely through the latest climax, Viet Nam, important though that seems to be to most youth, as the immediate cause of the trouble.

It will take some doing to retool teachers and counselors in junior colleges to help students understand the sources of depersonalization in crowded urban conditions—sources which will not be eliminated merely by raising taxes or changing political parties. Every junior college student should have some systematic, firsthand learning experiences working in a poverty area; existing voluntary programs are not numerous enough nor organized enough to contain the kind of firsthand learning experienced in the Peace Corp. Students need to learn how we have depressed human beings—black and yellow and white and red—into inhuman kinds of relationships. Such perceived degradation in others is a very rude awakening for many students. Those who themselves come from ghettos may come to see themselves more objectively and therefore more hopefully, and may be induced to help innovate societal reconstruction constructively.

All our students are citizens who must therefore be educated to assume intelligently and optimistically the direction that the future will take in our democracy. One of the best ways to develop a sense of direction is to study the worst and best conditions close at hand, and to discuss in rational ways in the classroom and elsewhere outside of class the possible courses of action open to us. Such a sobering review of possible solution is, in itself, a very difficult task for the teacher as well as for the students. We need to use rational methods to replace violence, and there is no better place to learn rational analysis of controversial societal problems than in the college itself. Students need to learn how to separate fact from fancy and from irrelevancy and untested assumptions. What I am suggesting are discussion classes, retreats, meetings, and debates, based on firsthand learning experiences—a new form of total learning in and out of the classroom. I am bold enough to suggest it for junior colleges because they are not tied to the Middle Ages as are many four-year colleges and therefore are freer to deal with contemporary unsolved problems. This function of a college would not have been new to John Dewey or William James or Thomas Jefferson, because all of them had in mind that we have a *participative democracy* in which everyone worked for the good of all and did not merely use schools and other social agencies for their own personal economic job advancement.

Junior colleges should not only teach students how to analyze societal problems rationally but also how to organize new forms of participation in the management of the colleges themselves. One of the long-delayed reforms in higher education in America calls for a redefinition or realignment of the relationship between the institutions and their students. We still lecture *down* at students as in the Middle Ages. It is a rare institution that gives students an *active* significant learning role of participation in problems related to college management. For example, I refer to the unsolved problem of how to deal with controversy when there are political groups ready to pounce upon the college if it takes sides on any issue.

It is possible for junior colleges to contribute to the reconstruction of society and still not weaken their role in accomplishing traditional worthwhile objectives for students for whom these objectives are relevant. One set of objectives need not be given up for the other, but rather added to it; what is required is a flexibility of organization and openness to change without abandoning goals of the past.

Students must be aided in learning effective ways of resolving highly controversial issues. As educators, we should teach them how to participate by rational discussion and well-planned actions which discard violence, hatred, bigotry, and ignorance for the method the school understands best —the use of reason in working for social good for all members of our society.

Making Programs Relevant **2**
for the College and Community

While student development programs must march to the drum of student needs, they are also influenced by professional guidelines, governmental policies, community pressures, and attitudes of faculty and administration. Part 2 considers these forces and suggests ways in which the college can integrate them, not only to serve students but the larger community for which the college is a primary avenue toward self-realization.

Influences From the Outside

CLYDE E. BLOCKER

President, Harrisburg Area
Community College

JAMES A. ODOM

Dean of Students and Executive
Assistant to the President,
Harrisburg Area Community College

Student personnel programs are affected by a variety of external influences on the national, state, and local levels, as well as by less formal but powerful trends in the larger society. A complete catalogue of such influences would cover many pages; therefore, the authors intend to select what they consider to be significant external influences, and to explore two questions: How is the influence brought to bear, and what have been the results? These questions will be examined by considering the varied but interrelated factors which affect student personnel programs.

TRAINING PROFESSIONAL PERSONNEL

After World War I the vocational guidance movement began. This first attempt at professional personnel work, aimed at secondary level students, somewhat mechanistically matched individuals with occupations. In the 1920s and '30s, a few universities were seriously interested in preparing professionals in the newly emerging guidance movement.[15] During this era, however, little serious consideration was given to the need for explicit professional preparation for such personnel. On the whole, only after World War II did universities and professional organizations recognize the need for systematic professional preparation.

After 1946, graduate schools continued to prepare primarily secondary and elementary school guidance workers. However, universities did begin to develop more widespread and responsible interest in college level student personnel services. Qualitative and quantitative expansion of training programs for such personnel finally gained momentum in the early 1950s, and continues today.

Unfortunately, university interest in training student personnel workers for two-year colleges has lagged behind the times. As a result, substantial numbers of such trained professionals were needed about a decade before the majority of universities even became aware of the need. Since only a few universities attempted to develop a meaningful sequence of graduate courses designed to prepare college level guidance personnel, trained professional personnel who came into two-year colleges during the last quarter century came from a background of secondary school education and experience.

Prior to the enactment of the Higher Education Act of 1965, the primary thrust of university training was for secondary schools. The availability of federal funding since 1965 has stimulated the development of somewhat stronger programs for preparing college level personnel workers; but the national effort, taken *in toto,* still has serious deficiencies. For example, "basic training" workshops and seminars, often with depressingly similar formats, are available only for relatively small numbers of practitioners and graduate students. At the same time, universities have generally failed to commit their own resources, both financial and administrative, in generous amounts to these programs, with the result that university leadership in the student personnel movement has, with a few notable exceptions, shown a curious lack of imagination in program structure and content.

The two-year college's attempts to find and retain qualified student personnel workers are further complicated by at least two factors. First, university personnel seem reluctant to recognize that college level personnel workers should be qualified in one or more subject matter disciplines if they are to function effectively in an academic setting. Similarly, university personnel must also grasp the relevance of the humanity and social science disciplines in the training process, for a firm grasp of these disciplines adds depth and meaning for student personnel workers who must interact in a highly complex, scientific society.[3] Second, the continuing dearth of executive talent in higher education tends to channel the most capable personnel workers into first and second level administrative posts, for the education, experience, and personality characteristics of these professionals seems to qualify numbers of them for such positions.[22]

FINANCIAL SUPPORT

Any discussion which centers upon training professional student personnel workers must eventually consider the question of finance, since without adequate financial support professional programs will not be available, with the result that trained student personnel workers will not be available in sufficient numbers to assure that services reach the student.

At the federal level, certain specific guidelines emanating from the United States Office of Education have had a direct bearing upon student personnel programs. Federal legislation has been even more influential in providing financing and staffing for student personnel programs. The National Defense Education Act, Title V-2, was a major step toward improved student services, since its specific mission was to assist colleges in establishing and maintaining guidance, counseling, and testing programs. Similarly, sections of the Educational Professions Development Act of 1967 Part D and E, the Higher Education Act of 1965 Title III and Title V, in the Higher Education Amendments of 1968, were set up specifically to provide for training counselors and other qualified student personnel workers. Thus both new colleges and established institutions have been able to plan more valuable student personnel programs, with the assurance that sufficient personnel to administer such programs can be trained.

Since 1960, several philanthropic foundations, four of the most responsible being the W. K. Kellogg, Danforth, Esso, and the Carnegie Corporation, have shown interest in student services in community colleges, primarily by providing financial support for training personnel in research and experimental programs. Even though projects funded by these and other groups have, with few exceptions, been aimed toward goals other than student personnel services, such projects have indirectly encouraged the improvement of student services in one way or another. Thus while the total financial contribution from foundations has been relatively modest in relation to the tasks which should be done, their contributions should not be underestimated.

More adequate financial resources for personnel services were provided when a smattering of states enacted community college legislation.[24] Legislation enacted in New York in the middle 1950s, for instance, established realistic financial support for two-year colleges. Equally important, it enabled individual colleges to allocate financial resources on the basis of specific institutional needs. Subsequently, legislation, illustrated by action in Michigan, Pennsylvania, Illinois, and Missouri, made it possible for colleges to provide more adequate finances for student services.[13]

At the local level, adequate financial support of student personnel services obviously determines whether or not these services reach the students, since it is at this stage where the level of effort is determined by high level administrative and policy decisions which allocate institutional resources, regardless of origin, and which in time shape the quality of student institutional interaction. In addition, until about 1965, most public community colleges were legal administrative appendages of public school districts. Thus financing and staffing of student personnel services followed the well-established secondary school pattern. This administrative arrangement further tended to perpetuate the myth that community college students could be educated at the same annual operating cost as could high school students. The result was that the very limited resources available to two-year colleges were used to shore up the most glaring weaknesses in the instructional programs, leaving few resources for other purposes.[16]

The deleterious effects of subordinating community colleges to public school traditions and administrative practices cannot be overestimated, for not only were student services underfinanced and understaffed, but their conceptual basis, operational principles, and relationships with students could hardly be called educationally positive.[6] Fortunately, most two-year colleges are now emancipated from public school control, enabling them to emerge from the shadow of the secondary school, and gain acceptance by other collegiate institutions. They are also enjoying somewhat more equitable financial treatment by local taxpayers, state legislators, and the federal government.

PROGRAM DEVELOPMENT AND IMPROVEMENT

Improvement and changes in student personnel services are stimulated by all the groups listed on page 114.

Such external influences vary in importance, depending upon explicit conditions and timing. If we trace, for example, the influence of federal activities we might well start with congressional hearings on federal legislation. As the legislative process continues, laws are enacted and the Office of Education is directed by Congress to set up federal guidelines and regulations. These administrative responses to legislation range from the general to the specific, and in the past have required that states utilizing federal funds develop state plans that will meet the requirements of legislation and regulation. Subsequently, this body of law, and administrative directions from both the federal and state levels, have explicit effects upon how student personnel programs will function.

There has also been considerable influence upon student personnel programs through professional organizations at the national level. Such organizations as the AACRAO, the APGA, and the ACAC have been instrumental in setting up training programs for professional staff and in exchanging information to make student personnel programs more effective. For example, these organizations have exchanged junior college-senior college articulation data, as well as information regarding more efficient utilization of electronic equipment, thus providing better services to students by freeing student personnel workers from many clerical tasks, enabling them to spend more time relating face-to-face with individual students. In addition, the national organizations were instrumental in assembling information regarding special programs for the disadvantaged,

SOURCES OF EXTERNAL INFLUENCES
UPON STUDENT PERSONNEL PROGRAMS

National Level	*State Level*	*Local Level*
Federal Executive, Judicial, and Legislative Branches	Executive, Judicial, and Legislative Branches	Executive, Judicial, and Legislative Branches
U. S. Office of Education	State Department of Education	Students
American Association of Collegiate Registrars and Admissions Officers (AACRAO)	Colleges and Universities	Parents
	Professional Education Organizations	Community
		Advisory Committees
American Association for Higher Education (AAHE)	State Boards of Control	Local Power Groups
	Educational and Management Consultants	Trustees
American Association of Junior Colleges (AAJC)		
American Council on Education (ACE)		
American College Personnel Association (ACPA)		
American College Testing Program (ACT)		
American Education Research Association (AERA)		
American Personnel and Guidance Association (APGA)		
College Entrance Examination Board (CEEB)		
Educational Testing Service (ETS)		
Association of College Admissions Counselors (ACAC)		
Philanthropic Foundations		
Universities		
Regional Accrediting Associations		

in this way enabling institutions from coast to coast to keep abreast of what is happening in such programs, both within their own state and at the national level. Finally, these organizations have been active in exchanging and disseminating financial aid information, as well as federal regulations concerning selective service and veterans administration certification.

Of the national professional organizations, AAJC and ACPA have been the most vigorous and effective proponents of qualitative improvement and quantitative expansion of two-year colleges, particularly during the last decade. They have stimulated interest and effective responses by federal and state governments, local sponsoring groups, the business community, labor unions, and philanthropic foundations to the needs of these institutions. In addition, they provide a number of much needed services not otherwise available, for instance, consulting services for developing colleges.[12]

Specifically the student personnel commission of AAJC has been a significant factor in calling attention to the role of student personnel work in the junior college. Through the Commission, AAJC encouraged the Carnegie Project, and more recently, has sponsored convention programs and has been responsible for a series of position papers which should prove influential in the further development of student personnel programs. Similarly, the Commission on Junior College Student Personnel Work of ACPA has provided national focus for grassroot student personnel workers to work together toward developing the profession. Recently, this Commission sponsored the first national conference of junior college student personnel workers, and since that time has sponsored national conferences each year that are held prior to the national convention of ACPA. This Commission cooperates with AAJC in producing the *Junior College Student Personnel Newsletter,* which goes to every junior college in the nation. Through a special interest section, junior college student personnel workers are able to participate in national programs and Commission activities throughout the student personnel higher education profession. In the near future, the Commission will publish a new monograph for ACPA entitled, *New Directions in Community College Student Personnel Programs.*

In summary, the primary contribution of the national professional organizations has been a systematic exchange of information regarding all phases of student personnel work. The result has been a further strengthening of student personnel programs in higher education.

Another very important influence has been the standardized testing program provided by national testing services. Both ACT and CEEB have shown interest in the two-year college. ACT tests and research reports have provided an enormous amount of usable academic and socioeconomic data on community college students, which have been of particular value to student personnel services. CEEB has developed materials usable in the admission and subsequent counseling of junior college students.[2, 26]

When one turns from national to state level influences, the most persistent and impelling influence felt by two-year colleges proves to be the state legislatures and boards of control. State legislation not only sets the legal limits of the institution, but it also dictates patterns of institutional control and, in a few instances, it explicitly defines educational services to be provided. Thus one finds the proscription of college-parallel education, occupational education, remedial education, and guidance services in some state statutes.

Similarly, state rules and regulations promulgated by both federal and state legislation are quite explicit in their influences upon student personnel services. Such regulations often decree that newly established colleges submit a five-year plan of development, including a detailed explanation of student personnel services.

Other influences from the state level include master plans for higher education, state certification requirements for teachers and counselors, and a wide variety of research studies designed and completed by professional staff employed by the state.[10] The state and regional chapters of the national professional organizations have also had a very decided influence upon student personnel programs, since it is at the state and regional level that many of the national projects are administered and worked out in more detail. Similarly, much information "filters up" from the state or regional level to the national level, often influencing the policies of such organizations and, indeed, in the long run influencing federal and state legislation concerning student personnel programs.

Finally, one must consider the influence of the regional accrediting associations for secondary schools and institutions of higher education. The efforts of these associations to upgrade college level student personnel services are well known. The Middle States Association of Colleges and Secondary Schools requires that two-year colleges provide such services, indicating that there must be clearly stated admissions policies, complete academic records, and student services which will stimulate efficiency of learning and student achievement. "Expressions of intent do not produce results. There must be definition, organization, and responsibility." [25] Although couched in different terms, all regional accrediting associations have similar requirements for the provision of student services.[14]

Local influences come from many directions. The trustees, through policy formulation and budgetary controls, play a critical role in the shaping of student personnel services. Community advisory committees representing government, business, industry, and other special interest groups also contribute to the types and kinds of student services. Often these committees stimulate the extension of testing programs, financial aids, part-time employment, and other services beyond the campus and into the community. They provide an ideal avenue for feedback, evaluation, and improvement of student personnel services.

Because students at two-year colleges generally live at home, parents exert both indirect and direct influence upon the interactions of the professional staff and students, for as the student develops greater maturity and a sense of independence, which in many instances is related to his experiences with a counselor or faculty advisor, the possibility of conflict between parents and students increases. Although such influences may have little effect upon the types of student services offered, it is entirely possible that the quality of such services can be adversely affected by undue parental concern and influence upon either the student or the professional staff.

Locally, perhaps the most pervasive influence upon student personnel services comes from the student himself.[23] In many ways he mirrors his family, community, and school background. Thus the primary thrust of student personnel services in a college drawing students from an urban ghetto, a poor rural area, or an affluent suburban setting would unquestionably be influenced by such external forces. It is clear that the kinds of programs necessary for community college students from Harlem or Watts would bear little resemblance to those appropriate to students in the center of Iowa. It is apparent, too, that the student body of many colleges seldom contains a preponderance of students from any geographic area. Indeed, the typical pattern would be a mixture of rural-urban-suburban students, all exerting an influence upon the direction the student personnel program will take at any given institution. Perhaps the failure to differentiate the various elements which make up a typical student body is the most striking weakness of student personnel programs in community colleges today. We have, to a large extent, built our student services upon middle-class concepts, ignoring the fact that the nature of the student body has changed radically in the last five to seven years, now including larger numbers of students from the large city ghettos and from rural areas who do not necessarily share middle-class values.

There is a subtle influence upon student personnel services which comes neither directly from the student nor from his parents, but from the community at large. The fact that most community colleges have the word "community" in the title means that the community at large often feels that it has the right to influence college policy. Obviously, the student personnel administrator must be able to distinguish the legitimate from the false, since a viable student personnel program cannot bow to community pressures and requests, but neither can it ignore them altogether.

What have been the results of all of the influences—national, state, and local—that have been brought to bear on student personnel services? At the federal level, the additional money appropriated and the guidelines emanating from Washington have tended to encourage institutions to strengthen their existing student personnel programs or, in the case of a developing institution, to be able to place a priority on such programs. Similarly, professional organizations at the national and state levels have enabled developing institutions to capitalize on successful programs from other institutions and to avoid programs that have proved to be failures.

At the state level, chaos has often been avoided from the very outset since the state sets down certain specific guidelines. The regional accrediting associations have had the same effect, that is, they have enabled student personnel programs at new institutions, and at institutions that are fairly well established, to have some appropriate guidelines toward which to strive.

Finally, at the local level, through local influences, student personnel programs have had to be tailored to fit the unique and specific needs of the given community. Thus while a certain amount of order may be exerted from the federal and state levels, it is at the local level that the programs are carried out. Often the unique needs of the community have been met by having information work up through state and regional associations to the federal level, thus affecting legislation (for example, the Higher Education Act of 1965 was amended in 1968 to provide certain specific services which had not been provided in the original act, services which came about through the influence of AAJC, and other educational associations.

RESEARCH

To date, there has been a paucity of research in the area of student services. Specific dimensions of student services, for example, administrative organization, role definitions of professional personnel, extracurricular activities, students and program evaluation, have been subjected to scattered, mostly superficial research.

As pointed out by Cross,[11] "Research on the junior college student is a new phenomenon; emphasis in this review, therefore, was placed on recent research. Almost half the references cited bear the date of 1968 and 1967." Her study is the most comprehensive synthesis of research on two-year college students to date. By reviewing eight dimensions or characteristics of students, Cross points the way toward research-based information and understanding which community colleges must have if they are going to begin to make realistic decisions.[11] It is essential that college counselors and teachers be encouraged to utilize information of this type in an effort to improve the quality of student services.

Several other lines of research are of value to personnel specialists. Of particular interest is the work of Pace [17] who has developed a method of matching student abilities, attitudes, and expectations with institutional characteristics. The use of CUES, College and University Environment Scales, as Pace calls the instrument, and JCES, Junior College Environment Scales, developed by Pace and Hendricks, make possible the placement of students in institutions with environments most conducive to their academic and personal development. Astin [4] has also contributed to our understanding of the college environment, particularly as it is expressed by student attitudes and behavior patterns. Two additional studies of seminal interest relate to the educational and vocational development of students and student dropouts.[5, 19]

The most important evaluative study now available is that by Raines,[20] which tried principally, ". . . to evaluate present junior college student personnel programs and to study the preparation of junior college student personnel specialists." [8] Succinctly stated, the study showed that few student personnel programs in two-year colleges were of acceptable quality. Raines also found that, ". . . forty-five percent of student personnel workers in large community colleges, and sixty percent in small colleges, did not meet minimum training standards, e.g., thirty graduate hours in student personnel or cognate fields." [8] The most important contribution of this study was the development of a model detailing minimal professional qualifications and outlining the essential parameters of an effective student personnel program. Matson has recently completed a follow-up study to determine whether these findings have had any impact upon student services in two-year colleges; her findings are not yet available.

A number of other sources of usable research must be mentioned. ACT has published a series of research monographs devoted largely to a description of students, and educational and vocational choice processes.[1] CEEB and ETS continue to fund research studies on students and student personnel services.[9] The U. S. Office of Education has funded a number of projects through selected universities.

In addition, there are many doctoral dissertations which provide information and insight into this important area of study.[18, 21] The most recent and complete bibliography which covers student personnel and all other major aspects of community colleges is that of Burnett.[7]

SUMMARY

It is apparent that student personnel programs are the product of many influences, many of which are extra-institutional. A few are negative but most are positive.

The constructive impact of external forces is directly related to the attitudes of the college faculty, administration, and personnel staff. If student services have genuine acceptance and strong stimulation by these groups, students will receive the help they need. Conversely, if there is faculty rejection or lethargy, underfinancing, and unimaginative leadership by the college president and dean of students, outside influences will be of little or no value to the institution. There are, in the opinion of the writers, a few two-year colleges which have demonstrated the willingness and ability to mount really effective student personnel programs. Genuine reform and improvement in higher education, however, will require significant changes and improvement in student personnel services.

REFERENCES

1. *ACT Research Reports* (A Series). Iowa City, Iowa: American College Testing Program, Inc.
2. *Announcement: A Program for Two-Year Colleges 1969-70.* New York: College Entrance Examination Board, 1969. 30 pp.
3. ARMOR, DAVID J., *The American School Counselor: A Case Study in the Sociology of Professions.* New York: Russell Sage Foundation, 1969. 227 pp.
4. ASTIN, ALEXANDER W., *The College Environment.* Washington, D.C.: American Council on Education, 1968. 187 pp.
5. ———— and ROBERT J. PANOS, *The Educational and Vocational Development of College Students.* Washington, D.C.: American Council on Education, 1969. 211 pp.
6. BLOCKER, C. E. and H. A. CAMPBELL, JR., *Attitudes of Administrators Toward the Administrative Organization of Public Junior Colleges in Seven States.* Austin, Texas, 1962. 41 pp.
7. BURNETT, COLLINS W., ed., *The Community Junior College: An Annotated Bibliography with Introductions for School Counselors.* Columbus, Ohio: The Ohio State University, 1968. 122 pp.
8. COLLINS, CHARLES C., *Junior College Student Personnel Programs: What They Are and What They Should Be.* Washington, D.C.: American Association of Junior Colleges, 1967. 46 pp., note p. 17, 34-35.
9. *Counseling in School and College.* New York: College Entrance Examination Board, 1961. 71 pp.
10. *Creation of the Future: Priorities of Growth and Change, The Master Plan Revised 1968.* Albany, N. Y.: State University of New York, 1968. 45 pp.
11. CROSS, K. PATRICIA, *The Junior College Student: A Research Description.* Princeton, N. J.: Educational Testing Service, 1968, 56 pp., note p. 8, 47-53.
12. *Developing Institutions: The Junior College.* An Interim Report of the First Year of The Program with Developing Institutions. Washington, D.C.: American Association of Junior Colleges, July 1969. 96 pp.
13. *Establishing Legal Bases for Community Colleges.* Washington, D.C.: American Association of Junior Colleges, 1962. 43 pp.
14. *Guide for the Evaluation of Institutions of Higher Education.* Chicago: Commission on Colleges and Universities, North Central Association of Colleges and Universities, 1968. 22 pp., note pp. 19-20.
15. LLOYD-JONES, ESTHER McD. and MARGARET RUTH SMITH, *A Student*

Personnel Program for Higher Education. New York: McGraw-Hill Book Company, 1938. 322 pp.

16. McDANIEL, J. W., *Essential Student Personnel Practices for Junior Colleges.* Washington, D.C.: American Association of Junior Colleges, 1962.

17. PACE, C. ROBERT, *The Use of CUES in the College Admissions Process.* Los Angeles: University of California, December 1966. 54 pp.

18. PARKER, FRANKLIN and ANNE BAILEY, *The Community Junior College: Bibliography of 519 United States Doctoral Dissertations.* Austin, Texas: The University of Texas, 1964. 38 pp.

19. PERVIN, LAWRENCE A., LOUIS E. REIK, and WILLARD DALRYMPLE, *The College Dropout and the Utilization of Talent.* Princeton, N. J.: Princeton University Press, 1966. 260 pp.

20. RAINES, MAX R. (principal investigator), *Junior College Student Personnel Programs: Appraisal and Development.* A Report to the Carnegie Corporation, November 1965.

21. ROUECHE, JOHN E., *Salvage, Redirection, or Custody? Remedial Education in the Community Junior College.* Washington, D.C.: American Association of Junior Colleges, 1968, 67 pp.

22. SCHULTZ, RAYMOND E., *Administrators for America's Junior Colleges: Predictions of Need 1965-1980.* Washington, D.C.: American Association of Junior Colleges, 1965. 28 pp.

23. *The Beliefs and Attitudes of Male College Seniors, Freshmen, and Alumni.* A Study by Roper Research Associates, Inc. New York: Standard Oil Company (New Jersey), May 1969. 46 pp.

24. *The Comprehensive Community College System in North Carolina.* Raleigh, North Carolina: Department of Community Colleges, State Board of Education, March 1968. 50 pp.

25. "Two Year Colleges," *Middle States Document No. 4.60A.* New York: Middle States Association of Colleges and Secondary Schools, September 1968. 10 pp.

26. *Using ACT on the Campus, 1968-69.* Iowa City, Iowa: American College Testing Program, Inc., 1968. 50 pp.

Influences from the Inside

WILLIAM A. ROBBINS

Director, Two-Year College Student
Development Center, State University
of New York at Albany

An exemplary student personnel program grows out of the college climate, the ways of believing and behaving of those in the institution. The staff members of such a program see themselves and feel themselves part of the bone and marrow of the institution, constantly affecting and always being affected by the many influences within the college community. No matter how excellent the model used and how filled it is with features that have been eminently successful elsewhere, in the main it is the local college condition that determines the program's effectiveness.

Unfortunately, this simple truth is not easy to grasp. It is sad to see a new staff member attempt to institute in his community college what he has recently learned in graduate school or in another institution, without taking into consideration the matter of institutional readiness for his idea. It is particularly sad to see his discouragement, or anger, when the plan fails. The framers of a program or modifiers of one already in existence are aware—if they are alert—of the effects of many influences on the program. The influences from within the college, that is, the attitude of the president, or faculty, are of particular significance.

It is the task of this chapter to consider those influences within the community college that limit or contribute to the development of the student personnel program. The writer will review a number of selected significant factors, bearing in mind that a number, including the student, are discussed more thoroughly elsewhere in this book.

INFLUENCE OF THE PRESIDENT

It would be difficult to overstate the influence of the college president on the student personnel program. Even though he may no seem close to the program, the college will feel his concern for a vital student-oriented total college program, if that concern is there. Conversely, his lack of concern will also be felt. The extent of the president's commitment will be noted in his budget support, in the way in which he works with both academic and student personnel leadership, in his search for a constructive presidential relationship with students and his dependence upon student personnel workers to help him develop that relationship, in his total educational leadership, and in his search for a meaningful, relevant educational program, not one simply copied from the four-year college.

When one considers all the different matters demanding time of the president his influence might be thought to be diluted. Studies do not show this to be so. John E. Roueche summarized a number of studies dealing with the community college presidency by saying that, ". . . the junior college president is the key to innovation." The quality of his educational leadership represents ". . . one of the most important factors in determining whether American junior colleges will measure up to the expectations held of them." [10] This generalization applies to all programs within the college, and in particular to the student personnel program.

The influence of the president can be seen in both its positive and negative aspects. Some very able deans of students testify to the constantly surprising support of their presidents, indicating unusual vision and understanding regarding the mission of the student personnel program. Rather than having to argue for support, many feel that their president is way ahead of them.

Even though the junior college boasts an open-door policy and an equalitarian philosophy, many presidents do not understand the vital role the student personnel program plays in this mission. As one outstanding president put it, "The significance of student personnel services in the community college is many times not understood nor accepted." [6] The president who does not understand and accept student personnel work will not press for the necessary dollars and make them available. He will be satisfied with a mediocre student personnel dean who does not understand sufficiently what a community college program should be. He will assign student personnel a perfunctory role in the college, thus showing clearly to all concerned the order of priorities. Such a president is influential, but toward mediocrity, traditional practices, and static ideas and programs. Of course staff members suffer—but it is the students who really suffer! The large number of community college students who lack the self-sufficiency to make it on their own, who badly need a student personnel program shaped to their abilities and interests, need a president who understands how a student personnel program can provide for their development.

The able president, the outstanding one, will attract committed people to his college's student personnel program. He will expect a strong program of student services, and he will secure the necessary resources to build such a program. He will represent vigorously to the community and to the board of trustees the philosophy of the comprehensive, student-oriented community college—and will allocate sufficient funds to keep the college's promises to students, at least to the limit of the possible. He will influence the development within the college of a commonality of thinking and working, thus stimulating close cooperation between the instructional and student personnel areas.

THE INFLUENCE OF THE FACULTY

The teaching faculty should be expected to influence markedly a college's student personnel effort. If their institution seriously strives toward significant community college objectives, then those engaged in teaching should share in the commitment. The college has recruited them because they are primarily interested in teaching rather than research and publication.

What crass stupidity it would be for counselors to work in a compartment of the college, ignoring teaching faculty who may be equally dedicated and conscientious, and not allowing them to contribute constructively to the student personnel program! Unhappily, shortsighted and irresponsible deans of students and counselors sometimes act in just such a way. They do not, however, possess a monopoly on student growth and development, despite pretensions of some that they do. In particular, counselors cannot "do it all" in helping students experience the full range of their potential.

In the strong community college there is a team effort in which teachers and student personnel workers engage in continuous dialogue and cooperative activity. Together they work on committees to plan innovative programs, as in developmental or special education. They help review ongoing efforts such as orientation, student activities, and the academic advising program. They want to know whether or not student referrals are occurring (in both directions) and whether they are followed through carefully. They constantly explore new directions by asking the searching, "unthinkable" questions.

The influence of the teaching faculty is felt in an untold number of other ways, mostly informal, both on and off campus. The effect of such influence can be significant in developing an integrated program to accomplish the important objectives faced by the comprehensive student-oriented community college. Anyone concerned with whether or not the community college is actually achieving these objectives would most certainly appraise attitudes of teaching faculty toward the student personnel program, their understanding of it, their appreciation and cooperative endeavor, and their influence upon the student personnel staff.

Questions such as the following might be very appropriate for review by an accreditation committee, or a faculty self-study group: Do instructional personnel understand what it is that the student personnel worker is trying to do? Do they understand his role and accept it? Do they respect his work? If so, do they convey this attitude in their classroom contacts with students—and elsewhere—in nonverbal communications as well as verbal statements? Do they seek out or respond positively to opportunities for joint educational programming—so that the counselors become known in the classroom, and students see a team approach?

The controversy in some community colleges as to whether student personnel members should have professorial rank along with the teaching faculty, or even have faculty status, has behind it the hidden problem of role acceptance and role rejection of one group by the other. Instead of integration, teaching faculty sometimes reject student personnel colleagues, and the latter in turn struggle to achieve "separate but equal" status. Behind the turmoil, there is much misunderstanding, self-interest, and blindness by both groups. As a result an opportunity for exciting, cooperative programming is lost.

If teaching faculty are uncooperative toward or unconcerned with the student personnel program, their attitude might be largely attributed to the newness of the student personnel field. There is little history or tradition behind student personnel work to prove to the teaching faculty member that it warrants his attention and participation. Student personnel services have, in many community colleges, grown in a rapid, hit-or-miss fashion to meet pressing, immediate needs, and often the faculty member has not been included in the planning and growth process. Therefore, he might not feel it incumbent upon himself to venture out of the classroom into the new realm of student personnel once a program is underway. If the original establishment of a student personnel program served to relieve a faculty member of some responsibilities to the students, why then open the way to taking those responsibilities back?

Counseling is the focal point of a great deal of misunderstanding. To be of real value to the students, teaching faculty and counselors must work closely together in the counseling relationship. Melvene Hardee has cited six views held by faculty members who fail to be enthusiastic about counselors:

1. The view that the relationship between teacher and student is a near-sacred one, a private affair with no interference from the counselor.
2. The view that "anybody can counsel," and that "an occasional pat on the back" is all that is needed.

3. The view that students who are old enough to come to college are mature enough to have solved all their problems; thus, there is little need for any professionally trained counselors on the college staff.

4. The view that only a few students *really* need the professional counselor's help, and counselors might be using these as objects of clinical experiment.

5. The view that, since there are counselors on campus, the teachers can leave to them most student problems, especially concern for the "whole student." The faculty member can be concerned only with lectures, examinations, and scholarly papers.

6. The view that faculty advisement takes badly needed time away from teaching, and the teacher is too swamped trying to be a good teacher to be able to be an advisor to students also.[5]

Although Hardee's evaluation is directed more toward the four-year college than the community college, still many observations are pertinent to both. It will be noted that the attitudes of some faculty members have their roots in the view that faculty members alone should be involved with students and that the college's responsibility should stop with the classroom. Such a position makes it impossible for the counselor to function effectively. There are those who feel that their responsibility begins and ends with the instruction of subject matter in a given field, or with the student's intellectual development. Such a position is unfortunate, for it makes it impossible for the counselor to work cooperatively with the teacher toward the colleges' objectives of aiding the development and growth of the "total" student.

Hardee makes it clear that it is not the teaching faculty alone who impede a favorable faculty-counselor relationship. Counselors sometimes hold such disabling views as:

1. The view that the counselor alone has discovered the "total individual." Such counselors assume that the faculty member, immersed in his subject field, has no real knowledge of the student and no wish to acquire such knowledge.

2. The view that the counselors on campus represent a very select circle, who can communicate only within the group, and that outside this group are the other people—teachers, administrators, and so on.

3. The view that *all* students need counseling, regardless of whether they feel they do. A motto for this would be, "We will help you with your problem, even to finding one for you."

4. The view that faculty members are well-intentioned but misguided and inept and, therefore, mishandle student problems. Counselors need to "protect" students from them.

5. The view that there are only a small select number of students with interesting problems that can be fruitfully used in professional circles. The "run of the mill" stuff is not for them.

6. The view that the faculty should not be included in counseling or academic advisement, because students tend to think of them as counselors and in doing so hurt the counseling profession and its work.[5]

Views such as these have no place in the community college, and violate its spirit. The total staff of a community college should incorporate both counselors and faculty who are wholeheartedly committed to the realization of students' goals. Only then will the college be in a position to develop a meaningful student personnel program, in which all staff members develop a common goal of aiding the student.

Another impediment to effectiveness of both teaching and student personnel faculty in the two-year colleges is the tendency to base their work on the standards of the four-year college model. At the present time, there are few graduate level programs for two-year college personnel; therefore, many two-year college faculty members are oriented toward the goals and standards of the four-year institution. They argue that as a "collegiate" institution, only those students should be admitted who can handle "college level" work. In short, such faculty members are advocating a selective admission policy. The natural effect of such a bias leads these faculty members to place highest value on transfer-oriented programs, according secondary value to "terminal," career-oriented programs. It is only natural, then, for these faculty to prejudice their student relationships on the basis of these views. A cogent example of such a bias is a situation described in a recent Educational Testing Service survey, where faculty on one campus characterize career students as "second-class citizens." Success was measured "in terms of how many career program students were moved over into the transfer program." [9]

Community college teaching, just as student personnel work, is also new, and has "few precedents or guidelines from the traditional structure of higher education." [3] In his study of the junior college faculty member, Roger Garrison emphasized the special, unique preparation needed for the teacher in the community college.[2] In addition, the solving of student problems faced by the teacher, especially the problems of the disadvantaged student, demand that the teacher be "for real" in the eyes of his students; be honest and sincere in ways that will come across to the student, learning to establish a confidence that will be helpful in working on future problems. The respect that will follow an honest interchange may lead to this confidence. Of course, this applies also to all those working with the student: the dean of students, the counselor, and the student activities coordinator.

Student personnel workers cannot help but be heavily influenced by their teaching colleagues. Sometimes the influence is negative, in the form of faculty bias and self-interest practices that undermine good student personnel programs. At other times faculty members provide powerful support and challenge. Only out of the cooperative interaction of both student personnel and teaching faculty will the total resources of the college be committed toward meeting the needs of students.

Administrative personnel in many offices of the college affect the morale of the campus by the ways in which they handle student contacts. For example, the business office may announce that it will only cash checks or make small loans between certain hours of the day to minimize interruption in its work. Those working in the registrar's office may seem cold and impersonal to students constantly besieging them on communications that need to go to the draft boards, or the registrar may resist changes in procedure that are desired because the "machine" can't do it. The food service, security office, and buildings and grounds office are also familiar trouble spots because of occasional insensitivity. If these departments operate without consciously trying to understand students and without providing maximum help within their area, campus frustrations can accumulate into sizable problems. When this happens, the skills of student personnel staff members are tested in their ability to handle crises, and to work cooperatively with students and faculty.

THE INFLUENCE OF THE BUDGET

How does the amount of the budget influence the student personnel program? This writer suggests that the answer is not as obvious as some would make it. A prevailing view for years has been that "in education you get what you pay for," or, "the more the money, the better the program." In one sense, this would be hard to deny. For example, where a rehabilitative and restorative student personnel program has been established in an urban situation, it obviously would be disabled by a large, crippling budget cut, and just as obviously be immensely aided by a large budget increase. However, the situations and choices are seldom this clear. In the broader sector of public education, reappraisals are now declared in order. The Coleman Report shocked and disturbed the policy makers by presenting data that seriously questioned the popular thesis of "more money—better program."

This is not to say that a level of budgeting is not needed which respects and supports a proper program. Community colleges define themselves as student-centered institutions, yet the Carnegie Report [7] identified student personnel programs in the large majority of community colleges in the country as poorly developed, poorly supported, and poorly administered. Community colleges speak of the availability of counseling that students in need can get, yet many provide as few as one counselor to 1500 full-time students, and none to the vast number of adult, part-time students. While recognizing the urgent financial problems that their students face—causing large numbers to leave—many small or new community colleges assign only a part-time staff member to the financial aid service—a staff member who has so many functions and duties that he can allot only a minimal amount of time to any specific problem. Without question, money restrictions, translated into staff restrictions, limit student personnel development and the means of serving students properly.

It is critical, however, that student personnel leadership look not only at money formulas but at the kind of program that will deal effectively with student development at the community college. The program needs to be imaginative, practical, significant, and tied in closely with the philosophy and goals of the institution. It needs to grow out of the thinking of student personnel staff members, teaching faculty, and students. It needs to be converted into costs, plans, and operational procedures. The program should then be presented in the kind of way that will earn it the most serious study by top college leadership and by the board of trustees. Such an approach should shape budget preparation for the student personnel program, rather than a rigid formula approach.

However, some student personnel leaders do argue for a formula approach rather than a program approach. They feel that for statewide planning, a formula basis would assure at least minimum adequate quality to the various community colleges, and it would even out inequities. For example, it would guarantee a "proper" numer of counselors per thousand students, and would take away the year-to-year, sometimes frenzied struggle for staff places and a cut of the pie. If the institution is relatively well established or only slowly changing, its set of formulas may satisfy all department budget claimants. Many administrations are utilizing formulas of 8 to 15 percent or so of the total budget as appropriate for student personnel services. State community and technical college systems frequently use the formula approach.

Other arguments, however, must also be considered. Community colleges are characteristically engaged in rapid growth, both in absolute size and in development of services and programs. The program needed in a community college is the one that can best do the job, and the one that can be financially supported regardless of formula figures. Developmental programs, particularly, are almost impossible to budget on a formula basis, for they vary strikingly accordingly to their nature. New and developing institutions are also unable to be properly appraised in the formula fashion. Priorities constantly have to be readjusted with effort and money allocated accordingly. Furthermore, there should be a range of programs, operations, and procedures that cannot be neatly pigeonholed in a budget category. The more imaginative programs to suit new needs will tend to be integrated, that is, reading clinics with teachers serving both in the classroom and in group counseling, and experimental, nonstructured curricular approaches.

Finally, the program approach to budgeting motivates and challenges each department of the community college, including student personnel, to develop what is needed—to refine it, write it up, and push hard for it. The effect, if carried out appropriately and with a needed view of the whole, will characterize a vigorous institution.

THE INFLUENCE OF FACILITIES

Some of the same considerations governing budget apply to the relationship between facilities and a strong student personnel program. As a good tool is to a cabinet maker, adequate physical facilities and equipment can help members of a professional staff to be effective in their work. Without the facilities that are needed or with facilities poorly suited to a program, the work is bound to be operating at a handicap. The problem is often acute in the counseling and student activities areas.

Counselors' offices, for example, often lack privacy, or are just not conducive to an openness of interaction between student and counselor. When the counselor wants to administer any of the various tests available to him he often must use makeshift quarters. Students dropping in to browse among vocational materials and college catalogs have to do this in a corner of the waiting room, or in the counselor's office itself. Occasionally, the counseling center is located far away from the beaten track, inconveniently distant from the normal traffic flow. A visitor to the counseling centers of various community colleges will not find these illustrations exaggerated.

Student activity programming suffers too because of facility problems. The visitor will see some community colleges without adequate rooms, in which student groups can meet, because classes preempt every available space day and evening. It is true, of course, that commuting pressures discourage normal student organizational planning, and student interest seems to be moving away from traditional group activity. Nevertheless, the lack of facilities for active student organizational purposes is frustrating.

A plan for developing and utilizing physical facilities to serve the student personnel program was developed by members of a special conference, sponsored by the American Association of Junior Colleges. Conference members directed their attention to the need to plan for facilities that can complement strong, ongoing, and innovative student personnel practices. It was emphasized that the philosophy and objectives of the community college must always be related to those physical facilities that support student personnel work:

The nature of the student personnel facilities and their geographic pattern will carry an implicit, perhaps unconscious, yet, loud message to the students, to the faculty and to the student personnel workers themselves. If student personnel is housed in the administration center, the message is "student personnel is part of administration." If the counselors are isolated in a warren of cubicles to which admission is controlled, the message is, "that is where you go to have your psyche fixed."

There is no way to avoid the media carrying a message. However, the message doesn't have to be a bad one, or inaccurate. The facilities and their patterning can carry in truth what many community college catalogs carry only in words: "This college is student centered." [1]

Research data offer little concrete evidence of increased effectiveness of student personnel staff as a result of adequate facilities in counseling, student activity and other student personnel areas. When adequate facilities are made available, however, increased satisfaction on the part of staff members is obvious. It also seems clear to this writer that securing and utilizing proper facilities complements other factors in the development of a strong student personnel program. It would be unthinkable and irresponsible long-range planning to ignore the facilities needed to provide effective services to students. The small, poor, developing program, as well as the larger, well-established one, needs the right kind of "facility tools" with which to work. In a small college or one in a special situation, however, adequate facilities may be almost impossible to secure. The challenge is great to carry on conscientious work with students in such a situation, to build morale and commitment despite limited facilities, just as the Peace Corps, Vista, and the Job Corps have done with their volunteers.

THE INFLUENCE OF THE PHILOSOPHY AND CLIMATE OF THE COMMUNITY COLLEGE

Throughout this chapter much attention has been given to the mission of the community college—its goals and philosophy. In very direct and also very subtle ways, these values will influence student personnel work. Staff members on a student personnel team should periodically review their college's aims and objectives to assure that the program is in accord with those aims and objectives. In addition to the harmony this would create within the programs of the institution, such a review would enable staff members to interpret adequately the college's character and the nature of the developing student personnel program.

Admissions work obviously is geared to the extent of the college's commitment to the philosophy of a comprehensive open-door community college. So also is each other element of the student personnel program. The test comes when the implications of this philosophy become clear, and there is demand for a forthright implementation of an entire program.

Meaningful development assistance to the disadvantaged student is now seen as one obligation of an opportunity-centered community college, where providing appropriate assistance is part of a total integrated college plan of support in the student's struggle to succeed.

College goals and philosophy never stand alone to influence the individual staff member. They affect him through a myriad of stimuli within and without the institutional community. Primarily they affect him through people who represent or who struggle against the ideas and traditions of the college. They also affect him as he learns about the history of the college and how its philosophy developed.

In some situations the community college's goals may be unclear, confusing, or even self-contradictory—indeed they are, if the college tries to become all things to all people. When this is so the student personnel program cannot become a strong one, relevant to student needs, unless it exerts appropriate pressures upon the college to help bring its goals into focus.

It is now widely recognized that college environments differ. In so doing, they affect, or "press" students differently, and also affect student personnel staff members as well, leading to wide differences in programs. The works of C. Robert Pace and George Stern have utilized sophisticated measurement instruments to identify the elements of his environment, in order to better understand the nature of the campus influence. Recently, Pace has reported a modification of the familiar CUES instrument to assess appropriately the junior college environment. He indicated that "the differences among junior colleges are not nearly as large as among universities or among liberal arts colleges." [8] Results have been reported based on the test's use in Los Angeles City College. Students spoke of this community college as one "where students are expected to do many things for themselves, where more emphasis is placed by both students and faculty on world affairs and culture than on campus activities, where the instructors are competent and businesslike, although sometimes difficult to approach, and where considerable learning takes place outside the regular classroom program." [4] The student personnel professional must work within the framework of the environment of his institution, or, if that environment is not conducive to an effective student personnel program, he is obligated to serve as a catalyst for change.

This chapter has focused on many influences within the community college that affect the student personnel program, noting both those that strengthen and those that weaken. It is the firm opinion of the writer that there must be adherence to and constructive use of influences that facilitate and resistance to influences that restrict and diminish. In this way, and only in this way, can a strong student personnel program develop in concert with the urgent mission of the community college.

REFERENCES

1. COLLINS, CHARLES C., *Premises: Planning Student Personnel Facilities.* Washington, D.C.: American Association of Junior Colleges, 1967, note p. 7.

2. GARRISON, ROGER H., *Junior College Faculty: Issues and Problems.* Washington, D.C.: American Association of Junior Colleges, 1967.

3. ———, "The Teacher's Professional Situation," *Junior College Journal,* March, 1967, note p. 16.

4. GOLD, BENJAMIN K., *The Junior College Environment—L.A.C.C. Student and Faculty Preferences, Student Perceptions of L.A.C.C.,* ERIC ED 018 204, February, 1968.

5. HARDEE, MELVENE D., *The Faculty in College Counseling.* New York: McGraw-Hill Book Company, 1959, note pp. 20-21, 22-23.

6. LAHTI, ROBERT, "A President's View—Student Personnel Services in the Community College," *GT 70,* Student Personnel Workshop, William Rainey Harper College, 1968, note p. 19.

7. PACE, C. ROBERT, *Explorations in the Measurement of Junior College Environments,* ERIC ED 014 972, January, 1967.

8. RAINES, MAX R., *Junior College Student Personnel Programs: Appraisal and Development: A Report to the Carnegie Corporation,* November, 1965.

9. SEIBEL, DEAN W., *Testing Practices and Problems in Junior Colleges—A Survey,* Field Studies Report FSR-2. Princeton: Educational Testing Service, September, 1966, note pp. 30-31.

10. "The Junior College President," *UCLA Junior College Research Review,* ERIC Clearinghouse for Junior College Information, American Association of Junior Colleges, June, 1968, note p. 1.

Curriculum Development
and Instruction:
A Proposal for Reorganization

ERNEST H. BERG

President, Indian Valley Colleges
College of Marin,
Kentfield, California

Even a cursory examination of the organization charts of various community colleges reveals that the functioning of these colleges is commonly divided into two parts, representing the cognitive domain on the one hand and the affective domain on the other. Although such a division of functioning involves some oversimplification, it is sufficiently valid for the purposes of the discussion which follows. An instructional administrator (usually the dean of instruction) assumes responsibility for the cognitive aspects of the education program, and a student services administrator (usually a dean of student personnel) assumes responsibility for the affective aspects. Except in the larger colleges, the two deans report directly to the president.

It is difficult to tell at this point in time whether the bifurcation of the institutional functioning was the result of a rational decision about the nature of organizational structure or whether it was a pragmatic solution which recognized the essential differences between and needs of the cognitive and the affective domains. In any case, it would be difficult to conceive of an organizational pattern which would more effectively isolate the bifurcated fragments from each other and, indeed, place them in an almost competitive position vis-a-vis the chief administrator.

The tragedy, however, lies not in the effect that the division of functioning has upon the deans or even the chief administrator, but rather in the effect that it has upon instructors, counselors, and students. The counselors are effectively isolated from the instructional staff. The instructors, who relate directly to the Dean of Instruction and only peripherally, if at all, to the Dean of Student Personnel, tend to teach as though the affective needs of the students were none of their concern and that such needs should be satisfied in another part of the institution. The students, on the other hand, possess only a very limited ability to divide their lives into cognitive and affective segments; they tend to respond as whole persons to the college environment. One might well expect that students would complain about a lack of relevance and the depersonalization of higher education. It does then appear that there exists a separation of the cognitive and the affective components of the community college program.

Although the literature of the community college indicates that some attention has been given to the problem of the relationship of the student personnel program and the instructional program, one seldom hears or reads about counselors being actively involved in the organization, development, or evaluation of the instructional program. In a recent issue of the *Junior College Journal,* Roberson wrote about a *unique* situation in which counselors worked with instructors in the development of the curriculum of a new college. He stated that, "Traditionally, a college's curriculum exists prior to a counseling staff; consequently, counselors have not influenced its content." [11]

It appears that the most frequent and closest approach made by counselors to the instructional program is in the area of the "remedial" program. In this definitive work on the junior college Medsker stated that

If an institution is to perform multiple student services which should be interrelated, they must be coordinated. In fact, the services should not only be coordinated with each other but also with the instructional program.[8]

Medsker recommended that:

There should be a plan for close coordination between those who perform student personnel services and those who teach, so that the curriculum and the instructional program are strengthened by information and ideas from those who work closely with students outside the classroom. Student personnel services cannot operate in a vacuum.[8]

Evidently, insufficient attention has been given to Medsker's recommendation.

In another publication Medsker again drew attention to the relationship of the student personnel worker to the instructional program.

. . . counselors and others may find themselves the gatherers, interpreters, and evaluators of student characteristics data for the entire college staff, both in advising and otherwise working with individual students and in working with faculty and staff in curriculum development and revision and in overall planning. Student personnel workers may assume the role of the conscience of the junior college . . .[9]

In a more recent work Blocker, Plummer, and Richardson explained the necessity for concentrating all nonacademic and nonbusiness functions within the sphere of the student personnel services and under the direction of a single administrator.[2] At the same time, however, they stated that,

The dissociation of the instructional program from student-personnel services constitutes a serious problem which operates to the detriment of both areas. Academic personnel may view the student-personnel program as an unnecessary bureaucratic adjunct to the college, lacking academic respectability and interfering with the basic purposes of the educational processes.[2]

The ideal relationship, they say, "can only result from a merger of thought and action on the operational level." [2] Their solution for accomplishing such a merger: Counselors should teach a class, and some instructional personnel should be assigned responsibilities for academic advisement.[2] Unfortunately, experience seems to indicate that such a solution has not produced and will not produce the desired result.

Forty-nine delegates at a research development conference were asked to respond to proposed developmental guidelines for junior college student personnel programs. The following was one of the items in the inventory. The numbers in parenthesis indicate the number of delegates who inserted "must," "should," "might," or "need not," respectively.

2.0.2 *Curriculum Development.* Student personnel workers (26-24-3-1) be actively involved with faculty members in continuing efforts to identify needs for additional courses and curricula or for revisions in curricular requirements.[1]

Obviously, the great majority of the delegates recognized the need for a close working relationship between the instructional and the student personnel programs.

In a California study, Jane Matson directed a task force which identified desirable essential elements of a student personnel program. Three of those elements are significant for the purposes of this discussion. The task force stated that,

Representatives of the student personnel staff are voting members of each of the standing faculty committees which act in an advisory or consultative capacity to the college administrators.

Members of the student personnel staff are considered to be members of the faculty with full rights and responsibilities, including eligibility for membership in the faculty senate or similar body.

The faculty demonstrates its understanding and acceptance of the objectives of the student personnel services through cooperation and willingness to contribute their time and skills. There is a mutual respect for the complementary roles of the teaching faculty and the student personnel staff in achieving the overall objectives of the junior college.[4]

Dr. Matson and the task force obviously were concerned about the relationship between instructors and student personnel workers.

In the report to the Carnegie Commission by the National Committee for Appraisal and Development of Junior College Student Personnel Programs, Fordyce, Shepard, and Collins constructed a taxonomy of junior college student personnel services. Although their taxonomy is comprehensive, it refers only tangentially to the relationship between the student personnel and the instructional programs. For example, they state that test data should make it possible to provide "curricula programs that are meaningful for the students involved." [3] But nowhere does the taxonomy include a more specific reference to the participation of student personnel workers in instructional planning and evaluation.

In the same report Raines [10] examined selected variables used to identify strong and weak programs. One variable is concerned with faculty support. No other direct reference is made to the relationship between the student personnel program and the instructional program. Evidently, Raines did not consider that such a relationship was of significance in determining the strength of a student personnel program.

However, again in the same report, Hoyt stated that the conference participants were agreed that,

. . . isolated efforts by faculty and student personnel workers were much less potent than consciously integrated approaches.

but

. . . concern was expressed that the mutual acceptance and respect which underlies such cooperation was too often lacking.[5]

Hoyt concluded that research was needed to investigate what personal and situational variables are associated with faculty acceptance of student personnel workers.[5] It is significant that Hoyt's recommendation is concerned not with how student personnel workers and instructional workers might cooperate but, rather, with how student personnel workers might go about gaining the acceptance of the faculty. Evidently, that is the central problem.

It is necessary, then, to be concerned with the problem of why community college instructors have not accepted student personnel workers as equal partners in the educational process. McConnell probably provided the answer to that question when he stated,

. . . when measured against criteria of scope and effectiveness, student personnel programs in community colleges are woefully inadequate.[7]

It appears that student personnel workers are not certain what their function is, or who should perform it, or how to evaluate what they have done when they have done it. Even in the area of guidance theory, student personnel workers appear to be navigating in troubled waters. Katz commented that,

Theoretical writing in guidance is like a wind-harp activated by ideas that are in the air at a given time, such as behaviorism, existentialism, statistical decision theory, McLuhancy, etc.[6]

Why, indeed, should instructors who believe that they know what their function is and that they perform this function well, consider student personnel workers as equals?

It seems reasonable, then, in times of expanding enrollments and shrinking funds, to reduce or eliminate those services which cannot stand the scrutiny of cost-benefit analysis. Exhortation, based on the widely accepted theoretical aims of the community colleges, has not convinced instructors that student personnel programs are essential. Administrators, who traditionally have given the greatest support to student personnel programs, find it increasingly difficult to defend and support a service which defies evaluation. McConnell suggests that,

It is possible—even likely—that as community colleges reach for higher academic status their faculties will be less sympathetic with the wide range of purposes and functions which the community colleges in theory should profess, and be less ready to lend enthusiastic support to comprehensive student personnel programs.[7]

It does seem probable, at least, that as community colleges have matured they have become more conscious of their academic status and have become less concerned about such services as the student personnel program. If that is the case, student personnel workers face a difficult problem. They must now begin to gain the confidence, acceptance, and support of instructors. At the same time, they must clearly indicate in what ways they can be of assistance to instructors in the educational process.

One of the problems student personnel workers must face is that, in terms of the operational or actual goals (as opposed to the theoretical or philosophical goals) of the community colleges, the central business of the institution *is* instruction. Colleges can and do operate without comprehensive student personnel programs, but they cannot operate without an instructional program.

As they exist today, student personnel programs are not an integral part of the educational program. Rather, they are *supplementary* programs which serve the institution by supplementing an academically-oriented instructional program which does not attempt to provide for the affective needs of students. Unfortunately, unless some counter force is brought into play, there is little reason to believe that the operational goals of the community college will change. Indeed, as McConnell suggests, community colleges will become even more academically-oriented as they mature, and student personnel programs will be even less enthusiastically supported.

It does appear that instructors are either unconcerned about the affective needs of students and do not believe that such needs are the business of the college, or they feel that such needs are adquately met in the classroom. One might even draw the conclusion that the very presence of a separate student personnel program which is designed to serve the affective needs of students tends to relieve the instructors of any similar responsibility. In any case, the bifurcation of institutional functioning that appears at the top levels of the administrative organization pervades the whole institution.

Thus, the immediate task of student personnel workers is not to continue their efforts to bolster the organizational integrity and independence of the services they perform within the framework of the operational goals of the community college, but rather to work toward the institutionalization of the broader goals of the community college which are concerned with the education of the whole student. It must be obvious that only within an institution committed to such broader goals will the student personnel program become an integral and essential part of the educational program and will be accepted as such by the instructors. The changing of goals always has proven to be a rather slow process in education, therefore, student personnel workers should also seek other methods which will make it possible for them to relate to and cooperate with instructors.

It was suggested earlier in this discussion that the organization of the student personnel services within the administrative structure of the community college might be a contributing factor to the inability of the student personnel program to relate effectively to the instructional program. For a long time student personnel workers have stressed the necessity of having a single administrator in charge of the student personnel program. They have also demanded that that administrator, usually the dean of student personnel, be on the same level administratively as the instructional dean. It has already been stated that most organization charts reflect both of those concerns. However, in actual practice it is doubtful that the two deans actually are at the same level. In the majority of cases the instructional dean takes precedence. For example, when the chief administrator is absent, the dean of instruction normally acts for him. The great majority of the members of the academic community, the faculty, do not consider the student services dean to be the equal of the instructional dean. Thus, although an attempt has been made to clothe the student services dean with the trappings of status and authority, in actual practice he has less of both than the organization chart indicates. It appears that the existence of a dean of student services has not produced the desired outcome—that of providing the student services program with status and acceptance. There is little reason to believe that additional time will change the situation.

It is certainly true that student personnel workers will not be able to relate to instructors if they continue to operate as a closed society under the supervision of the dean of student personnel who relates only to the president. In most community colleges counselors, in particular, are cloistered in their individual offices. Within the quiet confines of the cloister, however, they live frenetic lives vainly attempting to be the agents of behavioral change by using nondirective techniques during 20- or 30-minute appointments with individual students. They rarely have an opportunity to relate to the instructional staff. Obviously, then, if the student personnel program is to become an integral part of the educational program, both the organization and the operation of those services must undergo radical change. Student personnel workers must be provided with an environment which will make it possible for them to relate to and cooperate with instructors.

One solution to the problem might be to organize student personnel services at the divisional level with the chief administrator designated as division chairman and with most of the counselors decentralized as division counselors. In such an organization the student personnel program would operate within the instructional organization and would exert pressure and extend influence upward to the dean of instructional services; and that pressure and influence would operate through the same organizational structure as is normally employed by instructional staff. The head of the division of student services normally would meet on a regular basis with other division heads. It seems probable that under such an organization student personnel workers would more frequently be placed on the important instructional committees, thereby increasing in number and effectiveness their opportunities to relate to and work with instructors. The net result could well be a far greater input into the instructional process of concepts and ideas generated by student personnel workers.

The detached division counselors would become members of the instructional division and, in addition to working directly with students, could also work directly with instructors in the planning and operation of the instructional program. Such counselors could be of considerable assistance to faculty members who might be engaged in academic advisement. The detached counselor would act as a liaison between the instructional division and the student personnel division with which he would, of course, maintain a close relationship. Again, the input of student personnel ideas and concepts directly into the instructional program could be increased significantly. It should be noted that a system of decentralized counseling would not preclude the possibility of having a few centralized counselors available for more intensive counseling with students.

Although a detached counselor in an instructional division might well become more knowledgeable about the problems students in that division might face, it seems that student personnel workers are somewhat concerned that students might not relate to their designated division counselor. Thus, the student's choice of a counselor would be limited. However, it would be possible to introduce a large measure of flexibility into the system by permitting students to consult the general counselors in the student personnel division or the detached counselors in other instructional divisions.

The whole idea of organizing student personnel services on a division basis is usually regarded as heresy by the majority of student personnel workers. They should be reminded, however, that the present organizational structure is not producing the desired outcomes and that student personnel workers ought to be the first to recognize such a dysfunction. Student personnel workers should, under those conditions, be the *first* group to indicate a willingness to experiment with other forms of organization. Since student personnel workers have worked for a long time to establish a unified program under a single administrator who is the counterpart of the instructional dean, they are concerned that a change to divisional structure would result in the loss of much they have gained. However, it should be noted that the concept of a single administrator supervising the entire student services program could exist even in a divisional organization. All the services commonly considered to be a part of student personnel services would be included in the division. In any case, it should be recognized that the present organization probably is viable only because it is continually propped up and bolstered by the administration. As faculty participation in decision-making gains strength, chief administrators, in particular, will find it increasingly difficult to support student personnel programs at even the present levels. To put it another way, unless student personnel workers can demonstrate a greater measure of effectiveness than they are able to at the present time, it is probably inevitable that they will lose much of what they have gained.

The question of whether or not counselors ought to be assigned a part-time teaching load has frequently been discussed in the literature. For example, Blocker, Plummer, and Richardson stated that the ideal relationship between the instructional program and the student personnel program would be achieved if counselors taught a class and if instructors were involved in academic advising.[2] Community college instructors often recommend that counselors should carry a part-time teaching load for the purpose of making them more aware of the problems of classroom instruction. Although some improvement in the relationship between instructors and counselors might occur, the whole idea seems to be based upon three assumptions. First, all counselors should be effective instructors. Second, all instructors should be effective counselors. Third, in the case of Blocker, Plummer and Richardson's recommendation, counseling can be fragmented. There is little, if any, evidence which supports any of the three assumptions. Unquestionably, counselors will gain acceptance by the faculty only when they are able to demonstrate that they are specialists in human development and that they have much to contribute to the educational process.

Of course, nothing that has been discussed here should preclude the possibility that at times and for special purposes a counselor working on a team with an instructor can perform an instructional role. Indeed, such cooperative efforts should be encouraged if the outcome is likely to be a more effective and relevant education for students. Conversely, it is conceivable that an instructor might assume a counseling role under similar circumstances. Although it has been stipulated that the most important outcome of such cooperative efforts should be more effective and more relevant education for students, a very important secondary benefit would be a significant improvement in the relationship between the counselor and the instructor.

Another method that some student personnel staff have employed to increase their involvement in the instructional program is to establish a series of courses which are under their control and which are taught only by counselors. It is difficult to understand how such a system could result in anything but a more clearly defined division between the student personnel program and the instructional program. In fact, the net outcome might conceivably be the establishment of a competitive relationship between the two programs which would inhibit the development of a cooperative relationship.

If counselors are to establish themselves as specialists in human development—or to use Terry O'Banion's designation, "human development facilitators"—they will have to demonstrate to instructors that cooperative efforts which unify the cognitive and the affective aspects of the educational program are actually possible—and even more important, are desirable and essential. The first priority then for counselors would be to break their monastic vows, leave the cloister, and begin to associate with instructors in the real world of the academic environment. The second priority should be to infiltrate, by whatever means necessary, the academic structure of the community college. The process of infiltration can be facilitated by one-to-one relationships between counselors and instructors.

The latter must come to know the former as real people. Infiltration will also involve seeking membership on all of the important college committees. Of course, membership in this case means active, contributing membership. Parenthetically it should be noted that some system of decentralized counseling would appear to be the ideal vehicle for accomplishing the two priorities.

Once the process of infiltration is well advanced, counselors should begin to suggest to instructors many ways in which they might cooperate with each other. The initial emphasis should be on how the counselor can *assist* the instructor. The long-term goal should be to incorporate into the instructional program concern for the process of human development. Although the specific ways in which counselors and instructors can begin to cooperate will depend upon the characteristics of individual institutions, the attitude of the administration and the faculty, and the level of training and experience of the counselors, the following suggestions might be of some assistance.

1. Counselors should become actively involved in the construction of the class schedule. Too frequently schedules reflect what instructors want to teach rather than what students want and require. Counselors should act as resource personnel to the office of instruction in interpreting student needs and desires.

2. It has been stated that student personnel workers frequently live and work in a closed society. It is also true that in many community colleges individual instructional departments are closed societies. At the slightest sign of outside interest in their activities, the members of departments man the barricades. Counselors could perform a very useful role by bringing together members from different departments for the purpose of planning for and implementing interdisciplinary offerings which could effectively meet expressed student needs. Of course, the counselor should also seek ways in which he can become a participating member in such an instructional team.

3. Counselors could establish encounter groups which might include administrators, instructors, counselors and students. Although the encounter groups would be useful in generally making the participants more aware of personal and social relationships, initially the groups should focus upon, or at least be generated by, a specific and recognized college problem such as attitudes toward minority group students or, conversely, the attitudes of minority group students toward the college.

4. Instructors are chronically plagued by the inadequacy of measures of student learning. Counselors could be of considerable assistance to instructors in designing, using, and evaluating new and innovative methods of measuring learning. Central to the concern of counselors should be the measurement of not only the factual, cognitive outcomes but also affective

aspects of student learning. If instructors become more aware of the concept of measuring human development, it seems likely that their instruction would reflect a concern for the total development of students.

5. The relationship between many instructors and activist students is a matter of some concern. Counselors can be of assistance in helping each group to understand the attitudes and actions of the other, and in bringing the instructors and students together on neutral ground. By their intervention in such situations counselors can facilitate change.

6. Instructors often find that they are not able to motivate individual students in their classes and that frequently such students drop out. If instructors would seek the assistance of the counselor before intervention is too late, many students could either be helped to succeed in that specific class or to make program changes that would assure their continuance in college. Although some instructors presently seek such assistance, a great deal more can be accomplished. Since counselors often know about students who are likely to have academic problems, they should make a greater effort to follow up on such students and to offer assistance to instructors. Successful cooperative efforts on behalf of students will undoubtedly lead to a closer relationship between instructors and counselors, and such a relationship will probably make it possible for counselors to work more actively with instructors in the field of curriculum.

7. Counselors should be involved in the process of approving new courses and programs to be added to the curriculum. One of the important criteria for approval should be the degree to which new offerings meet some of the more recently expressed student concerns and demands. Another criterion should be the degree to which the new offering addresses itself to the concept of human development. Counselors should be recognized as the resource persons best equipped to evaluate courses and programs in relation to the two criteria.

8. Many of the traditional subjects which are frequently taught from an academic point of view could be vitalized and made more relevant for students if there were included in the instruction opportunities to explore and experience social and psychological relationships inherent in the subject. For example, a literature class studying *Hamlet, Moby Dick,* or *Soul on Ice* could involve a counselor in the discussion. In a sociology class a counselor could help the instructor and the students construct a classroom model which would assist them in actually experiencing the relationship between various social groups. There are undoubtedly many situations in which a counselor could be involved in the classroom.

9. Although the idea is fraught with danger, counselors could be of significant help to an instructor who is having difficulty in relating to students. With the consent and cooperation of an instructor, a counselor could visit several classes and have several counseling sessions with the instructor. If counselors can reach the point at which they are recognized

by instructors as specialists in human development, they could be regularly included on teams established for the purpose of evaluating and assisting new instructors.

10. The in-service training program in most community colleges is a disaster area. There is little question that the reason for the failure of such programs is that they are recognized as being dull, uninspiring, and practically useless. However, if it were possible for counselors and instructors to work together to establish a viable program of personnel development, something might be accomplished. The components of such a program should be developed only after the following questions are answered:

a. Can the educational program of this institution be improved?
b. Do we have the desire, the will, and the ability to improve the educational program?
c. Who should be involved in these discussions?
d. Which components of the educational program ought to be discarded?
e. Which components of the educational program ought to be revised or strengthened?
f. How do we accomplish change?

Undoubtedly, instructors alone could profitably engage in such a discussion. However, it seems probable that counselors, acting as human development specialists, could contribute much to the process and to the outcome.

11. In colleges which lack a department of institutional research, counselors should attempt to interest instructors in research involving the planning, operation, and evaluation of the instructional program. Counselors should offer their assistance in designing, conducting, and interpreting such research.

If counselors can assist and cooperate with instructors in many ways such as those suggested above, the immediate outcome should be a greater acceptance and support of the student personnel program by the instructional staff. There is reason to believe that such support and acceptance must be gained soon if it is to be gained at all.

In summary, it appears that there is wide agreement among student personnel workers that they should be involved to a much greater degree in the planning, operation, and evaluation of the instructional program of the community college. The most significant barrier to such involvement probably is the inability of student personnel workers to establish a cooperative working relationship with instructors. It is possible that the organization of student personnel services as a separate entity within the administrative organization may be inhibiting the establishment of such a relationship. One possible solution might be to organize student personnel services on the division level and to detach counselors to the academic divisions. The integration of the student personnel services into the mainstream of college functioning could result in a significantly greater input of ideas and concepts into the planning, operation, and evaluation of the instructional program. In the long run, student personnel workers operating as human development specialists might bring about the institutionalization of the broader, but still unrealized goals of the community college.

REFERENCES

1. "Appraisal and Development of Junior College Student Personnel Programs," *Proceedings of a Research Development Conference,* University of Chicago, April, 1964, Appendix F.

2. BLOCKER, CLYDE E., ROBERT H. PLUMMER, and RICHARD C. RICHARDSON, *The Two-Year College: A Social Synthesis.* Englewood Cliffs, N.J.: Prentice-Hall, Inc., note pp. 244-47.

3. FORDYCE, JOSEPH W., EUGENE L. SHEPARD, and CHARLES C. COLLINS, *Junior College Students Personnel Programs: Appraisal and Development: A Report to the Carnegie Corporation,* Max R. Raines, Project Coordinator. November, 1965, note p. 8.

4. *Guidelines for Student Personnel Services in the Junior College.* Prepared by a Task Force under the direction of Jane E. Matson, California State Department of Education, Sacramento, 1968, unpublished.

5. HOYT, DONALD P., "Research Needs in Junior College Student Personnel Work," *Junior College Student Personnel Programs: Appraisal and Development: A Report to the Carnegie Corporation,* Max R. Raines, Project Coordinator. November, 1965, p. 7.

6. KATZ, I., "Theoretical Foundations of Guidance," in *Review of Educational Research,* 30, No. 2 (April, 1969), note p. 134.

7. McCONNELL, T. R., "Foreword," to *Junior College Student Personnel Programs: Appraisal and Development: A Report to the Carnegie Corporation,* Max R. Raines, Project Coordinator. November, 1965.

8. MEDSKER, LELAND L., *The Junior College: Progress and Prospect.* New York: McGraw Hill Book Company, 1960, note pp. 146, 167.

9. ———, "The Junior College Student," *Junior College Student Personnel Programs: Appraisal and Development: A Report to the Carnegie Corporation,* Max R. Raines, Project Coordinator. November, 1965, note p. 22.

10. RAINES, MAX R., "Significance of Selected Variables in Differentiating Strong and Weak Programs," *Junior College Student Personnel Programs: Appraisal and Development: A Report to the Carnegie Corporation,* Max R. Raines, Project Coordinator. November, 1965, note p. 2.

11. ROBERSON, GLENN, "The Counselor and the Curriculum," *Junior College Journal,* 39, No. 6 (March, 1969).

Community Services:
Outdoor Student Personnel Work*

MAX R. RAINES

Professor of Higher Education,
Michigan State University

It is the purpose of this chapter to take some first steps in clarifying the range of community service activities in the community college, and in providing a method of conceptualizing the total community services program.

Service to community has long been a basic tenet of the community college philosophy. In the rural, agrarian society which gave birth to the community college, college transfer programs served a local community need unmet by distant senior institutions. Later, vocational-technical programs were developed in response to community needs brought about by rapid industrialization and urbanization. Since World War II, community colleges have become increasingly sophisticated in serving as a resource for manpower development.

In the decade of the 1960s, characterized as it was by sweeping social and technological change, renewed impetus and thrust was given to the community arena of service, and to a programming now becoming known as *community services*. Drawing upon adult and continuing education concepts and practices, and responding to the almost revolutionary pace of societal change, community services is the newest (and perhaps most exciting) dimension of community college development. In the current period of unrest and social ferment, many communities are looking to their community colleges for leadership in solving pressing social problems. The potential for service is great, but we must be reminded that exploration, rather than crystallization, expresses the present stage of the development of community services.

---

* This chapter was written in collaboration with my colleague, Gunder A. Myran.

Ervin Harlacher was the first to delineate, on a national scale, the range of community services activities in which various community colleges are engaging. One cannot read his book, *The Community Dimension of the Community College,* without sensing some of the vitality that comes with direct community involvement and the resultant institutional self-discovery and change. Also one cannot read the account without some feeling of a need for direction—a philosophical base by which to judge the appropriateness of a given community involvement activity. The philosophical base will come and hopefully it will be empirically derived. The need for definition and classification is apparent; practitioners who are exploring and discovering the "community dimension" need this to communicate within their profession and with their varied publics. An important step in this direction is Gunder Myran's recent American Association of Junior Colleges publication, *Community Services in the Community College.*[3]

Before launching into a discussion of the range of community services, it seems worthwhile to cite some of the commonalities of student personnel services and community services, and some differences between them. Conceptually both programs: (a) share a concern for human (self) development; (b) seek to adapt activities to the needs and interests of the clientele they serve; (c) acknowledge the importance of development of the whole person rather than single compartmentalized segments of personality; and (d) recognize the importance of creating environments that are conducive to individual and group development. In day-to-day practice both programs conduct similar activities and utilize similar human relationship skills. It is not surprising, therefore, that student and community services have already merged in certain programs in at least some community colleges. The essential differences between the two programs are more operational than conceptual. Student personnel programs focus on *campus* life and a more *traditional* clientele (though this is changing) while community service programs focus on *community* life and a *nonstudent* clientele.

As this writer has recently sought to comprehend the diversity and complexity of community services, it has been helpful to develop a taxonomy for classifying the remarkable variety of community service activities. It was at this point that a colleague, Russell Kleis, clarified the central focus of community services as encompassing both human and community development. With this concept in mind, the writer was eventually able to organize the various activities of community service programs into operational categories which were defined as follows:

I. *Individual Development Functions:* Those functions and activities of the college primarily focused upon the needs, aspirations, and potentialities of individuals or informal groups of individuals to help them achieve a greater degree of personal self-realization and fulfillment.

II. *Community Development Functions:* Those functions and activities of the college primarily focused upon cooperative efforts with community organizations, agencies, and institutions to improve the physical, social, economic, and political environment of the community.

III. *Program Development Functions:* Those functions and activities of the community services staff designed to procure and allocate resources, coordinate activities, establish objectives, and evaluate outcomes.

I. INDIVIDUAL-DEVELOPMENT FUNCTIONS

DEVELOPMENTAL COUNSELING

In most communities the opportunities for self-discovery through counseling are limited, particularly for adults. While adults may find agencies which can help them in times of crisis (that is, family service, child guidance, mental health, and so on) there are few agencies that concern themselves with helping nonstudents learn more about their potentialities and in identifying resources to develop those potentialities.

A mother whose children are well established in school and whose husband is caught up in his own career pursuits may soon find her daily responsibilities less than challenging. An opportunity to think through alternatives (part-time employment, career development, volunteer work, personal renewal, and so on) is seldom provided. If such an opportunity is provided for her by a guidance center, she is more apt to identify suitable alternatives to personal development.

Recently the writer was invited to evaluate a pilot guidance center [4] for women in the state of New York. This center is located in Rockland County and affiliated with Rockland Community College. It has provided counseling for three to four hundred women per year for the past three years. In addition it has had about 2000 requests for career information each year. The evaluation indicates that the venture has been a remarkable success and has led to recommendations for establishing such centers throughout the state. Here we see a merging of functions between the student personnel program and community services program.

Women are not the only ones who need such assistance. With the rapid technological changes, many men find themselves caught in "dead-end" jobs. Often these men are aware of their need for new skills and new knowledge, but are unaware of opportunities for job retraining. An adult counseling center can provide needed information, as well as the necessary encouragement to consider other career possibilities. The problem of recycling extends well beyond men who are faced with displacement resulting from automation. For example, many men who have built careers around a single corporation can find themselves locked into a junior executive position where their talents are not fully utilized. Some of these men succeed quite well if and when they find more challenging opportunities. Again, an adult counseling center can help.

Illustrations of the need for developmental counseling are manifold. It is quite apparent that some institution in our society must respond to the urgent need for personal and career development. The community college is particularly well suited to fullfill that role.

First, the community college is *there*. It is immediately available. As a college it has status. In addition it is constantly increasing its offerings to include a wider variety of educational and career development opportunities. The community college has *credibility* as an agency for personal and career development. Citizens readily accept its services in this area.

EDUCATIONAL EXTENSION

Those who have studied the history of the community college are acutely aware that it has made its greatest strides when it has sought to increase educational opportunities. Many community colleges now *extend* their regular program into evening hours and to other noncampus facilities (school buildings, church basements, industrial plants, and so on). Extension activities are a reflection of the willingness of the college to make opportunities more accessible by accommodating to the needs of students who may have responsibilities that prevent their participation in the more traditional, full-time collegiate life.

Oakland Community College in Michigan, for example, has established 28 extension centers throughout Oakland County and enrolls about 4500 students in this extension program. The extension program is frequently referred to as a "fourth campus." College staff members and other qualified personnel in the community are employed to teach the courses. Academic advising and educational counseling are provided by professional counselors at each center. A supervisory staff is employed not only to expedite administrative procedures but also to supervise the teaching process.

The extension approach of Oakland was adapted to the new Wayne County Community College in Detroit. This new college, with no campus facilities, managed to open its doors within six months to more than 8000 students (Fall of 1969) by implementing the extension concept in various school facilities throughout the district and to double the enrollment the following year. It is quite obvious that such centers do *extend* opportunities for self-development in a very visible way.

EDUCATIONAL EXPANSION

Even though counseling for individual development may be available and formal curricula may be extended to less traditional places at less traditional times, it is also vital to provide programs which adapt knowledge to the solution of specific problems. There are many needs for specific information and training. The needs may range from development of supervisory skills among plumbing foremen, to consumer buying among housewives, to management of small businesses in the ghetto. The medium for providing the needed knowledge or skill includes conferences, seminars, institutes, workshops, or short courses, depending on the nature of the problem and the clientele to be served. By avoiding the restrictions imposed by the college credit system, the content can be packaged to suit the immediate needs of the participants. The key elements in programming *educational expansion* activities are flexibility and relevancy.

CULTURAL AND LEISURE TIME ACTIVITIES

So much has been written about the increasing time available for recreation that it need not be elaborated here. It is apparent that finding satisfying ways of spending leisure hours presents a considerable problem to many people. Those who have been reared in the Protestant work ethic are inclined to uneasiness when they are not working and they need opportunities to develop *comfortable* attitudes toward leisure time. Those facing retirement need encouragement to develop avocational interests before they have retired. Cultural programs can be expanded to include people who may come from different cultures and ethnic backgrounds; for example, art festivals which encompass the many art forms of a culture contribute richly to a sense of social and personal dignity. Intercultural programs do much to build bridges of appreciation and understanding. The community college has an excellent opportunity to facilitate such programs and to endorse them by providing facilities, equipment, and staff assistance.

SOCIAL OUTREACH

Only within recent years have community colleges recognized their responsibility to the disadvantaged clientele of their areas. Some inner-city colleges are beginning to focus upon the needs of the deprived population. A recent study by Andrew Goodrich [1] has described the developing and emerging nature of inner-city community services in some of our large metropolitan areas. While additional experience and resources will be needed to produce programs with real impact on these large communities, the outreach effort remains as one of the most enlivening activities available to colleges. It can be expected that the egalitarian commitment of the community college will take on a deeper meaning as a result of social outreach efforts.

II. COMMUNITY DEVELOPMENT

Community development activities have generally received less emphasis in community college programs than the activities which we have classified as self-development. However, the urban crisis and the fading sense of community is bringing increased emphasis on community development. While it must be recognized that programs which foster individual development can properly be viewed as a basic community development thrust (people are the key resource in any community), community development may be viewed as focusing primarily upon cooperative efforts with community organizations, agencies, and institutions to improve the physical, social, and political environment of the community (for example, housing, transportation, air pollution, human relations, public safety, and so on). These activities represent efforts to understand the major forces and conditions in the environment which are shaping and affecting the lives of people and to plan programs of intervention and education which will make the forces and conditions more favorable to human development.

COMMUNITY ANALYSIS

Developing an awareness of needs and problems of a community can be accomplished informally through experience and interaction in the community. There are times, however, when a fuller understanding of the goals of persons and groups in the community, and their problems in reaching those goals, needs a more thorough analysis. Community studies can provide a thematic picture of community problems, and a careful analysis will suggest ways in which education can help in solving these problems.

We most often think of survey techniques in this regard; however, there are other sources of information which may be available without survey such as census tracts, manpower studies, resource analysis, and so on. In addition it is not at all unusual to find that major industries have developed an analysis of a community prior to locating a plant there. (Utility companies make outstanding projections in their demographic analysis which focuses on family development.) If one were simply to collect the studies that may have been made by both industry and government in a community, he could well identify many critical needs. Consequently, an early step in community analysis is to collect and analyze *available* data. Consultants are available to help college staff members interpret the data.

Another facet of community analysis is to identify the range and nature of various agencies that seek to help people. In a recent address, William Keim of Cerritos College in California noted that he had identified 126 separate agencies seeking to help the disadvantaged people in his district. Through community analysis the college can hope to determine the "gap-overlap problem" which may exist. Also the college may be forced to make intelligent but very private judgments as to which agencies are really performing the services they claim to perform. Armed with this knowledge a community services program can seek to foster community self-awareness by providing a common meeting place for interested groups to identify problems, issues, and needed resources.

INTERAGENCY COOPERATION

While the community college may serve as the catalytic force in bringing groups together, it soon becomes apparent that *many* different agencies have a stake in community development. Failure to recognize and respond to their specialized contribution can only alienate the college from sources of assistance. As a part of community analysis it is important to identify and map agency territories. What agencies exist? What is their major thrust? Whom do they serve? What staff resources do they have? Answers to these questions are the basis for establishing meaningful relationships that can lead to cooperative action in community development. While these agencies represent the established ongoing efforts of the community it is also vital to establish direct contact with the citizens themselves; potential agency bias must be recognized in the interpretation of community needs. College programs which can help in making agencies aware of changing viewpoints and conditions by facilitating direct interaction with citizens (not clients) can provide a partial basis for agency renewal. Also, simple matters of coordination among agencies is amazingly lacking (that is, calendar coordination, information exchange, joint committee work, and so on).

Interagency cooperation is as significant to community service programs as high school and university articulation is to the student personnel program.

ADVISORY LIAISON FUNCTION

As the college begins to develop its own responses to community problems through educational programming it may find advisory groups to be most useful. It must be recognized however that not all advisory groups are helpful. In some cases appointees may not be given a realistic view of their role and potential contribution; the wrong people may be selected; appointments may be made for some anticipated political gain; and in still other cases, the group may continue long after its usefulness simply because no mechanism was established for disbanding the group. These potential limitations can be counteracted if sound judgment is used in constituting advisory committees. Certainly the potential for increasing involvement and commitment to action is considerably enhanced in their use.

PUBLIC FORUM

As key issues emerge within the community, they are apt to block progress in community development. Community services programs can make a significant contribution in clarifying these issues. The community college is increasingly able to provide the open forum necessary for a full airing of viewpoints. There is no doubt that the path is a precarious one. The community services staff must be able to distinguish between *real* issues and the *facade* issues which community organizations will "adopt" to act out their power struggles. Providing a public forum is not the same thing as providing a "no-man's land" for organizational battles.

CIVIC ACTION

After the community analysis has been made and the major needs identified, after linkage has been well established with key agencies and organizations, after educational programs have been implemented to clarify problems or to provide new skills for dealing with them, the question of social and civic action remains. What is the role of the community college in collaborating with formal and informal groups to bring about change? Does the community college provide, for example, a community agent to work with a disenfranchised segment of the community such as found in poverty areas? What is the position of the community college if one of its community agents finds it necessary to lead a march on city hall to get the necessary attention to deplorable housing conditions? A short course in "how to live more comfortably with rats" (or even how to get rid of them) is begging the issue. In short, at what point does the college, as an integral part of the establishment, permit itself to function in a way that may be described by some community leaders as anti-establishment? There are no easy answers.

III. PROGRAM DEVELOPMENT

Finally the community services program will need some sense of order and unity. In fact there is no facet of the college which will have more difficulty in establishing unity. The program must be constantly interpreted to the community and to the staff of the college. The greater the involvement of staff, the more dynamic the impact of community involvement on the instructional program. It can be assumed that a teacher who is intensively involved in a community effort to solve the educational problems of the ghetto is likely to be more sensitive to the needs of his students than one who isn't—and he is also apt to teach a more stimulating course.

Campuses must be constructed that really facilitate informal as well as formal education. Where we might have thought of building student centers in the past, we should now think of community centers; the campus design should facilitate community use. Obviously, community use of the college auditorium that cancels the intramural basketball game will not always be warmly received by students. Yet such accommodations must be made, and if students become more actively involved in community programs as a result of a community-oriented student activity program, they may even welcome such use of college facilities. (At least their territorial indignation is apt to be tempered somewhat.)

Here then is a brief view of the potentialities and the dilemmas that the community services encounters. As a career student personnel worker, the writer has found the transition to community services work to be exhausting but enlivening. Certainly it is a stimulating arena for renewal. The decade of the '70s will undoubtedly see exciting and productive experimental efforts to fuse student and community services programs into unified, humanely oriented divisions within the college.

REFERENCES

1. GOODRICH, ANDREW, "A Survey of Selected Community Service Programs for the Disadvantaged at Inner City Community Colleges." Unpublished doctoral dissertation, Michigan State, 1969.
2. HARLACHER, IRVIN L. *The Community Dimensions of the Community College.* Englewood Cliffs, New Jersey: Prentice-Hall, Inc., 1969.
3. GUNDER, MYRON. *Community Services in the Community College.* Washington, D.C.: American Association of Junior Colleges, 1969.
4. RAINES, MAX R., *An Appraisal of the Rockland Guidance Center for Women.* State University of New York, Office of Continuing Education, 1970.

Articulation with High Schools and Four-Year Colleges, and Universities

JAMES L. WATTENBARGER

Director, Institute of Higher Education
University of Florida

If all levels of education were focused upon one single purpose and were under the policy direction and implementation of one board and one executive, there might be fewer problems which could be labeled articulation problems. Even if this circumstance were the case, however, any movement from one level to another would result in readjustments. This is the case because *problems* relating to the transfer of students from one level of the educational ladder to another level result largely from the fact that students change their goals, and quite often their goals do not coincide with those established by the institutions. The general inflexibility of institutions at all levels in accommodating individual goals is a major factor in the difficulties encountered by students which are discussed under the label "articulation problems."

A major portion of articulation problems are related directly to matters which may be characterized as "the bookkeeping of education." The bookkeeping policies often seem to be as related to concepts of "crime and punishment" as they do to any basic understanding of how persons learn. In fact, the bookkeeping problems may be symptoms of much more deep-seated philosophical positions. This chapter will not attempt to discuss all these factors, however. Major attention will be focused on those articulation problems which are centered around questions of institutional integrity, faculty competencies, restricted admissions policies, equivalency of courses, planning of programs, individual counseling procedures, student activities, and occupational objectives.

Articulation problems are never truly "laid to rest" because as soon as a workable procedure is reached and/or a decision made with clear and certain understanding on the part of all concerned, there are personnel changes; new individuals who have no common background in reaching solutions begin to make decisions and thereby to affect the entire process. A number of specific instances may be pointed out to illustrate this unsettled state. For example, in one state an articulation agreement was reached, after a number of meetings, that a course in mathematics offered in seven junior colleges was equivalent to a specific junior level course which was a required prerequisite for higher mathematics in the university. This decision caused no difficulties until a new counselor was appointed in the university's engineering college who began to require the students he advised to repeat the course. Result: loud protests, accusations of violating an agreement, and great unhappiness on the part of all concerned. When apprised of the earlier agreement, the counselor changed his requirements—but too late for more than 25 students who had been required to repeat a course.

A similar difficulty occurred when a new registrar was appointed in a state university. This state also supports ten community colleges and three state colleges. The new university registrar was unaware of the policies previously developed by his university regarding transfer students, and unilaterally established several new transfer policies based on his experiences in another state which supported no community colleges. These policies involved acceptance of credits, computation of grade point averages, and the total amount of acceptable credit for physical education. Almost a year passed before anyone realized that these new policies were adversely affecting many students transferring to the university. In some instances transfer students were being required to repeat a full semester's work. The agreements and previously developed articulation policies had to be redeveloped because the new registrar "refused" to acknowledge them.

Community colleges themselves often cause similar problems. A new business teacher in a community college became highly incensed over the refusal of a university to recognize the business law course he taught as equivalent to one the university offered at the senior level. This problem had been discussed and settled by mutual agreement several years prior to the junior college faculty member's employment. In fact the state law in this instance clearly specified that the junior college could not offer courses beyond the sophomore level. State regulations permitted courses usually offered as upper division courses to be offered only when required as a part of an occupational program. The new junior college faculty member learned of his mistake only after a number of heated exchanges.

These examples imply that there must be constant orientation, communication, and explanation of existing agreements and policies. These also should be continuous attempts to improve existing policies and procedures. The needs of the student should be considered more prominently in all discussions.

RESEARCH AS A BASIS FOR SOLVING PROBLEMS

A major essential consideration in achieving a sound procedure for solving articulation problems is to eliminate the difficulties caused by rumors and semantics. This can only be achieved through sound research, both institutional research and the more generally applied educational research. One of the most comprehensive national studies relating to articulation was the Knoell-Medsker study [2] which was published in 1965. This study conducted by the Center for the Study of Higher Education at the University of California, Berkeley, with an advisory committee representative of three associations, the American Association of Junior Colleges, the Association of American Colleges, and the American Association of Collegiate Registrars and Admissions Officers, became the basis for a number of conferences and policy statements. It stimulated a continuing attempt to achieve rational solutions within several states to the articulation problems identified by the study. State leadership in a number of states has assumed specific responsibilities in developing articulation procedures which are based upon the research findings in this and other continuing studies. States such as California, Florida, Michigan, Illinois, Pennsylvania, and New York have conducted research studies and published policy statements based upon research findings and articulation conferences. Other states are following this direction.

IMPLICATIONS OF RESEARCH

The Knoell-Medsker study emphasized a number of findings which have provided a basis for the development of sound procedures which can be used to alleviate articulation problems. From this study as well as from analysis of problems identified in other studies, the following important conclusions may be summarized:

1. In their academic work students may be expected to perform in a manner similar to that which has been typical of their past patterns of accomplishment. There are individuals, however, who will improve upon their past performance. It would, therefore, be prudent to avoid applying such generalizations to individual students in making decisions which determine their futures.

2. Policies regarding probation and dismissal sometimes reflect poor decision-making procedures in the university and discrimination toward transfer students. In many instances these policies are record-keeping decisions rather than educational decisions.

3. Problems such as financial support, inadequate goals, lack of self-confidence and similar difficulties which may have influenced students to

select a two-year college near home to begin their college work do not change when a person becomes a transfer student. These problems continue to affect his college work.

4. Students who complete a two-year associate degree program in a community college may be expected to be more successful after transfer than those who move prior to completing that part of their program.

5. In spite of the fact that a great amount of information regarding the numbers, the characteristics, and the problems of students who transfer from one institution to another has been made available, most senior institutions, both four-year colleges and universities, have done little to examine their rules, regulations, and policies to determine the ways in which they discriminate against the transfer student.

6. Academic bookkeeping procedures—that is, averaging grade point averages of all kinds of courses into a single mean and similar well-entrenched procedures—have little logical validity when compared with desirable outcomes for a college education.

7. If a successful system of higher education in a state may be measured by combining low attrition rates with high graduation rates, then those states where an effective articulation program is in operation may be said to be most successful.

8. Since in most senior colleges and universities restrictions on admission to the freshman class are often more rigorous than those for the junior class, the community college serves as a "second chance" institution for many young people who are highly motivated. Those who successfully complete their first two years are enabled to continue toward their baccalaureate degrees usually without reference to their high school work.

9. The articulation of programs in two- and four-year colleges is an exceedingly complex problem and will become even more complex as additional specializations are developed.

10. There is urgent need for constant contact between counselors in high schools, two-year colleges, and baccalaureate degree-granting institutions.

11. The college population is highly mobile. Large numbers of students transfer from one four-year institution to another, from university to junior college and back again, as well as the more generally expected pattern of transfer from junior to senior college.

AREAS OF CONCERN

Four areas of concern may be selected as the focal points for developing solutions to problems isolated by the implications listed above. These are: the student, the personnel services, the educational program, and the resources used in providing an educational program.

The student is often forgotten in the plethora of institutional problems which develop. He is the reason for institutionalizing the process of education; that is, the fact that he is multiple and he is complex makes it necessary to create institutions to provide for his educational needs. However, more often than not the development of tentative solutions to problems is conducted without concern for him. This concern should center around his goals, his personal characteristics, his previous experiences, his choices, his resources, and his humanness. If he were single rather than multiple, solutions would of course be more easily determined. If his goals were unitary rather than various, it would be easier to coincide them with those of the institution. If his abilities and interests were narrowed and less diverse, institutional goals could be more easily defined. If we were providing education for automatons, the entire process would indeed be more simple. Since none of these possibilities are correct, a major area of concern in working toward solutions for articulation problems must be the student himself.

The personnel services which are available or which should be available provide the focus for a second area of concern. Attention must be given to the role of those who are assigned the responsibility for these services: counseling, working with faculty, orientation programs, record-keeping and record transmittal, financial aids, student activities, student recognition and honors, and similar procedural activities. Currently considerable reorganization is under way in most colleges and universities which may release to a far greater degree the professional services of student personnel workers responsible for encouraging the development of services to students.

The educational program itself provides a major area of concern as solutions are considered. It is in this area of concern that institutional autonomy and faculty feeling become most prominently displayed. The imagined consequences and deduced logic which most often influence decisions relative to the educational program are in many instances refuted by research studies. This refutation is usually difficult to maintain, however, as a basis for policy decisions. Individuals forget the research findings and return to their process of internalized logic.

Some examples of problem areas may be briefly discussed in order to provide a basis for examining this area of concern:

1. Equivalency of courses. There is a great deal of discussion relative to the equivalency of one course to another. Scope and sequence statements, syllabi, course outlines, textbooks—all these and similar bases for judgment are used to determine whether the course a student takes at Institution A is equivalent to that offered in Institution B. A series or sequence of courses may be judged by titles and statements of intent and used to determine equivalency.

2. Grading standards may become a very important basis for developing judgments relative to a department, a division or an entire institution. The

tendency of a student to maintain a grade point average identical to or at least similar to his previous record is often used as a basis for decisions relative to other students transferring from the same institution. Articulation activities are quite often centered around the grading procedures and standards.

3. Grade point averages constitute a method of academic bookkeeping which is used in making basic decisions relative to an individual student's progress and prospects. Often his admission to the institution, his continuation in educational activities, his acceptance into certain classes, and his career decisions are based upon grade point averages. The acceptance of grades from other institutions as a part of a grade point average, the use of the grade point average in decision-making, and the unforgiving nature of the grade point averages reemphasize the fact that the policies related to the formulations of grade point averages are of special concern in any articulation study.

4. Prerequisites are among the most influential areas of concern in developing solutions to problems related to articulation. The sequential nature of many disciplines, that is, from simple to complex, provides an obvious basis for the procedures of using established prerequisites as a basis for further study.

5. The "balance" between general education and occupational education is also an example of a problem area which requires a solution. Each faculty arrives at a conclusion relative to this balance and becomes resentful at an implication that another faculty knows better than they what "ought to be." The student is quite often caught in the middle of this controversy.

6. The preparation of the faculty is an area of concern in developing solutions to transfer problems. Judgments are made on the basis of degrees held, areas studied, institutions attended, and similar quantitative information. These judgments affect the acceptance of the student's previously completed work as well as future directions of his study.

7. The procedures used in evaluating student progress is also an area of concern. Standardized tests, teacher-made tests, and related combinations of these constitute part of the problems. Other methods of student evaluation are also essential considerations in arriving at solutions to articulation problems.

The resources used in providing the educational program constitute a fourth focal point for developing solutions. The availability of facilities has a direct influence upon the decisions which an institution or a system of institutions must make relative to numbers of students. Quite often admission policies have evolved as a direct result of the limitations represented by the facilities which are available. Equally influential, however, are the differentiation of role and function among institutions. The calendars for academic year, the use of television, the provisions for individual work, the proximity of institutions, the accessibility of the programs—all these must be considered while solutions are developed.

MACHINERY FOR DEVELOPING SOLUTIONS

If real solutions to these concerns are to be developed, statewide, regionwide, and nationwide machinery must be developed. In the past, responsibilities for arriving at solutions have in the main been assumed by registrars and admissions officers who face these problems daily with students. Occasionally colleges and universities have added college relations staff members who attempt to alleviate the causes for concern.

More recently, however, there have developed in several states special committees and/or staff persons who have been assigned responsibility to work on articulation between junior and senior institutions. This development has accompanied the emergence of state-level coordinating or control agencies. A specific responsibility for articulation is placed upon the state-level coordinating or control agency.

A model organization (see Figure 1) for handling such a responsibility would provide for official articulation agreements which are implemented as policy statements by the respective governing boards. In the model these statements of policy are developed by professional people who represent all levels of education. There is also a place in the model to recognize the contributions of professional associations in suggesting solutions to articulation problems. Real and workable solutions must be implemented through regular legal channels, but contributions to policy development for solving these problems may be entirely outside the regular legal structure. The following may be used in developing the machinery for articulation.

1. A committee of professional persons representative of the several levels of education involved should be appointed by a state level agency which is responsible for overall coordination or supervision of the various institutions. If no such agency exists, then such a committee should be formed through a joint resolution of peer boards. It is important that the committee have official backing for its duties.

2. All intercollege agreements and activities should follow policies evolved by this committee.

3. The committee should draw heavily upon experts in various disciplines, representative of various institutions, students, lay representatives where appropriate, and other "grass roots" personnel in developing its statements of policy.

4. Articulation agreements and procedures relative to the various disciplines should be developed by special *ad hoc* task forces made up of persons who teach in those disciplines. Broad and diverse representation should be sought for membership on these task forces. Task force recommendations and reports should be received by the committee prior to sending the report into official channels for final approval and implementation.

5. Policy statements formulated by the committee should be received officially by presidents' councils or other committees which represent the institutions involved. At this point the policy proposal should be reviewed and modified where necessary. After this process, the policy becomes an official recommendation of the presidents' council and may be forwarded to the governing boards for implementation and the coordinating board for similar appropriate action.
6. Periodic review should be scheduled for all articulation policies and activities.

ROLE OF THE STUDENT PERSONNEL WORKER

No member of the community junior college faculty is more responsible for and more active in the development of solutions to problems related to articulation than is the student personnel worker. His major concern is the student and he must provide the student with an avenue for solving his problems. There are several specific roles that the student personnel worker must play in articulation activities.

First, he must serve as an instrument for identifying the students' problems. He is the person to whom the student should turn when he needs specific help. He is the one who often performs a liaison function with the high school on one side and the four-year college on the other for the student who may not be able to identify either his specific problem or its probable solution.

Second, the student personnel worker must serve as an interpreter to his own faculty. His function of faculty leadership is catalytic as well. He must also provide the faculty with a conscience which keeps institutional and faculty goals in a rational perspective to student goals.

Third, he serves as a major identifier of problems which require system-wide solutions. He will call to the attention of the state-level committees and responsible officials examples of problems which require solutions. He will make certain that students do not become victims of institutional rigidity.

Finally, he serves as a developer of policy. The student personnel worker in his capacity as a registrar and admissions officer has in many instances created problems of articulation as well as solutions to such problems. Active participation on the part of well-prepared student personnel workers will have direct influence on the specific solutions to many articulation problems.

GUIDELINES FOR IMPROVING ARTICULATION

Although major attention is most often given to those articulation activities associated with moving students from junior college to senior

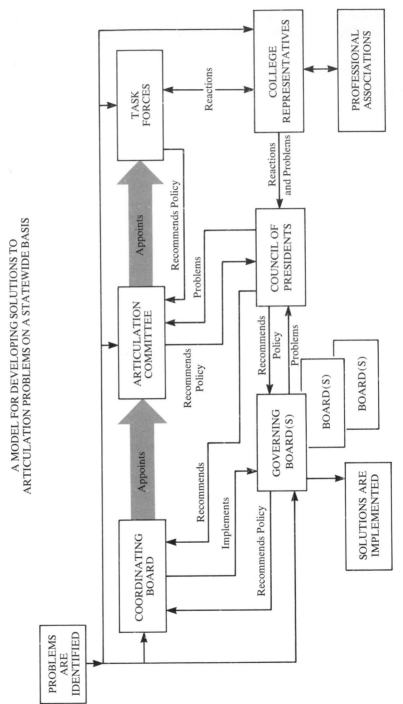

A MODEL FOR DEVELOPING SOLUTIONS TO
ARTICULATION PROBLEMS ON A STATEWIDE BASIS

institutions, equal concern should be demonstrated for the articulation between high school and junior college. In most localities, articulation with high schools should present fewer problems.

Most states have developed over the years fairly well understood procedures for alleviating articulation problems between high school and college. Stickler [3] reported in 1958 that more than half the states identified specific organizations and/or formal structures for articulation purposes. Others have no doubt developed since that time.

These organizations reported that their major activities included conducting research studies related to articulation problems, sponsoring conferences, publishing reports and brochures, organizing "college days," redesigning forms commonly used, preparing counselor handbooks, coordinating testing programs, and developing scholarship programs.

While many of these activities are related to statewide problems which affect all institutions in a similar way, there is still need for *each* community college to give specific attention to these and related problems within its own immediate area. Most public community junior colleges find that more than 80 percent of their students come from local high schools and therefore relationships with these schools directly affect the greatest portion of the junior college enrollment.

The local high schools often need the contributions which the community college faculty may be able to provide in assuring development of a continuous experience for the students. One of the advantages of attending local community colleges should be a continued and uninterrupted educational experience. There are numerous opportunities for subject matter scope and sequence planning with local high school faculties. There are unlimited opportunities to provide for gifted students to accelerate their educational progress while maintaining important contacts with their peer groups in social development. There are numerous ways in which the community college may share with the high schools in providing community services to the entire district served by the college. In all these activities the community college must assume a role of active leadership.

The attention which may be given to student personnel services are important enough to warrant a special mention at this point. Community colleges need to maintain close contact with local high school counseling staffs. Regularly established meetings several times a year, telephone contacts between counselors, and exchange of information relative to the program in both community colleges and universities and the high schools are a few examples of techniques which are useful. The records of students' progress should be returned to the high school to permit continuing evaluation of curriculum and teaching.

A technique often found useful in this interchange is for the community college to employ high school counselors during the summer months to serve on the college counseling staff. All methods of communication are valuable if they help improve the transfer of students from one level to another.

Since articulation problems are not limited to any specific level of education, the following guidelines should be applied in developing articulation activities for high schools, community junior colleges, and baccalaureate degree granting institutions.

1. In all matters, the welfare of the individual student is of primary importance. No decision or policy should be enforced merely for the convenience of the institution.

2. In counseling individual students, emphasis should be placed upon a realistic appraisal of demonstrated past performance and appropriateness of institutional and career choices.

3. Policies and standards should be clearly stated and objectively applied.

4. Procedures in evaluating and accepting credit should be uniformly and fairly applied to all applicants for admission.

5. There must be free, open, and continuing communication between institutions regarding programs of students, pending changes therein, and development of new requirements.

6. Generalizations about institutions and/or student groups should be avoided unless there is adequate research data which warrant such generalizations.

7. There should be recognition of the fact that students who have problems, such as financial or family responsibilities, and so on, will probably continue to have such problems and will need continued help.

8. In arriving at recommendations relating to solutions, all elements (high schools, community colleges, universities, coordinating agencies, faculty, students, and so on) should be represented.

9. Because articulation is both a process and an attitude, the machinery for achieving solutions to problems should involve voluntary and peer level participation on a collegial basis.

10. Since admission policies and similar regulations require official implementing action, boards of trustees or coordinating commissions should approve such policies and/or regulations only when recommended by committees of professional persons specifically assigned responsibility to develop such statements.

11. State-level action is not a substitute for local action. Each institution will need to provide specific feedback and other information to institutions within its own area.

12. Constant evaluation of procedures and other articulation machinery is necessary.

13. While systems of colleges or universities are generally public and therefore legal imposition of articulation activities is limited to public institutions,

privately supported institutions should be involved insofar as they are willing to participate.

14. There must be continuous attention given to articulation procedures. New personnel at all levels in all institutions will need constant orientation to the previous history in the state.[1]

In applying these guidelines there must be a statewide concern. All institutions must participate in the identification of problems, in the study of their effects, in the formulation of recommendations for solutions, and in the implementation of procedures which will alleviate or eliminate barriers to smooth transfer.

Many hours of committee work will be required. Many compromises will result. Many research studies will evolve. Much clarification and definition of terms must occur. The process of articulation must be continuous, and centered primarily around the student himself.

LOOKING TO THE FUTURE

During the latter years of the 19th century and the first half of the 20th century the public high school developed to a point where high school attendance and graduation have become almost universal. This fact has caused colleges and universities to accept freshman students on the basis of commonly accepted procedures which are applied in most all situations. Research studies such as the "Eight Year Study" and national policy statements of various professional organizations have substantiated and encouraged these procedures. During the latter part of the 20th century similar universal opportunity will occur at the post-high school level. Almost all persons will be involved in some type of education beyond the high school. It appears that most of this will be carried out in the setting of the community junior college. Trends in articulation which may be anticipated will probably develop as described herein.

The associate in arts degree will become the basis for admission to the junior level of the four-year colleges and universities. A student's program for graduation with a baccalaureate degree will be planned and developed without particular reference to course work which he has previously completed. Graduation from a community college will complete admission requirements to the junior class level.

Each state will appoint a special articulation committee which will be responsible for developing policy recommendations relative to transfer of students from one institution to another. This committee will be representative of all levels of education and will consider the specific needs of students rather than the convenience of institutions in developing policy recommendations.

There will be a considerable increase in research activities which provide information about student progress. Analysis of problem areas will require specific data which will be available as a part of management information systems. The use of computer technology will provide more information and better ways of analyzing it. As a result, decisions which are based on facts may be more commonly reached.

More emphasis on efficiency and effectiveness in education will result in more attention to the causes of student difficulties. Concern for the individual student will lead to increasing awareness that resources devoted to his educational development are apparently wasted when he does not reach some definable goal. While the definition of such a goal is not an articulation problem, it is obvious that the attainment of the goal may be directly affected by transfer difficulties.

The continued concerns evidenced in many places about the costs of education will make it even more necessary to eliminate articulation problems. The structure of post-high school education will be made up of a variety of institutions. Students will select one or more of these institutions as a result of a variety of reasons. Smooth transfer from one to another will be essential in order to conserve the available resources for productive activities. The person who provides support will not be satisfied with the failure rates and elimination procedures which have been common in the past, especially if such procedures can be eliminated through soundly developed articulation procedures.

REFERENCES

1. Joint Committee on Junior and Senior Colleges, *Guidelines for Improving Articulation Between Junior and Senior Colleges.* Washington, D.C.: American Council on Education, 1965.

2. KNOELL, DOROTHY M. and L. L. MEDSKER, *From Junior to Senior College: A National Study of the Transfer Student.* Washington, D.C.: American Council on Education, 1965.

3. STICKLER, HUGH, *A Survey of Policies and Practices Regarding Articulation of Public and Secondary and Higher Education in the United States: Fall, 1957.* Tallahassee, Florida: Office of Institutional Research and Services, Florida State University, 1958. (Mimeographed)

The Decade 3
of the Seventies

How far we have come, where we are now, and what the tasks are ahead provide the gist for this final section. Current trends and innovative practices are examined. A new focus for community junior college student development programs is described and developed as an emerging model. Lastly, solutions are sought for unresolved student personnel issues of the sixties.

Student Personnel Work
Four Years Later:
The Carnegie Study and Its Impact

JANE E. MATSON

Professor of Education, California
State College of Los Angeles

The junior-community college has always claimed as one of its major functions the provision of counseling and guidance services to all students. It is the only post-secondary education segment which has given full recognition to the critical importance of a broad spectrum of supportive services for students in the achievement of the purposes for which the college exists. As educational opportunity is extended to an ever-increasing proportion of the total population, these student services become even more crucial. Beginning with the recruitment of students to the college, the assessment or appraisal of their educational needs, and the design of appropriate educative experiences, the student personnel specialist's skill and knowledge is of primary importance. The students, many of whom have not yet acquired skill in making decisions nor developed adequate competencies to achieve success in education, need the help of the professional student personnel staff in acquiring understanding of themselves and the opportunities for self-development which the college offers.

In November 1965 the National Committee for Appraisal and Development of Junior College Student Personnel Programs presented its final report to the Carnegie Corporation. It represented the culmination of a two-year study of student personnel programs in junior colleges carried out under the sponsorship of the American Association of Junior Colleges and supported by a grant from the Carnegie Corporation. This report constitutes the first significant landmark in the history of student personnel work in the two-year college. It was an unprecedented attempt to evaluate the effectiveness with which the functions, commonly designated as student personnel services, were being performed in a representative cross-section of American two-year colleges. The precise effect of such a study is difficult to evaluate. It seems likely that the process of assessment carried on in the 125 colleges which constituted the sample had some impact on the student personnel programs in those institutions although it would be difficult, if not impossible, to determine results in precise terms. History may record that the most significant influence of this study was to focus attention on student personnel work as an integral and essential part of the total educational process and to provide increased visibility for these services.

The evidence revealed by the study was not encouraging to those concerned with the effectiveness of student personnel services in the two-year college. The chairman of the National Committee stated in the fore-word to the report,

The conclusion of these studies may be put bluntly: when measured against criteria of scope and effectiveness, student personnel programs in community colleges are woefully inadequate. The reports of the Committee's studies identify the principal deficiencies and point out where improvement is essential. The Committee presents its constructive recommendations for upgrading the services which, to a very large degree, will determine the extent to which community colleges discharge their very considerable responsibilities.

Among the areas in which specific recommendations were made were staffing standards, program interpretation, leadership development, counselor preparation, use of field consultants, establishment of demonstration centers, extension of community services, and development of evaluative criteria.

In the more than four years which have passed since the final report, significant changes have occurred in the junior college world which have undoubtedly affected the quality of the student personnel services provided. Among these developments are (1) a phenomenal growth in the number of students enrolled in two-year colleges; (2) a rapid increase in the number of two-year institutions, with an average of 50 or more new colleges opening in each of the past three years; (3) a developing focus in federal and state legislation on the role of the two-year college, evidenced by increasing availability of federal and state funds for junior college use. A review of apparent trends in several areas related to student personnel services may reveal some of the directions taken since the final report of the Carnegie Study in 1965.

ORGANIZATIONAL PATTERNS

There is an unmistakable trend toward centralization of the responsibility for all student personnel functions. The "umbrella" type of administrative structure which groups related student personnel functions is most common, especially in colleges with over 100 students enrolled. The chief administrator of these functions carries a variety of titles, for example, dean of students, dean of student services, dean of student personnel, vice-president for student affairs. There is an increasing likelihood that the position will involve supervision of most, if not all, of the services traditionally classified as student personnel. It is also increasingly probable that he will be directly responsible to the chief administrator of the college which reflects the recognition, at least in the administrative structure, of the senior partnership of the student personnel area with the instructional function.

What might be considered a counter-trend is occurring in a number of colleges. Student personnel specialists (most frequently counselors) are assigned to work with a particular instructional area or group of academic disciplines. This practice is often referred to as "decentralization" and usually represents an effort to facilitate a closer working relationship between the teaching faculty and student personnel staff. In some more recently established colleges, the physical location of the counseling staff is adjacent to or part of the office of a division or department. In the great majority of colleges, however, where decentralization has been attempted, the primary administrative responsibility for the student personnel functions remains with the chief student personnel administrator.

STAFFING PATTERNS

An increasing number of staff positions in the student personnel areas are full-time assignments. In smaller colleges it is common to find one position combining a number of functions until the college is of sufficient size and the program has been developed to the point where separation is warranted. The number of levels of supervision varies and is related to the overall pattern of the college administrative structure. It is common in larger colleges to find at least two levels of supervisory positions within the student personnel area with counseling usually the first function in which a separate supervisory position is created.

A development, embryonic as yet but growing rapidly and considered to have great promise, is the use of subprofessional or support personnel in student personnel areas. The tremendous shortage of well-qualified professional staff, which inevitably lies ahead, may be alleviated by the proper and judicious use of appropriately trained support personnel. Several junior colleges have begun or are planning two-year associate in arts degree programs to prepare workers for these positions. The design and implementation of such curricula presents a challenge and requires a reexamination of the variety of tasks performed in the student personnel functions. There is little doubt that the introduction of the para-professional can have great impact on the practice of student personnel work in junior colleges. The student personnel professionals now working in two-year colleges must assume a primary role in the definition of these new jobs and in the design of a curriculum to prepare people to fill them.

The assignment of prime responsibility for the academic advisement function to the teaching faculty remains a controversial issue. The practice of assigning staff as part-time teachers and part-time student personnel workers appears to be declining. But in many junior colleges faculty are given advisement duties in addition to a full-time teaching assignment. A pendulum or cyclical phenomenon may be involved in this practice. In some of the newer junior colleges, faculty are asked to assume this counseling-related function on the premise that there is insufficient money or staff to do otherwise and everyone must "pitch in and help" in order to get the job done. As the college grows in size and budget, it is not uncommon for the advisement function to be shifted entirely to the counseling staff. The next stage of development occurs when the faculty are again given the responsibility for academic advisement. At this point the rationale is likely to be that this arrangement facilitates good faculty-counselor relationships, or that it improves faculty-student communication, or that it is impossible to maintain a reasonable counselor-student ratio without resorting to a faculty advisement system. The argument is also used that faculty are generally better equipped than the professional counselor to provide superior advisement service. Perhaps each of these is a reasonable hypothesis, but neither has been well evaluated and, therefore, remains merely an hypothesis with only vague and questionable data to support it. What is needed is a good evaluative study of the advantages and disadvantages of the use of faculty advisers in a variety of college settings. Until this is done practice will continue to swing on a pendulum and will be justified on opinions, frequently more emotional than rational.

SELECTED FUNCTIONS

There is no doubt that counseling is considered to be the key student personnel service. To many it is synonymous with student personnel. It is the one function in which there are readily identifiable expertise and well-established training programs to provide the essential skills and knowledge. In this sense it is the most professionalized of all student personnel functions and thereby occupies a central position in the total student personnel field.

"Counseling and guidance" has been widely accepted as one of the basic functions of a junior college. Because "guidance" is a vague term subject to many different interpretations, it has been largely ignored in the public perception, and counseling has borne the major responsibility for implementing the counseling and guidance function of the junior college. Traditionally, counseling in the junior college has differed markedly from counseling in the four-year college. In the junior college, counseling has been defined generally as a service for *all* students—it is focused on vocational and educational decision-making and is the major means of accomplishing the appropriate distribution of students among the curricula offered by the college. The counseling center concept found in the four-year college has only recently appeared in junior colleges. The shortage of well-trained counselors and limited financial resources has forced some colleges to redefine the counseling function. Another factor contributing to this practice may be an almost over-professionalization of the counseling role, leading to the attitude on the part of counselors that such mundane, common problems as choice of curriculum or choice of college of transfer, or even choice of a vocational objective are not the best use of a truly "professional" counselor's time, which might be more appropriately spent in assisting students with in-depth investigations of personality aberrations of a more or less clinical nature. Attention to these problems is of course important and it is appropriate for a junior college to provide such assistance. But the question might be raised regarding the adequacy of a counseling service which provides *only* that kind of assistance and then only to a very small proportion of the student population.

The rapid and extensive spread of group work which has characterized the entire counseling field in the past several years has also been found in the two-year colleges. The administrator frequently perceives group work to be an economical method of spreading the available counseling talent and is seen by many counselors as the panacea to all their problems as well as those of their clients. In reality, group counseling in all its various forms is an effective technique when used by competent practitioners and can provide an important dimension to a counseling service. Continued exploration of its outcomes are essential if group processes are to achieve their maximum potential in the college setting.

Positions defined as involving strictly "vocational counseling" are appearing in a number of junior colleges. To some degree these arise from peculiar regulations regarding the use of federal and state funds and represent an expedient means of obtaining additional staff. In some colleges the creation of these positions represents an effort to force the attention of the counselor to the problems of vocational choice rather than what is perceived by some to be an overemphasis on emotional problems. Any attempt to compartmentalize the counseling process is probably doomed to failure since counseling involves communication with a total person who is unlikely to consider his problems as existing in water-tight compartments. It must be noted, however, that to some degree the trend toward placing an emphasis on vocational counseling is due to the failure of junior college counselors to deal adequately with students who need help in making decisions about vocations.

Out-of-class activities programs in most junior colleges have followed the traditional patterns of activities programs found in the four-year college. In too many instances, these programs have represented largely "fun and games" accompanied by a student government of questionable representativeness and severely limited autonomy. It is not surprising that in most junior colleges only a very small proportion of students are active participants in either the student government or in the various clubs and interest groups which constitute the activities program. There has been little effort to design and develop a program which demonstrates for the student a relationship between what he learns in the classroom and his out-of-class hours. There is need for cooperative effort of student personnel specialists, teaching faculty, and students directed toward the design and implementation of co-curricular programs which provide a laboratory for the learning and practice of attitudes and skills for everyday living.

The changing role of the student in the college environment is a hopeful sign in the development of more significant out-of-classroom activities. There is a rapid and marked increase in the number of colleges which are making some effort to involve students in the policy-making process and in the formal governance of the college. In a number of colleges students have become full voting members of official college committees responsible for policy recommendations in such areas as educational policy, facility planning, curriculum, student personnel, and in a few instances, faculty hiring and evaluation. In other colleges there is less formal student participation in many phases of college governance. A number of alternative models are emerging which provide for the involvement of students in the college-governing process. Longer experience with varying roles for students and more adequate evaluation will be necessary before any model or models can be recommended with either authority or conviction.

Few junior colleges have experienced the more serious confrontation between students and the college establishment. It would be unwise to conclude that some of the same forces which contribute to disruptive behavior on university campuses are not present on many junior college campuses. The fact that junior college students are, on the whole, less articulate, more conservative, and less likely to take strong partisan positions than their four-year college counterparts does not mean that they cannot benefit from the educational advantages of direct participation and involvement in the major issues confronting colleges and college students. The question of student rights and freedoms (and, of course, concomitant responsibilities) is being examined on many campuses. There is little doubt that students are asking and receiving more attention and more consideration, and are more actively participating in the day-to-day operation of many colleges. It is peculiarly appropriate that this should be occurring in the junior college which has long claimed to be "student-centered."

The student personnel professional has a facilitating role to play in this process of achieving student involvement in college governance. For many reasons, the junior college student needs help as he "tries on for size" his newly recognized rights and freedoms. Faculty and administrators also need assistance in developing the skills and knowledge which will enable them to make good use of the students' contributions toward achievement of the college's objectives.

GROWTH OF PROFESSIONALISM

There are hopeful signs of an increase in a sense of professional identity among the student personnel specialists in junior colleges. The American Association of Junior Colleges and the American College Personnel Association have each made key contributions to this development. Both organizations make use of commissions as the major media for accomplishing their professional goals. The American Association of Junior Colleges Commission on Student Personnel has provided leadership and guidance in the Association's work in the student personnel area. Statements defining positions in the areas of new models for student government, role of student personnel workers in education of the disadvantaged, role and function of student personnel services, and student rights and freedoms are in the process of preparation and will provide useful guidelines to colleges as they formulate policies in these areas.

The ACPA Commission on Junior College Student Personnel Work was established in 1962 as an effort to focus attention on the two-year institution as a special segment of higher education. The work of the Commission has provided benefits in two directions. Members of the Association who have been drawn largely from four-year college and university student personnel staffs have had an opportunity to become acquainted with the two-year college and its differences from and similarities to the senior institutions. Junior college members, who have increased markedly in number, have been able to establish an identification with a broadened cross-section of the student personnel profession. The one measure of increased visibility of junior college student personnel work can be found in the significant number of programs at local, regional, and national conventions which are directed to special problems of the two-year college.

Other professional organizations have also become aware of the growing importance of the community junior college. In 1967 the National Association of Student Personnel Administrators modified its constitution in order to accept two-year colleges as voting members. Other related professional organizations in the student personnel spectrum have increased their attention to the two-year colleges through such devices as special workshops, publications, and so on. It seems likely that, as junior colleges grow in number and enrollment with concomitant increase in staff, professional organizations will increase their efforts to serve them. It is the responsibility of junior college student personnel specialists to assume an active role in these organizations in order to improve the understanding of their role and functions so that the organizations can more adequately serve them.

The Junior College Student Personnel Services Newsletter is an admirable example of cooperation between two professional organizations. Jointly funded by the American College Personnel Association and the American Association of Junior Colleges, it is now in its third year of publication. About 2500 copies are distributed four times each year. It serves as a useful means of providing information of special interest to junior college student personnel workers.

SOME PROBLEMS TO BE FACED

In the final report to the Carnegie Corporation presented by the National Committee,[1] recommendations were made which were intended to develop and strengthen areas of weakness revealed by the committee's study. An additional grant of modest proportions was given to the American Association of Junior Colleges for the purpose of creating a staff position at the headquarters office to establish some priorities for the implementation of the recommendations made in the final report and to undertake some pilot or exploratory projects in areas of critical need. This position was filled from October, 1966 to August, 1968. In addition to providing staff services in the student personnel area, a number of special projects were undertaken. Among these were a conference to explore the relationships between the nature of physical facilities and effective student personnel practices reported in a publication, "Premises: Planning Student Personnel Facilities," a pilot workshop to identify and prepare a small group of specialists who might serve as consultants in the area of student personnel services, the establishment of liaison relationships with major service organizations, for example, the Educational Testing Service, College Entrance Examination Board, and American College Testing Program, so that the special needs of junior colleges might be served. It was hoped that a permanent staff position in the headquarters office of the American Association of Junior Colleges might be established following the expiration of the 1966 Carnegie grant. To date this has not been possible and the Association has continued its service in the student personnel area through a part-time consultant and the ongoing work of its Commission on Student Personnel Services. There is little doubt that student personnel work in the two-year college would benefit from the additional assistance which could be provided by full-time staff representation.

If student personnel work in the junior college is to make its maximum contribution to the achievement of the institution's goals and objectives, attention must be given to the following areas:

1. The role of the student personnel professional needs to be redefined in terms of clearly stated objectives related to the purposes of the two-year college. The rather hazy and sometimes almost invisible relationship between student personnel functions and the curriculum needs to be explored with vigor and skill. The integration of the work of student personnel specialists into the central activity of any educational institution, namely learning, is long overdue.

2. Once this role has been given form and substance, efforts must be directed to the identification of experience and training which is likely to provide a supply of professionals prepared to assume this role in all its dimensions. This will involve not only attention to appropriate pre-service preparation but a major emphasis on providing ongoing staff development which will enable the student personnel professionals to maintain and enhance their knowledge and competencies.

3. An area of critical importance to the effective implementation of the student personnel role is that of research and evaluation. It is of equal importance to the total effort of the college and, indeed, a strong case can be made for the position that evaluation of the student personnel function cannot be done outside the context of the entire system of the college program. Daily decisions are made which make important differences in the lives of all members of the college community. Too often these decisions are made with inadequate data or without consideration of information which is available. Educational decision-making is too likely to be made under conditions of stress or crisis without adequate consideration of the ultimate consequences to the students, actual or potential, who are presumably to be served. This is not necessarily because decision-makers are unskilled or poorly informed. In many instances, the data pertinent to the problems are simply not available.

Significant information about students is especially sparse. Many junior colleges do not describe their students in any terms other than number, sex, obvious identifying data, and academic ability level. Yet there is persuasive evidence which suggests that these are not the most pertinent items of information needed in planning educational experiences which will lead to success for students. Not only are more data needed about students but greatly increased information is needed about the community, its occupational structure, its socioeconomic dimensions, the important elements of the college environment, its impact on students—to suggest only a few factors which are all too rarely studied.

But data alone are not enough. They must be interpreted in the light of a particular situation or problem. There must be a willingness to use the data in the development of policies and procedures and to test continuously the hypotheses on which the decisions rest. Only with this kind of resiliency will the junior college be able to achieve its purposes or, perhaps, even to survive.

There is no doubt that significant changes have taken place in the practice of student personnel work in the two-year college since 1965 when the report of the Carnegie Study was presented. The nature and directions of those changes are seen only dimly and with vague dimensions. The extent to which these changes have resulted in *improvement* is even less well known. If the mistakes of the past are not to be repeated in the new colleges which are appearing at a rate unprecedented in the history of education, guidelines must be available which are based on a continuous process of appraisal and evaluation. Only by such vigilance and constant search for new models will the junior college be able to meet the challenge of extending educational opportunity to an entire society.

REFERENCES

1. *Junior College Student Personnel Programs: Appraisal and Development: A Report to the Carnegie Corporation,* Max Raines, Project Coordinator. November, 1965.

Exceptional Practices
in Community Junior College
Student Personnel Programs

TERRY O'BANION

Associate Professor of Higher Education,
University of Illinois

Identity for junior college student personnel workers came rapidly in the 1960s. The American College Personnel Association and the American Association of Junior Colleges appointed special commissions on junior college student personnel work. The first publications devoted exclusively to junior college student personnel work appeared. Special programs at conventions and workshops were offered. Several NDEA Institutes were developed for student personnel workers in the junior college. The Project for the Appraisal and Development of Junior College Student Personnel Programs (the Carnegie Study) was launched at the national level. A specialist in junior college student personnel work was appointed by the American Association of Junior Colleges.

In recent years an annual workshop for junior college student personnel workers has been sponsored by ACPA and AAJC. A national newsletter is issued quarterly. Several states have appointed student personnel specialists to state-level positions to coordinate and consult with student personnel staffs. Several states have developed their own newsletters, organizations, state evaluation projects, and state guidelines. Programs for the preparation of junior college student personnel workers continue to appear in major universities. Professional associations have organized special interest sections for junior college student personnel workers and appoint junior college people to most major committees.

These activities are dramatic evidence of substantial growth of junior college student personnel work as a profession. There is also evidence of substantial growth in the programs that have been developing during these ten years on the individual campuses of junior colleges.

Some of these programs may have been influenced by national activities; for the most part, however, they reflect the initiative and creativity of junior college student personnel workers who have responded with imagination and skill to the changing needs expressed by students.

Many junior colleges continue to support the time-honored structures and practices of student personnel programs. More and more, however, student personnel professionals are experimenting with practices that are exceptional, especially when compared with practices of the past. In a few colleges there seems to be commitment to experimentation and innovation to the extent that the total student personnel program can be described as exceptional; such programs are usually found in the newer colleges.

Recognizing these developments, the American College Personnel Association commissioned a study to describe some of the exceptional practices that have emerged in recent years in student personnel programs on junior college campuses. Junior college leaders (selected presidents, selected deans of students, directors of the Kellogg program, state directors of community colleges, professors of junior college education, and officers of appropriate professional organizations) were asked to nominate exceptional practices for possible inclusion in a monograph. Once nominated, the person having major responsibility for the practice in an institution was asked to follow a set of guidelines in preparing a two-page description. Only selected, exceptional practices in the area of organization and administration, academic advising, counseling, student activities, and orientation are described here. While exceptional practices do exist in other areas of student personnel, few were nominated in this study. In the monograph to be published by the American College Personnel Association, many more practices are described and in much greater detail; this chapter is only a brief review of a few selected practices.

For a few colleges, the new directions will have already been tried and incorporated as standard practice. For others the practices will provide encouragement for experimentation and innovative program development. Across the nation and even within many states, junior colleges are in different stages of development. No list of practices can provide alternatives for all student personnel programs in junior colleges. Neither can a list of practices reflect all the exciting new programs with which junior colleges are experimenting. The examples included here are illustrations of what exist. Hopefully they reflect areas of activity that members of the profession would agree are most generally innovative and exceptional.

It is not the purpose of this chapter to point out weaknesses of the practices described. Most of the practices are fairly new developments, and few have been subjected to evaluation. These practices were nominated by leaders in the field as exceptional; it will be some time before the slow process of evaluation sorts out the practices that survive the test of careful scrutiny. In the meantime, these practices can serve as tentative models for exploration and experimentation with new forms of student personnel functions.

ORGANIZATION AND ADMINISTRATION

In keeping with developments in four-year colleges and universities, a few junior college deans of students have been promoted to the level of vice-presidents. Titles that reflect this change include vice-president for student development and vice-president for student affairs. This appears to be a recognition of the importance of student personnel work in educational institutions; it remains to be seen whether student personnel vice-presidents will be accorded the same status as instructional vice-presidents.

Most organizational experimentation is taking place in the area of decentralized counseling services. These developments reflect several aspects of an emerging role of student personnel work. (1) In a decentralized system the counselor "goes out to" the students; he does not wait for students to come to his counseling cubicle. (2) In a decentralized system the counselor works in concert with the faculty, often sharing an office in an instructional division. (3) In a decentralized system the counselor works with all kinds of students, not just those who have "personal" problems.

If the student personnel program is to have a major impact on the institution it seems certain that counselors are going to have to leave the comfort and isolation of the counseling center. The student personnel program must be thrust into the heart of the institution—into the curriculum, into the instructional process, into the faculty conclaves, into the decision-making processes, and into the community. If the organization and administration of the student personnel program is structured to maintain a separate program, often housed in a separate building, student personnel work is in danger of even further isolation—isolation that may lead to obsolescence.

The major question is no longer, "Should the counselor work more closely with faculty?" The question is, "Should the counselor be literally moved out of the counseling office and housed with faculty members?" Blocker and Richardson [1] have suggested that counselors be assigned according to their competencies to divisions, housed in the divisions, and be administratively responsible to the division chairman. Harvey [2] has advocated that counselors be assigned to divisions but that they report to the dean of students or their chief administrative officer. In some colleges counselors are assigned to special divisions, attend divisional meetings, advise students in that division, spend some time in the division, but maintain their offices in the counseling center and report to the dean of students.

So far, decisions regarding decentralization have been made on philosophical considerations; no evaluation is available to test the merits of the various systems proposed. It seems quite clear, however, that many junior college student personnel workers will find it helpful to work more closely with faculty members—perhaps through the division—as they attempt to provide more meaningful programs for students.

William Rainey Harper College (Illinois) and Forest Park Community College (Missouri) have decentralized counseling services with some success. At Harper, counselors are housed in academic divisions and are assigned students for counseling who enroll in those divisions. Video terminals provide student information. The emphasis is on vocational guidance. Division counselors rotate on a regular schedule to provide some centralized services in the college center and to maintain their professional identity with counseling colleagues.

The decentralized counseling service at Forest Park is similar. The rationale for the Forest Park program is stated as follows: "We hope that by decentralizing our counseling system and by organizing our physical set-up to increase faculty-counselor relationships, we can prevent a schism from developing between the counselors and the faculty. Locating the counselors throughout the faculty makes them readily available for consultation, both by faculty and by students."

At Moraine Valley Community College (Illinois), the college facilities have been carefully planned to provide for decentralization. The facilities call for a "Main Street" intersected by educational subdivisions containing instructional facilities for occupational, transfer, and developmental classes. The intersections are called "Crossroad" and provide facilities for studying, relaxing, eating, conversing, and socializing. Work areas for student personnel workers and faculty members are located at each crossroad.

At each of the seven planned crossroads the student personnel staff consists of six to eight counselors, technical assistants, and clerical staff. All student data and information regarding job placement, financial aids, student activities, transfer and occupational programs are available at each center. Other functions are centrally located. A senior staff member coordinates the activities of each crossroad and reports to an associate dean of students. This associate dean, along with other administrators of the central functions, reports to the dean of students.

In this system at Moraine Valley student personnel staff are placed in the mainstream of student life on the campus where they come in close contact with the teaching faculty. In addition, they have opportunities to develop a team cohesiveness because of the smaller and more personal groupings of staff.

Another interesting practice in organization occurs at Fulton-Montgomery Community College (New York). The dean of students states, "Since the curriculum is one of the most significant aspects of the student's experience at college, the student personnel staff must be able to influence this aspect of the college, if it is to affect the student's collegiate experience." The student personnel program, therefore, has been organized as an academic division in the college. Student personnel staff members offer instruction and are represented on those committees responsible for making curriculum decisions. Developmental courses in reading and study skills have been shifted to this new division and new credit courses initiated in Personal Development, Educational and Vocational Exploration, and Seminar on College Life. In cooperation with other divisions, courses in Contemporary Issues and Seminar on Human Values are being developed.

ACADEMIC ADVISING

Practices regarding academic advising seem to revolve around three questions: Who does academic advising? When is it done? How is it done? Though the question regarding who should do it seems to have been answered in the universities in favor of the faculty, who should do academic advising in the junior college is still open to debate. The usual approach has been to assign responsibility to faculty members. At Portland Community College (Oregon), this concept is so important that the president even acts as an academic advisor to a small group of students.

A number of new colleges are experimenting with a variety of approaches to academic advising. El Centro College (Texas), Santa Fe Junior College (Florida), and William Rainey Harper College (Illinois) are examples of colleges that use professional counselors for the advising function. At Harper College it is believed that "academic responsibilities prevent the instructor from having the time to gather the information and to develop the skill to help the student bring into perspective the basic considerations involved in the selection of a program of studies." At El Centro, "Educational program planning is a highly personalized counseling service and rests upon the basic assumption that program planning is essentially a counseling problem."

At Illinois Central College counselors do the advising but faculty members are involved as consultants to counselors and students in areas of the faculty members' expertise. Meramec Community College (St. Louis) employs support personnel to perform much of the academic advising function, releasing counselors and faculty for other professional services to students. Support personnel, who are given the title of educational advisor, are selected on qualities of warmth, maturity, open-mindedness, and potential for working with counselors and students in the community college setting. Two measures of the value and effectiveness of the educational advisors have been completed with positive results. In a preliminary study educational advisors and counselors were viewed in a similar positive manner in regard to students' perceptions of their pre-registration conferences. In a second study there was no significant difference between the frequency of self-referrals for counseling in the fall semester between students who had been advised by counselors and students who had been advised by educational advisors. Initial student contact with educational advisors rather than counselors apparently has no adverse effect on the likelihood of students subsequently seeking counseling assistance.

New freshmen often get assistance in planning their programs only a few days before beginning classes. A number of colleges have initiated programs of summer advising by counselors or selected faculty members. At Monroe Community College (New York) students visit the campus during the summer and talk with a faculty member in their major area. Counselors are available for undecided students. At Fulton-Montgomery small group sessions are held daily throughout the summer. These groups are advised by specially trained faculty members assisted by student aides.

Numerous exciting practices in academic advising have been developed by various colleges. One of the most interesting is the use of video tape at Grossmont College (California). During the summer, students select a two-hour period to come to the college. In the first hour students view a 38-minute video tape that explains such concerns as how to read a catalog, how to understand course numbers, how to recognize prerequisites, how to read a class schedule, and how to complete a program form. Once the tape is viewed students complete their program. If students wish they can make appointments with counselors to discuss educational goals. By using this method Grossmont counselors are able to hold individual conferences with approximately 2500 freshmen during the summer. In addition, all freshmen will have received the same information of the programming and registration process.

COUNSELING: INDIVIDUAL AND GROUP

The sample of practices in this section also reflects aspects of an emerging role for student personnel workers. In these practices few counselors are isolated in their cubicles; counselors are thrust into the activities of the institution—counseling students in the cafeteria, counseling faculty members, and meeting in groups in many different places for many different reasons. Counseling emerges from therapy for a selected clientele to an educational process for all members of the educational and local community.

INDIVIDUAL COUNSELING

At Portland Community College (Oregon) counseling is viewed as an educational shopping center. Counselors are located wherever students are likely to congregate: in the library, study areas, faculty office areas, and even the cafeteria. Desks are arranged in a relatively open fashion similar to office areas frequently seen in banks. Semiprivate interview areas are located immediately adjacent for those occasions requiring such facilities. Staff evaluation indicates that counselors feel quite comfortable in their new locations and that instructors and students are dropping by for a variety of services.

A number of junior colleges provide counseling services for special target populations. Flint Community Junior College (Michigan) offers specialized services for adult women and for the physically handicapped. These programs are carefully coordinated by a counselor assigned to these special students. A similar approach is used at Danville Junior College (Illinois) for academically deficient adults. Since junior colleges have such a variety of kinds of students it may be necessary to provide specialized services for selected groups.

Evaluation of counseling effectiveness is always a difficult task. The counselors at Lane Community College (Oregon) explored their effectiveness as seen by instructors, division chairmen, students, administrators, and themselves by organizing a series of Thursday morning meetings to discuss counselor effectiveness. Representatives of the various groups were invited to talk with the counselors regarding counseling services. In an informal atmosphere over coffee, counselors listened to the observations of the visitors, asking questions of clarification but never defending their positions or their practices. From a list of critical observations developed at these meetings, counselors have initiated a number of new activities.

GROUP COUNSELING

The most exciting innovations in junior college student personnel programs are occurring in the area of group counseling. Dozens of junior colleges across the country are experimenting with the counseling process with groups of students. This trend is in keeping with what is happening on the national scene in industry, government, and the church. Recent articles in *Look* and *Life* magazines are an indication of the interest in group counseling. The term *group counseling* is seldom used to describe the process, however. Terms in vogue include: T-groups, sensitivity training groups, marathons, micro-groups, basic encounter groups, and human encounter groups. The names themselves suggest some flavor of the excitement and the experimentation involved in these activities.

Group counseling is used primarily for three purposes. Perhaps the most acceptable use of group counseling is in terms of working with students who have backgrounds of academic deficiency. The usual goal is that of satisfactory adjustment to college measured in terms of academic achievement. There are a number of excellent programs designed for this purpose with which most student personnel workers are familiar. Since the professional literature includes numerous references regarding this use of group counseling, little discussion is devoted to it here.

The second primary use of group counseling or the basic encounter is in orientation. Here the purpose is to use the small group process to help students focus on and understand their relationship to the college. The student and his college problems provide the primary content for these sessions. At Dodge City Community Junior College (Kansas), all freshman students are required to enroll for a one-hour credit course in educational and vocational planning. The purposes of the program are to provide students with close counselor assistance, to aid them in their adjustment to college, to help them develop educational plans and an understanding of themselves and their objectives. Students meet one hour a week in groups of 15 or less for the first semester. These groups are led by a staff of professional counselors.

At Mount San Antonio College (California), voluntary "personal assistance groups" are led by faculty members. Groups of from 15 to 20 participants meet for the year in an attempt to develop a climate in which ideas and feelings can be shared without the fear of being criticized or judged. Topics such as sex, money, religion, marriage, and work are discussed; evaluation indicates that both faculty and students benefit. As a result of these groups, curricular changes have occurred in psychology courses, guidance classes, and library orientation classes.

The commuting student is of special concern to the staff of the Springfield Junior College (Illinois). Halfway through the first semester, members of the student affairs staff look through the student directory and select names of students with whom they are unfamiliar. These students are invited in groups of ten to participate in a one-hour session in which they are introduced to the student personnel program of the college; introduce themselves to each other; and indicate their area of study, future plans, and their general reaction to the experience of college. While the meeting lasts no more than an hour, students have had an opportunity to meet student personnel staff and other students whom they did not know and to contribute ideas about how they might become involved in the life of the college. At least once, the student has been an individual in a social encounter with staff members and students in the college.

A third major purpose of group interaction in the community college is to help students develop sensitivity and awareness of self and others, to become more open and trusting, to learn to deal with the here-and-now, and to get in touch with one's own feelings. This is the human encounter at a more intensive level. Counselors who initiate these groups often have had special training at National Training Laboratories, Esalen, or the Western Behavioral Science Institute. Special consultants in group process are often used to work with student and staff.

A program of sensitivity training for students and staff has been developed at the Monterey Peninsula College (California). The purpose is, "To improve the skill of the counseling staff in group counseling techniques and to provide better opportunities for students to acquire more accurate self-identity and a personally, more relevant education." A consultant meets with the counseling staff twice a week. During the first meeting the consultant introduces various group techniques. During the second meeting the staff participates as an active encounter group. As staff develop competency, they offer "self awareness" groups to volunteer students. Groups of 12 students meet for one and one-half hours per week for one-half unit of college credit. Adult evening groups and faculty groups have also been formed. Evaluation indicated that a more open working relationship has developed among staff members. Students have reacted very positively to the experience and would like to continue their participation.

At Kendall College (Illinois), human potential seminars are available for students to help them increase self-motivation, self-determination, and affirmation of self-worth. "The human potential seminars are focused on the conviction that something is right for the participant rather than focused on what has him hung up." The seminars focus on individual discovery and immediate group reinforcement of the personal strengths, capacities, and success experiences of each participant. It is primarily an action system rather than an analysis system. Each seminar proceeds through seven phases that have been carefully developed by the Kendall staff along the lines of the work of Herbert Otto of the Stone-Brandel Center in Chicago. Group membership is limited to mentally healthy persons. The long-range goal is to help each person transfer his group learning to a living style outside the group.

At Fulton-Montgomery Community College (New York), a program of sensitivity training groups has been initiated. "Staff perceive the function of these groups as developmental and educational rather than clinical, and the students who join the groups are normal individuals who are interested in increasing their self-awareness and sensitivity to themselves and their environment." Groups of eight students meet for three hours a week, usually in the late afternoon, with a group facilitator from the counseling staff. Counselors are participants rather than leaders, and feel strongly that they must make the same commitment to openness and self-revelation that they expect from students.

At Santa Fe Junior College (Florida), all new students are required to participate in basic encounter groups of eight to twelve students. Students receive three hours transferable credit for the experience. Evaluations from the approximately 400 students who participate each term indicate that the program is meeting some important needs of students.

STUDENT ACTIVITIES

Another area of yeasty practice in junior college student personnel programs is that of student activities. The student activities program is difficult to organize in the community college for a number of obvious reasons: freshmen and sophomores do not have the leadership experience that juniors and seniors have on university campuses, many community college students work part-time, only two years are available to develop leadership ability, and many high school leaders with a background of leadership experience elect to attend the university instead of the junior college. Rather than settle for a token student activity program a number of junior colleges have developed some rather outstanding innovations.

With a Title III Developing Institutions grant the Rochester State Junior College (Minnesota) developed a three-phase student leadership training program. In phase one, faculty advisors, student senate members, and student presidents or designated leaders of clubs and activities participate in a weekend workshop under the direction of consultants trained in leadership dynamics. In phase two, faculty consultants and student consultants representing each of the major clubs and activities are brought to Rochester State Junior College from colleges throughout the country to consult with their counterparts at Rochester. In phase three, as a continuation of the leadership program, faculty advisors and newly elected student leaders return for a spring conference focused on group dynamics, communication skills, problem-solving, decision-making, and organization for management. The results have been rather dramatic on the Rochester campus. The student senate voted to provide special funds for training programs for the next year. Workshop leaders indicated that faculty members had a new understanding of the educational purposes of student activities in the junior college.

Fulton-Montgomery Community College (New York) has been restructuring the role of the student in the governance of the college. A new constitution spells out clearly the areas for which students have primary responsibility and indicates those areas of the college in which students have related responsibilities, such as the development of curriculum, budget, and the quality of instruction. Students serve as full voting members on faculty committees in a ratio of one student to two faculty members. Faculty members, after a one-year trial, have now guaranteed student involvement on faculty committees in their newly adopted bylaws. Recognizing that involvement is a two-way street, faculty members also participate as consultants in many areas in which students have major responsibility, such as orientation, student rights, discipline, clubs, publications, and student calendars. The faculty member is not an advisor to an organization; he is a consultant, and his role is carefully spelled out in a set of guidelines. Students assume ultimate responsibility for all clubs and activities, with the consultant providing the resources of his expertise.

The Student-Faculty Communications Laboratory is a significant new development at El Centro College (Texas). Student leaders have participated in the leadership development program by attending NTL sessions in Utah and through sessions on campus led by consultants. The Student-Faculty Communications Laboratory developed from a suggestion of a student who had attended one of the earlier programs. The purpose of the laboratory is to enlarge understanding of the nature of communication between inter-generational groups. The pilot program took place during a 48-hour period in which students, faculty, and administrators lived together at an off-campus site. Twenty-four participants, twelve students and twelve faculty and administrators, were separated into heterogeneous groups, each under the direction of a skilled group leader from outside the educational organization. The groups met in five small group sessions and in several large group assemblies, which were designed to explore the barriers to communication between students and faculty, faculty and administration, and students and administration. Since immediate gains in insight and understanding were reported, the college will continue to experiment with this and other group experiences.

✓ ORIENTATION

Orientation—helping students learn about college and about themselves—is a continuous process beginning in high school through articulation conferences and continuing through conferences designed to help students prepare for transfer to universities or to jobs in the community. Orientation occurs in small groups throughout the summer. Most colleges have a one- or two-day orientation session preceding the beginning of classes. Many colleges require students to attend orientation classes during the first term. Such classes may meet once a week for half a term on a noncredit basis; once a week all terms for one hour credit; or as regularly as other classes for three hours credit. In addition to these various patterns of orientation, some colleges provide special seminars for special groups of students (off-campus students, career students, married students, veterans, foreign students, and so on) designed to provide information for their special needs.

When orientation occurs is probably not as important as *how* it occurs. Most orientation sessions are a holocaust of information giving, in which administrators and student personnel staff members feel they have met the purposes of orientation when they have "told the students what they need to know." In this kind of orientation, students are exposed to the chief officers of the college in a series of speeches designed to make students feel welcome and to inform them of relevant programs offered by the college. These sessions are often followed by citations of rules and regulations which the student is supposed to remember and observe throughout his college experience. The "information blast" may also include an introduction to the dozens of clubs and organizations available to students. Finally, the student sits through an explanation of program tracks, course offerings, academic advising procedures, registration procedures, and a detailed account of where to place his parking sticker.

At least one college has tested the traditional model described above against an emerging model. The orientation program at Grossmont College (California) has been developed over a seven-year period. Originally conceived as a course, students were introduced to such topics as to how to take notes, how to adjust to college life, understanding the rules and regulations of the college, and how to use the college library. In 1964 a comparison was made of the students who took the course and a control group exempted from the course. At the end of two semesters it was discovered that the students who had not taken the course did as well on an objective test covering the items studied as did the students who had been through the program. As a result, the counseling department met with the faculty and students to develop new objectives for an orientation program focused on the student's need to become more responsible for his person and the total society in which he lives, and on his need to find other reasons for education in addition to potential financial gain. A new course required of all freshmen now meets twice each week for 12 weeks. The meeting each week is a large lecture for 120 students; the second meeting is a seminar composed of 18 or fewer students. The lecturers deal with important issues, often controversial, which include such topics as alienation, student rights, human rights, war and peace, and personal commitment. During the seminar which follows, students assume responsibility for expressing themselves and encountering the ideas discussed in the lecture. Evaluation indicates that the course may have had a part in lowering the attrition rate, which has been reduced from 13 percent to 3 percent since the inauguration of the new program. Student, counselor, and faculty feedback indicate that the course has been quite successful.

At Rochester State Junior College (Minnesota), a freshman orientation camp is available for a three-day retreat for the first 150 freshmen who sign up. The purpose of the camp is to unite the various groups in the junior college, to develop positive attitudes toward the college, to stimulate a desire in the student to be active in the life of the college, and to encourage the student to explore what a college education really means. Sophomore counselors and volunteer faculty members help lead the camp activities which include buzz sessions, coffee house activities, and recreational activities. More faculty members volunteer to serve at camp than are places available. A written evaluation indicates that 99 percent of the campers are overwhelmingly enthusiastic about the experience.

While the purposes of orientation at Flint Community Junior College (Michigan) are similar to most institutions, the approach stresses both contact with a counselor and the small group experience. Each student's orientation session varies with the division of the college he plans to enter. As soon as a student is admitted to the college, a counselor personally notifies him by letter of the time and place of his orientation session. During the session counselors review information regarding courses and curricula and help students complete their program. In addition to these activities, students participate in a micro-group in order to explore and clarify their purposes for coming to Flint and to share their concerns about attending college. Some divisions utilize the micro-group approach more extensively than others. One division uses a video tape, another involves faculty and students in an orientation followed by a luncheon, and in the Applied Sciences Division orientation continues throughout the first semester.

These are only a few of the exciting and exceptional practices that junior college student personnel workers have developed in recent years. They foreshadow, in part, the emerging role of the student personnel worker described in this book.

Unfortunately, as with most educational practices, there is a decided lack of evaluation of the effectiveness of practices. Because of their need to respond to pressing demands of students, colleges have responded on a trial-and-error basis rather than on a careful and thoughtful plan of evaluation and research. It is hoped that colleges will more carefully evaluate the new practices they are now initiating. Through planned evaluation, colleges will be able to determine which practices provide for the greater facilitation of student development. Once that is determined, what is considered exceptional today may become essential tomorrow.

REFERENCES

1. BLOCKER, CLYDE E. and RICHARD C. RICHARDSON, JR., "Teaching and Guidance Go Together," *Junior College Journal,* 39 (November, 1968), 3.

2. HARVEY, JAMES, "The Counseling Approach at Harper College," *Junior College Journal,* 38 (October, 1967), 2.

Student Development
in the Community College

W. HAROLD GRANT

Director of Student Development
Services, Auburn University

Man's history is the chronicle of a continuing search for the realization of his personal and social potential. He structures institutions such as churches, hospitals, family, business, and schools as tools to facilitate this "becoming." Each institution concerns itself with a primary area of human behavior, but there is usually one that serves as an integrating force for the others and gives direction to the total process of human development. The church fulfilled this role in the first millennium of the Christian era. Thus, in the middle of the community one found the church building which was more symbolic of the central force in man's struggle to beome than a physical structure that contained the function of religion, for religion permeated the community and all men were religious men as well as fulfilling other specific roles in community life. The second millennium saw religion dispersed throughout the community as just another institution while business took over the center of the community, geographically and as the integrating force. While man's development was judged by his movement toward religious perfection in the first millennium, in the second his progress was judged by his upward movement in the socioeconomic structure. As we move into the third millennium we find education moving toward this central integrating role. The community school and the community college movement is an example of the changing role of education in the community. While it was just another institution in the past 2000 years, education now seems to be the principal midwife monitoring the birth of human potential in each individual and in the community as a whole.

Previous attempts in educational reform in this country have been more attempts at renewal of education's response to its basic purpose. The land grant movement, the progressive education movement, and other such reform movements in their infancy have harkened education back to the philosophy of dealing with every individual, being concerned about all his behaviors, and continuing this concern throughout life. As each reform movement waned in its impact and ceased to be a viable force for renewing this basic view of education, another reform movement, another effort at renewal, emerged, but each has always had the same basic purpose. The community college movement today is another effort to turn education toward a broader view of its role. Education has tended to see itself as being concerned with intellectual life primarily and sought to accomplish this through the transmission of knowledge and the creation of new knowledge. The community college movement is again extending education to all people and attempting to be concerned about all their behaviors, not just their intellectual life, and to extend this concern from birth to death. This is particularly necessary for education to fulfill its newly acquired integrative function in human life.

Student personnel programs in colleges, as a child of the progressive education movement, attempted to implement a point of view about education that included these concepts of serving all people throughout their life and being concerned about all their behaviors. Just as other movements have not been totally successful in bringing about the completely successful reform of education, neither has student personnel been totally successful in implementing its point of view. It would seem inappropriate, therefore, to be content with any particular model of student personnel work that we have used in the past. It seems particularly appropriate within the context of the community college movement to seek new forms and new models so that student personnel work along with other aspects of higher education will more truly speak to this yearning in each man to become what he can be, to realize his potential for perfection, to develop a repertoire of behavior that enables him to meet any challenge his environment provides.

This chapter is not an attempt to develop a complete model, but rather suggests directions that model development might take.

If we view education as an attempt to structure experiences of persons so that their behavioral development is facilitated in the most efficient and effective manner possible, we must be concerned with both the content of behavior and the process by which it is developed. In higher education we have tended to focus almost exclusively on content; thus the structure of the college is based on behavioral contents. The rewards that students and faculty receive are based on the quantity and quality of their behavioral content. Persons who staff colleges, whether they be administrators, faculty, or are called by any other name, generally receive very little assistance in developing expertise in the process of behavioral development. Since we have found it necessary to specialize in various areas of the content of behavior, it would seem unfeasible to expect someone to master an area of content and in addition be expert in behavioral development process. It would seem reasonable, therefore, to include process experts in the staffs of colleges. We generally view the faculty as the content specialists. Each of them by virtue of their past experiences are viewed as persons who have already developed certain behaviors to a high level of expertise. They, therefore, can serve as models for students who seek to develop these same behaviors. They also serve as sources of knowledge and evaluators of the level of expertise that a student has been able to achieve in his attempt to become a colleague to the faculty member. The student personnel administrator because of his previous point of view about education and his present role could very easily become the chief process specialist in higher education. Rather than a manager appointed to control student conduct, or a coordinator of various services to meet student needs, or a co-curricular specialist who has another curricular area parallel to the sciences, the arts, and applied fields, the student personnel worker is needed in the community college today as a student development specialist.

When a student first enters a college, there is an immediate need for a behavioral description of this student so that his present status of behavioral development will be known to those who seek to assist him in furthering this development. In addition to this behavioral profile the student also needs to be assisted in formulating in operational terms his behavioral objectives for attending college. The development of the behavioral profile and the behavioral objectives appears to be a suitable role for a student development specialist to perform as an admissions process.

The behaviors which are the variance between the behavioral profile and the behavioral objectives become the student's curriculum for his college experience. Hopefully, the community college will continue to move toward individualized instruction so that in the future it may be possible for a student to have an individually designed curriculum. He will not have to be involved in processes that are designed to develop behaviors he has already acquired, and he will not be deprived of activities that are needed to obtain his objectives as is the case today in the normative curriculum. However, even with an individualized curriculum constructed by the faculty, there will still be a need for the student to have an opportunity to help to structure some of his own activities in an ad hoc manner. This ad hoc curriculum which fills in the gaps of his formal curriculum should be the area of concern of the student development specialist instead of our present program of student activities in the student personnel program.

Just as our activities become institutionalized and normative so that a single program is provided for all students, so do we tend to treat all students the same in providing other student personnel services such as financial aids. However, there is reason to believe that various forms of financial aid such as loans, grants, and part-time work may have differing impacts on different kinds of students. While a grant may be the salvation for one student, it may be the damnation for another. Rather than contributing to his behavioral development and the fulfillment of his self-concept, it may have negative impact and lower his self-esteem and interfere with his continuing development. The student development specialist responsible for the financial aid program is as interested in providing the right kind of aid for the individual student so that it facilitates his continued behavioral development as he is providing money that will enable the student to remain on campus.

Sometimes direct intervention in the behavioral development of an individual student is necessary in order for that student to continue his development, that is, a student becomes anxious when he has to speak before a group or take an exam or approach another person. Sometimes he is not able to change this behavior by his own efforts and yet this behavior prevents him from developing the ability to speak to groups, to be assertive, to take exams successfully. Student development specialists with the knowledge and skills necessary for such intervention in collaboration with the student are needed to handle such problems that will arise in the normal, everyday life of the student. These are not illnesses or breakdowns but rather behavioral problems that inhibit normal, behavioral development. This would be the role of the student development specialist who would succeed our present counselor in student personnel work.

We know, today, that an ideal educational environment must provide the student with meaningful peer group opportunities as well as territorial integrity. In other words, the student must have a physical and human environment over which he exercises some control in a mutual way with other members of the peer group or others who share his common territory. Student development specialists who understand the territorial need of man, and its role in the development of identity and its necessity for behavioral development, would succeed our directors of housing. These specialists must also be expert in group dynamics and its application to the educational environment so that the student may be assisted in entering a group immediately upon arrival at college and maintaining effective group membership throughout his study, for the peer group filters the impact of the total environment upon the person and is also a potent force in his achievement of identity. Most community colleges do not include a housing staff in their student personnel program. While students may not sleep on campus, there is still a need for student development specialists concerned about the physical and human environment of the students.

While education may become the integrating institution in society, it certainly will never replace all the other institutions we presently have or ones we may devise. Therefore, the community college will not be the only environment the student will have throughout his life. Student development specialists, therefore, need to be aware of the nature of other available environments so that they may assist the student in selecting environments that can supplement or replace the college. These environments would be chosen on the basis of being most conducive for a particular student at a particular time for his continuing behavioral development. These student development specialists would thus be performing a placement function but it would go beyond the introduction of employer to prospective employee.

Higher education has not been unsuccessful in the past. It has been one of the principal facilitators for individual human growth and the growth of our societies. Because the colleges have been successful in the past, the people of our nation expect even more from these colleges today, thus the number of colleges continue to grow rapidly and the percentage of the population attending college is spiraling. An ever-increasing amount of our national wealth is allotted to the educational enterprise. Attempts at educational reform such as the community college movement should not be construed as a condemnation of education in the past or in the present but rather an attempt to more completely realize the hope and the faith that human beings have in education.

Likewise, student personnel has not been a miserable failure. It is similarly growing by leaps and bounds and its practitioners are continuing to upgrade their competencies in order to provide an even better service. The suggestions presented in this brief paper are not an attempt to supplant student personnel but to fulfill it. The student personnel point of view which is the basic philosophy of the profession is a dedication of the profession to be catalysts to facilitate student development. We must develop new models that offer means whereby this point of view can be more fully realized and hopefully will be a natural outgrowth of our present models. Perhaps, if we did become student development specialists, then students would no longer need their own SDS that points up higher education's failure to practice what it preaches. We may never be above criticism, but perhaps the student development specialist in higher education is the natural next step for a profession that is seeking to develop its potential to be a facilitator for the becoming pocess for all people.

Junior College Student Personnel Work: An Emerging Model

TERRY O'BANION
Associate Professor of Higher
Education, University of Illinois

ALICE THURSTON
President, Garland Junior College

JAMES GULDEN
Director of the Experimental
College, College of Du Page

If we don't change our direction, we are likely to end up where we are heading.   Chinese Proverb

The junior college is at a critical crossroads in its history. Can it make meaningful its commitment to the inner city? Can it respond to the manpower needs of business and industry? Can it participate in higher education as a respected partner with the university? Can it rehabilitate where so many others have failed? And in all these valiant efforts can the junior college provide the climate and the encouragement for individual students to feel more keenly, experience more deeply, live more fully—to encounter a fuller range of their human potential? Can the junior college be many things to many people?

The junior college—claiming to be dynamic, innovative and responsive—has risked its future on an affirmative response to these questions. Yet, like other facets of higher education, the junior college has tended to cling to an outmoded educational model appropriate to a society coping with economic scarcity rather than abundance. In this model, which is paternalistic at best and autocratic at worst, the educational process has been *educare* "to put into"; students have been the passive recipients of education as a product.

With rapid changes in society, however, the old educational model is becoming obsolete. Martin Tarcher says, "The times call for new social goals, new values and assumptions, new institutional arrangements that will allow us to complete our unfinished war against scarcity and move beyond production to the development of human potentialities." [16] Nevitt Sanford writes, "The time has come for us to control our zeal for imparting knowledge and skills, and to concentrate our efforts on developing the individual student . . . By education for individual development, I mean a program consciously undertaken to promote an identity based on such qualities as flexibility, creativity, openness to experience, and responsibility." [14] Thus, the dimensions of a new model begin to emerge: education becomes *educere* "to lead out of," so that education is not a pouring into, but the means of providing a learning climate in which the greatest possible development of potential and fulfillment can take place.

In response to this emerging model the junior college is struggling toward educational innovation and change. Its doors are opening wider yet—to the handicapped, the factory worker, the high school dropout, the impoverished ghetto youth with serious learning disabilities. If the junior college is to be truly the people's college, it must provide its increasingly diverse student population with meaningful learning experiences. Lock-step scheduling, instruction primarily by the lecture method, ill-defined and poorly evaluated instructional objectives, and ineffective student personnel programs are being gradually abandoned in favor of new goals and new approaches. Junior college educators are breaking down outmoded inter-disciplinary boundaries, utilizing the new technology of the systems approach, retooling grading practices, and setting specific educational objectives toward which students can move at their own pace. The focus is shifting from instruction to learning. What is known about bringing about behavioral change is gradually being put to use. Cohen describes this kind of junior college which is to evolve by 1979:

At the core of the college's processes will be the deliberate practice of instruction. It will be built on a definite teaching-learning paradigm and employ a built-in system of evaluation. Student learning—predictable, measurable, definable—will be the college's *raison d'etre*. The college will predict and accept accountability for its effects. No longer slavishly following the university, it will take the lead in experimenting with instructional forms—not by innovating for the sake of innovation, but by setting hypotheses, introducing changes, and assessing their impact . . .[2]

Any hope of achieving even a modicum of success in fulfilling these goals depends, to a very great extent, on the student personnel program. Jane Matson points out, "Student personnel workers must assume appropriate responsibility in this monumental effort. This may require almost complete redesigning of the structure or framework and even the content or practices of student personnel work." [8] In the last years of the decade of the 1960s, student personnel workers are examining with great seriousness the status of the student personnel profession. Student personnel work has developed for half a century as a series of services reacting to forces within the college community rather than as an action program for shaping forces. The wave of student discontent and open disruptions has forced an examination of educational practices, and student personnel work along with most other factions of higher education has found itself woefully inadequate to respond to the needs and demands of students. Existing models of student personnel work—regulatory, servicing, therapeutic—are inappropriate to needs of students in a changing society.

EXISTING MODELS

One of the historical models for the student personnel worker is that of *regulator or repressor*. The student personnel profession came into being largely because the president needed help in regulating student behavior. In the early 1900s student personnel workers were given the titles of "monitor" and "warden."

In this model the student personnel regulator works on colonial campuses as a mercenary of the president at war with students. He is the president's *no-man*. He tends to behave in ways that regulate, repress, reject, reproof, reprimand, rebuff, rebuke, reserve, reduce, and even remove human potential. In this system all the negative aspects of *in loco parentis* are practiced as staff members attempt to maintain a strict supervision over the affairs of students.

This model has been more prevalent on residential campuses and, therefore, on four-year college and university campuses; but junior colleges have been much too eager to copy the style. Perhaps the continued existence of this model contributes to much of the student distress evident at such places as Berkeley, Harvard, and Columbia. Under such repression students have had to develop their own bill of rights in the historical tradition of all repressed minorities.

Perhaps the most prevalent model of the student personnel worker is that of *maintenance or service man*. In this model the student personnel program is a series of services scattered around the campus: financial aid, registration, admissions, student activities, academic advising, and so on. The student personnel worker provides services for students who seek them. In 1963 the Carnegie Corporation contributed $100,000 to the American Association of Junior Colleges for an evaluation of this maintenance model. Thirty-six different student personnel functions or services were isolated for study; the findings were disillusioning to those who had committed themselves to student personnel programs in junior colleges. T. R. McConnell, Chairman of the National Advisory Committee for the study stated, "The conclusion of these studies may be put bluntly; when measured against criteria of scope and effectiveness, student personnel programs in community junior colleges are woefully inadequate." [10]

A third model of the student personnel worker is that of *therapist*. In this model the student personnel worker behaves as if he were a psychotherapist or a counseling psychologist. His contribution to the educational program is to provide therapy for a few selected students who have intense personal problems. He is often disdainful of other student personnel functions such as academic advising and student activities.

In this model counselors become isolated in their counseling cubicles which become identified in the perceptions of students as places to go only when you have serious problems. If the dean of students is also a practitioner of "early Rogers," he becomes confused regarding his responsibility for educational leadership. The program is likely to remain safely constricted in the therapeutic confines of the counseling center.

In recent years several states have endeavored to develop statements of models as guidelines for junior college student personnel programs. Perhaps the most thorough state report has been that of California entitled "Guidelines for Student Personnel Services in the Junior College." [9] While the basic philosophy expressed in the California guidelines represents an emerging model of student personnel work, the functions, or implementation of philosophy, are those of the Carnegie Study and, therefore, reflect the model of service. Other state studies in New York, North Carolina, and Maryland also reflect an orientation that perceives student personnel work as a series of services designed to meet student needs. Out of the Maryland guidelines, however, came a statement that has significance: "Many of the old, cherished ideas that guided student personnel workers are being questioned, remodeled, or cast aside as no longer 'relevant' to this day." [13] The Maryland guidelines begin tentatively to identify some of the dimensions of the new and needed model for student personnel workers.

AN EMERGING MODEL

As the student personnel profession enters the decade of the '70s, there is a clear call for a new model for the profesison—a new model for the role of the student personnel worker. The call is for a new kind of person, a person who is hardheaded enough to survive the battles that rage in academe and yet a person, warmhearted, and deeply committed to the full development of human potential.

As old concepts of human nature and of education are uprooted, it is a precarious venture to attempt to articulate new directions when they are so dimly perceived. Educational Don Quixotes are likely to fabricate models out of their own dreams and frustrations. The authors openly admit that the fragments of an emerging model presented here represent their own hopes of what might be, but hopes that are buttressed by a growing number of educators, student personnel workers, instructors, and administrators who believe in and who have begun to provide opportunities for the full development of human potential. *The emerging model described, then, is only a tentative statement. It needs considerable modification. It needs testing out in practice. It needs rounding out with the concepts of others.*

While student development has historically been defined as development of the whole student, educational practice has focused with few exceptions on development of intellectual capacities and skills that have been narrowly defined. At the present time, however, a growing number of educators, supported by the humanistic psychologists and a developing Humanistic Ethic, are beginning to define *student development* in some creative and exciting ways. Fundamental to the new definition is a belief that man is a growing organism, capable of moving toward self-fulfillment and responsible social development whose potential for both has been only partially realized.

In the new model of student development there are implications of climate and outcome. A student development point of view is a behavioral orientation in which educators attempt to create a climate of learning in which students have:

1. Freedom to choose their own directions for learning;
2. Responsibility for those choices;
3. Interpersonal interaction with the learning facilitator that includes:
   a. Challenge, encounter, stimulation, confrontation, excitement;
   b. Warmth, caring, understanding, acceptance, support;
   c. Appreciation of individual differences.

Through such a facilitative atmosphere the outcomes of student development would be increases in:

1. Intellectual understanding,
2. Skill competencies,
3. Socially responsible behavior,
4. Flexibility and creativity,
5. Awareness of self and others,
6. Acceptance of self and others,
7. Courage to explore and experiment,
8. Openness to experience,
9. Efficient and effective ability to learn,
10. Ability to respond positively to change,
11. A useful value system,
12. A satisfying life style.

This student development model, only briefly described, requires a new kind of person for its implementation. Terms that have in the recent past attempted to describe the student personnel worker in this emerging model are the counselor as catalyst and the counselor as change agent. More recently, model builders have talked about the student personnel worker as student development specialist.

A term that may reflect more accurately some of the special dimensions of the emerging model is that of the *human development facilitator*. *Facilitate* is an encountering verb which means to free, to make way for, to open the door to. The human development facilitator does not limit his encounter to students; rather he is interested in facilitating the development of all groups in the educational community (faculty, secretaries, administrators, custodians and other service workers, and board members). In the community college his concern extends into the community.

THE HUMAN DEVELOPMENT FACILITATOR

One way of describing the model that needs to be developed is to present an idealized prototype of the student personnel worker as a person. While it is helpful to have a model as a goal, it is to be understood that individuals exist in a process of becoming in which they reflect only certain degrees of attainment of these characteristics. The kind of person who is needed has been described by Maslow as self-actualizing, by Horney as self-realizing, by Privette as transcendent-functioning, and by Rogers as fully-functioning. Other humanistic psychologists such as Combs, Jourard, Perls, Moustakas, and Landsman have described such healthy personalities as open to experience, democratic, accepting, understanding, caring, supporting, approving, loving, nonjudgmental. They tend to agree with the artist in Tennessee Williams' play *Night of the Iguana* who said, "Nothing human is disgusting." They tolerate ambiguity; their decisions come from within rather than from without; they have a zest for life, for experiencing, for touching, tasting, feeling, knowing. They risk involvement; they reach out for experiences; they are not afraid to encounter others or themselves. They believe that man is basically good and, given the right conditions, will move in positive directions. They believe that every student is a gifted person, that every student has untapped potentialities, that every human being can live a much fuller life than he is currently experiencing. They are not only interested in students with intense personal problems, they are interested in all students, in helping those who are unhealthy to become more healthy and in helping those who are already healthy to achieve yet even greater health. They understand the secret the fox told the little prince: "It is only with the heart that one can see rightly; what is essential is invisible to the eye."

The human development facilitator has a high degree of self-confidence and self-acceptance out of which emerges a strong trust in others. Jack Gibb puts it this way:

The key to emergent leadership centers in the high degree of trust and confidence in people. Leaders who trust their colleagues and subordinates and have confidence in them tend to be open and frank, to be permissive in goal setting, and to be non-controlling in personal style and leadership policy. People with a great deal of self-acceptance and personal security do trust others, do make trust assumptions about their motives and behavior. The self-adequate person tends to assume that others are also adequate and, other things being equal, that they will be responsible, loyal, appropriately work-oriented when work is to be performed, and adequate to carry out jobs that are commensurate with their levels of experience and growth.[5]

The model student personnel worker, however, must not only be committed to positive human development; he must also possess the skills and the expertise that will enable him to implement programs for the realization of human potential. He must be able to communicate with other administrators in the college, and he must be able to keep the functions and services under his responsibility operating efficiently. In the new model, present services and functions would not be disregarded. These are needed because they serve students in important ways. The emphasis of the program, however, would be different. *The program would be focused on positive changes in student behavior rather than on the efficient functioning of services.*

In order to develop and implement a humanistic program in his institution, the student personnel worker must understand the social system in which all members of the academic community live and work as well as the ecological relationships of those members in the academic setting. He must understand the nature and complexity of bureaucracy and how it affects student development. He must understand and appreciate the diversity of student subcultures, and learn to use those subcultures in the development of an institutional climate that allows for full growth and development in the collegiate community. He must learn to conduct relevant research on student behavior to evaluate the success of the student personnel program and to communicate to his colleagues what the program is accomplishing.

To provide focus for the program the chief student personnel administrator would ask, "What kinds of programs can we build that will allow great numbers of students to explore the dimensions and potentialities of their humanity?" Or he might ask, "Can we create an environment for the student in which he can search out his identity, grapple with the problems of commitment, and become attracted to and involved with the health-engendering aspects of life?"

Within what kind of an organizational structure can student personnel workers develop a program which facilitates the release of human potential? How do they function to implement philosophy and goals?

ORGANIZATIONAL STRUCTURE

The most appropriate organizational structure would be decentralized, with responsibility and authority shared throughout the college. A climate of "participative administration" set by the president should permeate the institution. Gibb describes this concept as follows:

It seems to me that joint, interdependent, and shared planning is the central concept of the kind of participative, consultative leadership that we are considering. . . . Our assumption is that the blocks to innovation and creativity are fear, poor communication, imposition of motivations, and the dependency-rebellion syndrome of forces. People are innovative and creative. The administration of innovation involves freeing the creativity that is always present. The administrative problem of innovation is to remove fear and increase trust, to remove coercive, persuasional, and manipulative efforts to pump motivation, and to remove the tight controls on behavior that tend to channel creative efforts into circumvention, counter-strategy, and organizational survival rather than into innovative and creative problem-solving.[5]

A chief student personnel administrator deeply committed to the facilitation of human development will offer his own staff participative leadership. However, if he attempts to create a democratic staff island amid a network of rigid bureaucratic controls, he does so at considerable psychic cost, both to himself and to his staff, and with a corresponding loss of creativity. The autocratic president is the antithesis of the democratic dean of students; when they attempt to work in the same institution, neither they nor the institution can function effectively. The problem is just as acute when an autocratic dean of students is employed or inherited by a democratic president. Unfortunately, many "new model" presidents have become disillusioned with student personnel work because they have known only "old model" deans of students.

In line with the concept of "participative administration," the dean of students should function as a full member of the administrative team. President Samuel Braden of Illinois State University calls his administrative team "the president's see." As a member of this group, the chief student personnel administrator functions not only as a student personnel dean, but as an official of the college working with other administrative officers and hopefully with representatives both of faculty and students, to solve problems confronting the entire college.

The administrative officers responsible for student personnel services and for instruction should be on the same administrative level, and should work closely together. Joseph Cosand says:

As president of a comprehensive junior college, I believe strongly that the student personnel program on the campus must be given the same status as the instructional program. For that reason I feel that the administrative structure should have a dean of student personnel services and a dean of instruction at the same level in the organizational chart, both of whom would be responsible to the president of the college.[3]

The chief administrator of a student personnel program works democratically with his staff to develop plans which will assist in implementing the goals of the college. As an administrator he delegates and defines staff responsibilities and coordinates the work of the staff, helping each staff member to see how his work relates to the total institution. He conducts planned, in-service programs for professional and personal development. The larger his staff, the greater the proportion of his time is spent in integration, communication, and coordination, rather than in performing direct services to students. He is necessarily both task-oriented and people-oriented.

Most student personnel programs are clustered in a single building, often next to the central administration or in the student union. Thus, student personnel staff members often become isolated from the rest of the college. There is little interaction with the faculty. Students are seen only in the safety and security of the counselor's office. To obviate the problems of such isolation, several recent writers have suggested the deployment of student personnel workers to divisions. Blocker and Richardson [1] advocate that counselors be assigned to instructional divisions and report directly to the chairman of the division to which they are assigned. Because of the conflict of multipurposes, divided loyalties, and professional backgrounds this proposal may not work out in practice. Harvey [7] proposes that counselors be assigned to instructional divisions but that they continue to report to the dean of students.

If the human development facilitator is to be effective in accomplishing his purposes, he must work closely with faculty and students *where they are*. Student personnel staff members can extend the impact of the student personnel program by serving as liaison persons with instructional divisions in terms of their interests or backgrounds. They should attend divisional meetings, participate in projects and workshops, and assume responsibility for informing the other student personnel staff members regarding developments within the divisions. The student personnel worker should become acquainted with each faculty member in his area to insure continuing communication and liaison with the student personnel program. It would strengthen relationships if the student personnel worker was assigned to advise students enrolled in the division and had responsibility for acting as a resource for the faculty advisors of the division. He should also encourage the development of student activities that reflect the special interests of students in the division.

When the student personnel program is extended into each instructional unit of the college, and when such activities are carefully coordinated by an effective student personnel administrator, students and faculty alike become more aware of the significant impact that student personnel can have on their development. When the president of the college coordinates the student personnel program with other programs in the college, when he provides equal status for student personnel workers by appointing them to faculty committees and granting them faculty rank and tenure where these exist, he sets the tone for a college climate in which lines of demarcation can disappear and teams of devoted and excited professionals can work closely together with and for students.

ROLE AND FUNCTION

Student personnel staff members should offer student development courses not usually available in instructional programs. Such a course is not a psychology course in which the knowledge of facts and principles concerning psychology form the subject matter. It is not a traditional orientation course in which the student is introduced to the rules and regulations of the college and given "tips" on how to study. Nor is it an introduction to vocational development in which the student sifts through occupational information and writes a paper on a career. This is not the old, first generation adjustment course of the 1950s that had as its major purpose helping the student make a satisfactory adjustment to college and to the society.

Such a course is a course in introspection: the experience of the student is the subject matter. The student is provided with an opportunity to examine his values, attitudes, beliefs, and abilities, and an opportunity to examine how these and other factors affect the quality of his relationships with others. In addition, the student would examine the social milieu —the challenges and problems of society—as it relates to his development. Finally, such a course would provide each student with an opportunity to broaden and deepen a developing philosophy of life. Such a course would be taught in basic encounter groups by well-prepared human development facilitators. In many cases sensitive instructors can work with student personnel staff to develop and teach such a course.

The student personnel worker should also move directly into contact with the community beyond the campus if his impact is going to be significant. He must arrange community laboratory experiences if he is to encourage the development of a growing student social consciousness. Working with faculty members in appropriate divisions the student personnel worker should seek opportunities for students to participate in recreational and educational programs for the socioeconomically disadvantaged, tutor the undereducated, campaign in elections, contribute time to community beautification programs, and explore and question the structure of community government.

Another role of the new student personnel worker is to participate actively in getting students involved in the life of the college. New alternatives for student involvement should be explored: special task forces, *ad hoc* groups, town meetings. If the traditional committee system is to be used, then students should be on all the committees of the college. This should extend far beyond the old worn-out student government association in which students play sandbox government and spend their time quarreling over student activity fee allocations. Students should be on the curriculum committee of the college, they should be on the administrative council that makes all major decisions, they should have representation on the board of trustees, they should be constantly involved in teacher evaluation, they should have responsibility for helping to relate the college to the community, and they should participate in the planning of new buildings. Students will also need educating in "academic and bureaucratic dynamics" so they can function effectively as contributing members of committees. Student personnel workers in concert with interested faculty members can provide these experiences for students.

The student personnel worker should also consider the means of getting students involved in the education of other students, and in this way, to discover new and creative learning experiences for students and teaching faculty and student personnel staff. Students with special skills should be identified to assist in courses requiring their expertise. Work-study programs should be designed to utilize students in instruction, curriculum development, and student services rather than as menials.

Another important role for the student personnel worker in the junior college is to be a guardian against the oppressive regulations that tend to develop unquestioned in most institutions. Junior colleges notoriously and often unconsciously borrow repressive rules and regulations from the catalogs of four-year colleges and universities. It is the role of the student personnel worker to question at every turn the traditional rules and regulations. Hopefully he can convince the college that every rule and regulation needs to be examined carefully for its basic rationale and its applicability to the community college and the community college student.

The junior college needs to examine carefully whether or not it needs academic calendars, probation and suspension regulations, F grades, social probation, dress codes, regulations regarding work load, and final examination periods. These traditional educational trappings may hinder the development of human potential more than they help. The student personnel worker must help ferret out the sometimes repressive philosophy that has become associated with such rules and regulations as he assists in the development of a total institutional climate conducive to the development of human potential. He must function with a sound rationale, however, so as not to appear the standard-wrecker to faculty members.

If instructors are freed by the new technology from the role of transmitting knowledge to a role of assisting students in integrating and applying knowledge, the student personnel worker will relate to instructors in important ways. With his background of preparation in psychology, human relations, and learning theory, the student personnel worker can assist instructors in a team effort to help students examine the personal meaning their education has for them. Student personnel workers can conduct group discussions and organize experiences for students to apply what they have learned. They can also help students evaluate their progress and make decisions about further learning.

Cooperative work-study programs should be planned so that the student's work for pay is also a planned learning experience. Student activities programs should be developed to provide leisure-time learning experiences as a basis for later leisure activity. The focus of the financial aids office should be to supply students' financial need in ways which contribute to their personal and social development. High priority should be given to health counseling and to preventive and compensatory health programs for students with special health problems.

These are only a few of the dimensions of an emerging role for the junior college student personnel worker. A number of years will be required for the role to be developed, tested, and finally evaluated for effectiveness. In the meantime, student personnel workers will continue to develop particular aspects of the role for practice on their own campuses.

AN "OPEN DOOR" TO STUDENT PERSONNEL WORK

New models of student personnel work should have good opportunities for imaginative development in the junior college. The climate for acceptance of student personnel work in the junior college is quite positive. In no other post-high school educational institution is student personnel work considered as important as in the junior college, where it is recognized and proclaimed as a function that is equal to instruction, curriculum, library services, and the management of the college. Fordyce has said,

I am convinced that student personnel work can and must come to full fruition in the comprehensive junior college. No other educational institution can afford the broad expanse of educational opportunities that provide a setting in which students' choices can be so fully implemented. By the same token students have generally reached a level of maturity in a time of life when most important decisions can and must be made. Opportunities and necessities then combine to make the junior college the ideal setting for the most effective student personnel programs.[4]

Noting one of the important roles of the student personnel program in the junior college Medsker has said, "One can predict that if a junior college does not properly distribute students among programs, the whole idea of the junior college will fail and that a new structure for education beyond the high school will emerge." [11] The Executive Director of the American Association of Junior Colleges has described the role of student personnel work as "a senior partner in the junior college." [6]

The basic rationale that supports the importance of student personnel work in the junior college is that the "student personnel point of view" and the "junior college point of view" are one and the same. From *The Student Personnel Point of View,* first published by the American Council on Education in 1937, the following statements are indicative of student personnel philosophy: "students as individuals"; "optimum development of the individual"; "preservation of basic freedoms"; "renewed faith in an extensive use of democratic methods"; "development of mature citizens"; "The individual's full and balanced development involves the acquisition of a pattern of knowledge, skills, and attitudes consistent with his abilities, aptitudes, and interest."

Any one of these statements could have come from the list of purposes and objectives of almost any junior college. From the purposes of one junior college comes the following declaration that is repeated many times in junior college catalogs throughout the nation:

The educational offerings of Santa Fe Junior College are based upon the belief that development of the individual for a useful and productive life in a democratic society is the chief obligation of the public educational system. This philosophy implies a deep and abiding faith in the worth and dignity of the individual as the most important component of a democracy. This faith and this recognition of need for responsibility suggests that the college must find appropriate programs and effective educational techniques to help each student discover his abilities and interests and develop them to the fullest extent, consonant with his own goals and capabilities and the needs of the society.[15]

The philosophy that is common to the junior college and to student personnel work is based on a foundation of democratic-humanitarian principles. It is the upward extension of the American ideal of equal opportunity. Without doubt, student personnel work and the junior college rank among the most important of American educational inventions. As such, they reflect the basic pattern of American democracy with its concern for individual opportunity.

An important historical parallel also exist between the two movements. According to some, the junior college movement began with the founding of the first public junior college in Joliet, Illinois, in 1902. Nunn,[12] in the first complete history of student personnel work in American higher education, suggests that student personnel work as an organized movement began about 1900. Regardless of the exact date of origin, both movements had their major beginnings in the early 20th century, and both reached a mutually high point of recognition and development in the present decade. The junior college has now become the community college. The student personnel point of view has now become the student development point of view. There exists today a claim of one upon the other—a bond of mutual purpose. Both movements are young, both have critics, and both have high aspirations for meeting and fulfilling the needs of students.

Because there is philosophical and historical congruence between student personnel work and the junior college, however, does not necessarily mean that creative programs flourish. At the present time junior college student personnel work is in a state of confusion similar to that expressed by Alice in Wonderland when she meets the Cheshire Cat in the woods.

"Cheshire Puss," she asks, "would you tell me, please, which way I ought to walk from here?"

"That depends a great deal on where you want to get to," replied the Cat.

"I don't really care where," said Alice.

"Then it doesn't matter which way you walk," said the Cat.

So long as junior college student personnel workers do not know where they are going, it doesn't really matter, as the Cheshire Cat points out, which way they walk. However, with a clear sense of direction, junior college student personnel workers can assume their role as significant participants in the humanization of the educational process. If student personnel workers do not develop a clear sense of direction they are likely, as the Chinese proverb warns, to end up where they are heading.

REFERENCES

1. BLOCKER, CLYDE E. and RICHARD C. RICHARDSON, JR., "Teaching and Guidance Go Together," *Junior College Journal,* 39 (November, 1968), 3.

2. COHEN, ARTHUR M., *Dateline '79: Heretical Concepts for the Community College.* Beverly Hills, Cal.: Glencoe Press, 1969.

3. COSAND, JOSEPH P., quoted in TERRY O'BANION, "Student Personnel Work: A Senior Partner in the Junior College," May, 1966. (Mimeographed)

4. FORDYCE, JOSEPH W., quoted in TERRY O'BANION, "Student Personnel Work: A Senior Partner in the Junior College," May, 1966. (Mimeographed.)

5. GIBB, JACK R., "Dynamics of Leadership," in *In Search of Leaders,* ed. G. K. Smith. Washington, D.C.: American Association of Higher Education, 1967.

6. GLEAZER, EDMUND J., JR., "Student Personnel Work: A Senior Partner in the Junior College." Paper presented at the First Annual Junior College Student Personnel Workshop, Dallas, Texas, April, 1967.

7. HARVEY, JAMES, "The Counseling Approach at Harper College," *Junior College Journal,* 38 (October, 1967), 2.

8. MATSON, JANE E., "Trends in Junior College Student Personnel Work," *GT-70 Student Personnel Workshop,* ed. James Harvey. William Rainey Harper College, 1968.

9. ————, *Guidelines for Student Personnel Services in the Junior College.* Sacramento: California State Department of Education, 1967.

10. McCONNELL, T. R., "Foreword to," *Junior College Student Personnel Programs: Appraisal and Development: A Report to Carnegie Corporation,* Max Raines, Project Coordinator, November, 1965.

11. MEDSKER, LELAND L., "The Crucial Role of Student Personnel Services in the Junior College." Paper presented at the American Personnel and Guidance Association Convention, Denver, Colorado, March 28, 1961.

12. NUNN, NORMAN, *Student Personnel Work in American Higher Education.* Unpublished dissertation, Florida State University, August, 1964.

13. RAVEKES, JOHN E., *Functions of Student Personnel Programs in Maryland Community Colleges.* Maryland Association of Junior Colleges, April, 1969.

14. SANFORD, NEVITT, *Where Colleges Fail.* San Francisco: Jossey-Bass Co., 1967.

15. Santa Fe Junior College, *Bulletin of Santa Fe Junior College.* Gainesville, Florida, Catalog Issue 1966-67.

16. TARCHER, MARTIN, "Leadership: Organization and Structure," in *In Search of Leaders,* ed. G. K. Smith. Washington, D.C.: American Association of Higher Education, 1967.

The Decade Ahead

ALICE THURSTON

President, Garland Junior College

The Sixties were a time of great expectations: The war on poverty would be won. Man would reach the moon. Peace would be achieved. Education would heal and reshape society. Junior colleges would become people's colleges, offering university education beyond high school to all who could profit from it.

The Sixties were also a time of confrontations: doves against hawks, blacks against whites, the turned on against the turned off. Some also felt that the conflict was between generations. Students who lost faith in the colleges tried to destroy them. Others worked for needed reforms, forcing changes in instruction, curricula, admissions, grading practices, and governance. Paternalism in the college lessened; subtle racism was exposed.

Junior colleges were relatively untouched by confrontation—and also, relatively unchanged. With typical American myopia they confused bigness with success. They built imposing campuses, often facing inward, on neighboring hills or pastures. At conventions, presidents asked each other, "How many students do you have?"—and those who had 2000 envied those who had 4000, and everyone knew it was really better to have 8000. By the end of the decade more freshmen entered junior than senior institutions. And a new community college, however briefly gestated, was born every week.

At the close of the decade about 4 percent of the students entering junior colleges were black.[12] Despite the avowed policy of the American Association of Junior Colleges "to assume an expanding role in helping the poor," [1] only about 7 percent were at or below the poverty line.[12] In the major cities thousands of youth who might profit by attending college did not do so.[10] Was the strength of junior colleges flowing more into buildings and bigness than into programs which discovered and nurtured human potential?

Student personnel workers in the junior colleges, not liking their reflection as mirrored by the Carnegie Study,[5] tried to make their programs more effective. But effective in doing what? By the end of the Sixties a new role was emerging, articulated by Grant,[7] O'Banion,[13] and others: the goal of student personnel work was to unlock and nurture the development of all students. This goal was, in fact, the goal of the junior college, always stated, now coming into sharper focus. Implementation was the responsibility of everyone who dealt with students. Leadership should come from student personnel workers who would function as catalysts, change agents, and teachers of students and faculty and administrators in how to create a climate which permitted all members of the academic community to discover and develop the richness of their humanness.

As the Seventies begin . . .

We have been to the moon. But the war on poverty has not yet been won, nor peace achieved, nor universal educational opportunity beyond the high school assured. Higher education as the great panacea has lost some of its magic appeal. Mounting costs and dwindling public support are forcing junior colleges to reexamine some of their priorities. Few junior colleges are able to expand their student personnel services; some are hard pressed to maintain them.

Against the backdrop of shrinking resources and escalating societal pressures, student personnel workers in the junior colleges are attempting to resolve the many issues which emerged in the late Sixties.

GROUP WORK: FAD OR FUNDAMENTAL CHANGE AGENT?

Encounter groups, micro-labs, human potential seminars, and a variety of sensory experiences are being used to help students, faculty, administrators, and clerical staff relate more openly and honestly with each other. Is the human encounter, at worst, a dangerous tool, and at best, a kind of fortifying of the human condition with artificial closeness in the same way dry cereal is fortified with vitamins? Or is it a healing, shared journey? [14] If, in the hands of an expert, it has demonstrated its capability of becoming the latter, criteria for "expertness" should be stated. Ethical considerations must be examined and a code of ethics developed. As with other aspects of the student personnel program, evaluation is needed to assess the kinds of changes which occur, their degree of permanence, and the type of leader-group configurations through which desirable changes are most likely to take place.

DECENTRALIZATION COUNSELING: TO WHERE?

As the orientation of counselors changes from helping a few troubled students cope with their problems to facilitating the development of all students, there is a rather general agreement that counselors must leave their cubicles to go where the students are. Should counselors be attached to academic divisions? Or at least housed there? Or is the most appropriate spot a table in the cafeteria or a corner of a lounge? Should divisional assignments be on a permanent or rotating basis? Is there still need for a central counseling staff? Other questions relate to the assurance of counseling privacy when it is needed; availability of records; maintaining professional relationships among members of the student personnel staff for the sake of their professional growth as well as for the cohesiveness of their program.

MEANINGFUL STUDENT INVOLVEMENT IN CAMPUS GOVERNANCE: HOW CAN IT BE ACHIEVED?

Professional educators have devoted considerable discussion to the role of students in campus affairs. As a result, there has been a widespread movement among junior colleges to put at least a few students on at least a few committees. The extent to which meaningful involvement has been achieved is unknown. On many campuses, some students are still willing to play the student government game, without real responsibility or purpose. The other students step over them to go to class or work. Like their four-year college and university counterparts, junior college students feel they should have a major voice in curricular design.[12] Yet they have not insisted that their voices be widely heard. New participatory models have been suggested which would permit all members of the academic community to share in its governance. Should the organization be bicameral [17] or unicameral? [6] Or, as Hodgkinson suggests, what may be needed is more decision making by ad hoc groups, because "different problems require different structures for their solutions." [8]

IN MULTI-UNIT JUNIOR COLLEGE SYSTEMS, IS THERE A CENTRAL STAFF ROLE IN STUDENT PERSONNEL ADMINISTRATION?

Multi-institutional junior college districts are developing rapidly in metropolitan areas where demands are greatest for educational opportunities beyond high school. Student personnel services, which are urgently needed in inner-city colleges, are caught in the cross fire of the battle for campus autonomy. When ranked against pressing instructional and administrative needs, student personnel programs are likely to receive low priority; in competition with computers and new facilities and instructional equipment and faculty demands for pay increases, student personnel is apt to lose. Should there be a person on the central staff who serves as spokesman, leader, or coordinator?

In a recent study by Kintzer, Jensen, and Hansen, there was disagreement among respondents as to whether admissions, bookstore, housing, research, and financial aid should be central staff or campus functions. Counseling, health services, student activities, and discipline were generally viewed as campus matters.[9] Some functions such as research and financial aids should probably be shared; admissions and records are of necessity linked by the computer. Some degree of coordinating among the campuses seems desirable, to assure cooperation and sharing of resources, while at the same time stimulating college creativity and innovation.

OLDER STUDENTS: WHAT CAN WE DO FOR THEM?

Under the strange illusion that most junior college students came directly from high school, student personnel workers have been mainly concerned with "the kids." Yet the typical student population, especially in the large comprehensive institutions, is a mix: veterans, housewives, married students, police enrolled for special training, welfare mothers, practical nurses working toward associate degrees in nursing, transfers, and students who have worked for several years before attending college. Older students are liberally represented in day as well as evening programs. Yet they are offered psychodelic dances, sports car clubs, and other experiences geared to the 18 to 21 year olds who are rapidly becoming a minority. Even financial aids are typically planned for young adults presumed to live at home where families provide room and board. Older students want to grow occupationally and as persons or they would not undergo the sacrifices required in attending college. Unlike the lovely ladies in the ads, junior college students are *not* forever young; student personnel workers need to assess the needs of older students and plan experiences which speak to these needs.

THE TECHNICAL-OCCUPATIONAL STUDENTS: WHAT CAN WE DO FOR THEM?

Most junior college student personnel workers have a strong academic orientation; their egos were nourished in the university and their knowledge of occupations other than their own limited largely to summer jobs and occupational monographs. How many counselors understand or even appreciate the intricacies of air frame mechanics or hotel and restaurant management or inhalation therapy? As a result, the career programs have been used as dumping grounds for the academically inept or unprepared. Moreover, lack of information about occupational opportunities coupled with the old notion that there is such a thing as vocational counseling per se still causes some counselors to feel that students' personal concerns are unrelated to their choice of program and that only the former is the proper domain of a professional counselor. Technical-occupational faculty can be asked to orient the student personnel staff to their programs and to help in securing up-to-date information about job opportunities and salaries within the community.

STUDENTS AND THE STUDENT PERSONNEL PROGRAM: WHAT IS THEIR ROLE?

Student personnel workers, while championing student involvement in campus affairs generally, have devoted surprisingly little attention to student involvement in shaping the student personnel program. Does the answer lie in the creation of student advisory committees for the various student personnel functions? Or should students have a stronger voice? Perhaps the role of the chief student personnel administrator is emasculated because he attempts to serve two masters, top administration and students.

INNOVATING WITHIN TIGHT BUDGETS: CAN IT BE DONE?

Many chief student personnel administrators in the junior colleges report that their most pressing problems are insufficient staff and budget.[18] Yet some innovations take more imagination than money, and can be undertaken by a reallocation of existing resources. Others can be conducted by the professional staff if support services are used for more routine tasks.

As Collins suggests, it is time we look at the kinds of things counselors do which can as well be done by supervised, trained para-professionals. Collins and others believe that counselor aides can be trained in community colleges, through a core curriculum, specialized courses, and internship experiences.[4] Why not use the same core curriculum but vary the internship in order to prepare aides to also assist in other phases of the student personnel program?

New media (TV, tapes, film loops, dial access) can take over the information-giving aspects of orientation, academic advising, transfer, and vocational counseling. Our present methods of disseminating information are as out-of-date as the classroom lecture, although we are quick to criticize teaching colleagues for being similarly unprogressive.

STUDENT PERSONNEL WORK AND THE NEW
INSTRUCTIONAL TECHNOLOGIES: DO THEY GO TOGETHER?

As the systems approach becomes increasingly commonplace and students learn at their own pace, through a variety of media, the traditional testing devices are becoming obsolete both for placement and prediction. Learning labs, like laundromats, will probably be open round the clock, on the campus, in store fronts, or in mobile classrooms. Some students will learn in their own living rooms and others in "wet carrels" equipped with buttons, knobs, TV monitors, computer keyboards, and earphones. Will the new learning approaches, as Arthur Cohen predicts, make student personnel work obsolete? [3]

Group work is an important antidote to the loneliness of learning on one's own, as well as an opportunity for students to learn to work together with others. Counselors are needed to help students pace themselves realistically and evaluate their progress. Counselors should serve as members of instructional teams, helping instructors write behavioral objectives which express the affective aspects of subject matter learning.

IN-SERVICE TRAINING: WHOSE RESPONSIBILITY?

Most student personnel workers—counselors, college nurses, student activity directors, admissions and financial aids directors—learn their special skills on the job. They come primarily from positions in secondary schools or perhaps from residence hall work. Most deans are educated either in the fields of educational administration or counseling and guidance, neither of which prepares them to fulfill a dean of student's role. Frequently they are promoted to the deanship because they are good counselors, rather than because they know how to develop and administer a program which facilitates human growth and at the same time effectively handles day-by-day operations.

More regional and state short-term workshops should be developed, particularly for new deans. In turn, knowledgeable deans could conduct continuing in-service training for staff. Left to sink or swim, new student personnel workers are apt to sink—or float in safe mediocrity.

STUDENT UNREST: BLESSING OR CURSE?

With scattered and painful exceptions, junior colleges have remained relatively peaceful. Various explanations have been offered: junior college students are vocationally oriented; faculty and students communicate well; many students work and therefore have a stake in the establishment; older students help keep the campuses cool; parents exert a calming influence; there is a time lag before junior college students adopt the ways of students in the university. Perhaps the explanation is simply that, even more than other educational institutions, junior colleges reflect the communities which surround them; the many small two-year colleges in rural or suburban areas are quiet, while those in the cities are turbulent. The great majority of junior college students are apathetic, a state which is comforting to presidents and boards who fear that student activism would lead to withdrawal of community support. Most students appear to be more interested in coping with things as they are than in changing them. Yet, for lack of student pressure, community colleges are clinging to traditional programs and policies. And at a time when society needs the concentrated action of concerned people, junior college students appear to be swelling the ranks of the silent majority. If activism spreads to the junior college campuses, will the response be crisis-oriented and repressive? Meanwhile, to what extent should we stimulate student concern for educational reform and for greater responsiveness to the human condition?

EDUCATING THE DISADVANTAGED: CAN WE DO IT?

Federally funded programs such as Upward Bound, Talent Search, and Special Services for Disadvantaged Students are encouraging colleges to work with high risk students. High risk, however, is a relative term; the selective institutions, which now include many state universities, define it in terms of the characteristics of current students. Thus only the junior colleges are likely to seek out and enroll the great majority of disadvantaged students, who are educationally crippled. Compensatory education has so far been generally less than successful. Yet the Council of the Society for the Psychological Study of Social Issues states:

. . . the major failure in so-called compensatory education has been in the planning, size, and scope of the program. We maintain that a variety of programs planned to teach specific skills has been effective and that a few well-designed programs which teach problem-solving and thinking have also been effective.[16]

Subtle racism and snobbery still haunt the junior colleges. White counselors and black students make each other uncomfortable. Many faculty and administrators have difficulty accepting students who are different in skin color, length of hair, values, and modes of expression. Student personnel workers need first to work through their own attitudes and then to assume leadership in developing experiences which sensitize all members of the college staff to cultural differences in perceiving and responding.

WORKING WITH OTHER PROFESSIONAL GROUPS: WHAT ROLE TO PLAY?

Many professional organizations are now giving at least token recognition to junior college student personnel specialists. Among such groups are The Association of College Unions–International, The American College Health Association, The National Association of Women Deans and Counselors, The American Association of Higher Education, The National Association of Student Personnel Administrators, and of course, The American College Personnel Association. Since junior colleges now enroll too many students to be ignored, student personnel representatives are being included on national commissions. Are we now mature enough to serve without the old defensiveness which has too often made us obnoxious? Junior college student personnel workers need the resources and support of these groups, just as they need ours. The onus is on junior college representatives to participate effectively toward common professional goals.

BRIDGING THE GAP BETWEEN STUDENT PERSONNEL AND INSTRUCTION: HOW?

This gulf, which appears to exist on many campuses, has been of great concern to student personnel people. It seems to be based on the false notion that learning is primarily concerned with content and takes place only in formal settings. Student personnel services are therefore ancillary; the real business of the college is to teach. Faculty, who are largely recruited from high schools, bring a limited perception of the place of guidance services. And despite their talk, junior college student personnel workers have done little to change the image. According to American College Testing Program institutional research, students generally rate student services as of little value.[11]

Student personnel workers must themselves be convinced that they also teach and that their work is an integral part of the total educational program of the college. They are then in a better position to establish a working relationship with faculty, especially as they design services which students and faculty alike perceive as of value. Whether the communication problems are a matter of organization, as Berg [2] and others have suggested, or of human relationships, student personnel must contribute in more significant and tangible ways to the educational process. Perhaps student personnel workers should be less concerned with what they are called and where they appear on the organizational chart and more concerned with the nature of their contribution.

PUBLISHING: HOW IMPORTANT?

For too long junior college student personnel workers have lived in an isolated practitioner's world. University professors and presidents, who no longer face the daily problems of the student personnel specialist, do most of the writing. Perhaps the question is not so much who writes but who reads? In a recent survey chief student personnel administrators gave low priority to professional activities, including keeping up with the professional literature.[18] Is there any reason to believe that staff read more than their supervisors?

Junior college student personnel workers will not perish because they do not publish. They are overworked and oriented toward doing. But what they do well should be shared with colleagues in four-year colleges and universities as well as in other junior colleges. Graduate students in neighboring universities can be induced to lend their research skills to implement a coordinated research plan. Regional editorial assistance boards could be set up by the Student Personnel Commission of the American Association of Junior Colleges or by Commission XI of the American College Personnel Association to help young writers prepare manuscripts for publication.

Because of the dearth of basic literature in student personnel work generally, we have all been accused of being a "profession stillborn." [15] Profession or not (and does it really matter?), we need to show other educators that we are very much alive.

As the Seventies continue . . .

How well the issues of the early Seventies are resolved will in large part determine the shape of things to come. How we go about decentralizing counseling or reacting to student unrest or involving students in campus governance or educating the disadvantaged should be decided on the basis of a coherent philosophy and purpose. If we believe that man's essential nature contains a core which, when unfettered and unencumbered, grows toward self-actualization, we will then make decisions in terms of what facilitates or does not facilitate the development of creative humanness in all students.

Human development facilitation is oriented toward the growth of all students rather than toward problem-solving with a few. It focuses on the creation of conditions and experiences which help persons become more free to self-actualize. It involves what White described as the patience of the husbandman rather than the hasty tinkering of the mechanic.[19] How to implement this concept is the basic task of the Seventies.

As the Seventies continue, junior college student personnel workers will have some stark realities to face. They can continue as they are, their services generally perceived as of little value. In time they will probably disappear quietly from the scene, pushed out by the new instructional technologies and higher budget priorities. Or they can make meaningful contributions to the lives of students, by their being as well as by their actions, and thereby become an indispensable part of the educational process.

Like Janus, this book looks both backward and forward. It outlines what should be, *new,* and looks ahead to what could be. It describes new roles, foreshadows new organizational structures, and voices concern for individuals as well as for the society of which they are a part. It assigns student personnel a central role in making the junior colleges what they have always said they want to be. Only with the unique contribution which junior college student personnel workers can make to the development of persons will the junior college become a leader of society rather than its reflection.

REFERENCES

1. "AAJC Approach," *Junior College Journal,* March, 1969, p. 9.

2. BERG, E. H., see article, p. 134, this volume.

3. COHEN, A., *Dateline '79.* Beverly Hills, Cal.: Glencoe Press, 1969, p. 39.

4. COLLINS, C., "Giving the Counselor a Helping Hand," *Junior College Journal,* May, 1970, pp. 17-20.

5. ———, *Junior College Student Personnel Programs: What They Are and What They Should Be.* Washington, D.C.: AAJC, 1967.

6. DEEGAN, W. L., "Student Government and Student Participation in Junior College Governance—Models for the 70's." Position paper presented to the AAJC Student Personnel Commission, Hawaii, March, 1970.

7. GRANT, W. H., see article, p. 194, this volume.

8. HODGKINSON, H. L., "The Next Decade," *The Research Reporter.* Center For Research and Development in Higher Education, UCLA, Vol. V, No. 1, 1970.

9. KINTZER, F. C., A. M. JENSEN, and J. S. HANSEN, *The Multi-Institution Junior College District,* ERIC Clearinghouse For Junior College Information, American Association of Junior Colleges Monograph Series, Washington, D.C.

10. KNOELL, DOROTHY, "Who Goes to College in the Cities?" *Junior College Journal,* September, 1969, pp. 23-27.

11. *Manual For The ACT Institutional Self-Study Survey.* Iowa City, Iowa: American College Testing Program, 1969.

12. *National Norms for Entering College Freshmen, Fall, 1969, ACE Research Reports.* Creager, J., A. Astin, R. Beruch, A. Bayer, and D. Drew, pp. 30-31.

13. O'BANION, TERRY, see article, p. 180, this volume.

14. ———— and O'CONNELL, April, *The Shared Journey.* Englewood Cliffs, N. J.: Prentice-Hall, Inc., 1970.

15. PENNEY, J. F., "Student Personnel Work: A Profession Stillborn," *The Personnel and Guidance Journal,* 47, No. 10 (June, 1969), 958-62.

16. "Psychologists Comment on Current IQ Controversy, Heredity Versus Environment," *IRCD Bulletin,* Publication of the ERIC Information Retrieval Center on the Disadvantaged, V, No. 4 (Fall, 1969), 6.

17. RICHARDSON, R. C., see article, p. 51, this volume.

18. THURSTON, ALICE, T. NEHER, and J. INGRAHAM, *Community College Deans of Students.* ERIC Clearinghouse for Junior Colleges, in press.

19. WHITE, R. W., *Lives in Progress,* New York: Dryden Press, 1952, p. 364.

Index